Phonology for Communication Disorders

Phonology for Communication Disorders

MARTIN J. BALL • NICOLE MÜLLER • BEN RUTTER

Psychology Press
Taylor & Francis Group
New York   Hove

MW

Psychology Press   Psychology Press
Taylor & Francis Group   Taylor & Francis Group
270 Madison Avenue   27 Church Road
New York, NY 10016   Hove, East Sussex BN3 2FA

© 2010 by Taylor and Francis Group, LLC
Psychology Press is an imprint of Taylor & Francis Group, an Informa business

Printed in the United States of America on acid-free paper
10 9 8 7 6 5 4 3 2 1

International Standard Book Number: 978-0-8058-5761-0 (Hardback) 978-0-8058-5762-7 (Paperback)

Library of Congress Cataloging-in-Publication Data

Ball, Martin J. (Martin John)
    Phonology for communication disorders / Martin J. Ball, Nicole Müller, Ben Rutter.
        p. ; cm.
    Companion v. to: Phonetics for communication disorders / by Martin J. Ball & Nicole Müller. c2005.
    Includes bibliographical references and index.
        ISBN 978-0-8058-5761-0 (hardcover : alk. paper) -- ISBN 978-0-8058-5762-7 (pbk. : alk. paper)
        1. English language--Phonology. 2. Speech disorders. I. Müller, Nicole, 1963- II. Rutter, Ben. III.
Ball, Martin J. (Martin John). Phonetics for communication disorders. IV. Title.
        [DNLM: 1. Phonetics. 2. Speech Disorders. WV 501 B187pb 2009]

RC423.B285 2009
616.85'5--dc22   2009016073

Visit the Taylor & Francis Web site at
http://www.taylorandfrancis.com

and the Psychology Press Web site at
http://www.psypress.com

6/30/10

CONTENTS

PREFACE

This book is a companion volume to our *Phonetics for Communication Disorders*, and just as that text aimed to introduce all the relevant areas of phonetics to the student and practitioner of speech-language pathology, so this book aims to describe those approaches to phonology that we have deemed most relevant to communication disorders. Indeed, to understand the arguments presented in the book, readers will need to be familiar with phonetics. Phonetic symbols and terminology are used, and we do not stop and explain all of these as we go along. Just as a theory of phonology presupposes a detailed phonetic analysis of the data concerned, so a book on phonological theories presupposes familiarity with the concepts and terms used in phonetics. For readers who need to access current phonetic symbols for normal and disordered speech, relevant charts are included in the appendix at the end of the book.

It is important for the reader to realize, however, that this is not a book on *clinical phonology*, as that term is generally understood. In other words, we don't provide clinical assessment methods based on a particular variety of phonology; there are no test sheets showing how to categorize particular errors or patterns of errors. There are numerous publications available that take this route. Rather, we look here at schools of thought in theoretical phonology, and their relevance to description, explanation, and remediation in the clinical context.

Naturally, we have not been able to include every approach to phonology that has developed over the last 50 years or so in this book—and no doubt some in the field will regret the exclusion of a particular theory. Phonology has been a particularly fruitful area of linguistic research and theory development since the 1970s, and it would not be possible to cover all these innovations.

We have tried to include those aspects of phonological theory that either have been applied to clinical data or—in our opinion—could usefully be so applied. The beginnings of generative phonology in the 1960s also saw the first attempts to apply modern phonological insights to the analysis of disordered speech, so the first few chapters of the book take a historical tour through the main developments in generative phonology up to the present. Most of the advances from classical generative phonology, through nonlinear phonology, up to the present dominant paradigm of optimality theory have had clinical applications, so it is important to cover these areas both to clarify where modern phonology currently is (and how it got there) and to point out the applications of these developments to communication disorders.

However, we do not restrict ourselves to developments within the generative paradigm, as several recent approaches to phonology are, arguably, of more potential use to clinical applications. Some of these seem closer to speech production than more abstract formulations; in this regard we would highlight articulatory phonology. Other theories may seem more closely linked to acoustic and perceptual aspects of speech, for example, government phonology. Natural phonology has a developmental basis, and prosodic phonology and systemic phonology are both polysystemic with a functional aim. Finally, we can note the move toward a cognitively based phonology, which attempts a psycholinguistically adequate description of phonological storage, production, and perception.

This last point brings us to a recurring theme throughout the book, that is, the distinction between phonological theories that attempt elegant, parsimonious descriptions of phonological data, and those that attempt to provide a psycholinguistic model of speech production and perception. Clearly, if we are confronted with speech data from a highly unintelligible client, then an analysis that sorts the data into clear patterns will be extremely useful. (However, we can note here that if the data include nonnative or atypical speech sounds, the phonological feature systems of many more abstract theories may well not account for them.) Such an analysis may not explain why such patterns arose, or how best to remediate them. Analyses derived from more phonetically concrete or psycholinguistically valid phonologies may well provide just that extra information. The problem is that approaches within the overall generative paradigm are not always clear as to the status of their formalism; while overtly it is usually stated that these models aim for descriptive economy, the resultant analyses are often treated (within theoretical and clinical phonology) as if they described a psycholinguistic state.

As the field of phonology develops, so the application of phonological models to clinical data will also expand. This need not be a one-way street, however. We see clinical phonology as both applying the insights of theoretical advances and acting as a testing ground for such theories. If disordered data can be accounted for well within a particular model, this provides extra evidence to support the claims of the model. In particular, if the model not only accounts for the data but also provides principled explanations for the error patterns and insight into intervention, then we may well value such a model more highly than others that do not do so.

1

INTRODUCTION AND BACKGROUND

PHONETICS VERSUS PHONOLOGY

This book is about phonology, but to understand phonology we also need to know about phonetics. Phonetics is the study of the production, transmission, and reception of speech sounds in natural language. In other words, phoneticians are interested in how speech sounds are made using the vocal organs, the acoustic properties of speech sounds in air, and how the sounds are converted from acoustic signals into mechanical and then electrical activity in the ear. All the sounds of natural language are of interest to the phonetician, but the behavior and function of specific sounds in particular languages are outside the bounds of phonetics: These are part of the field of phonology.

Phonologists, then, are interested in patterns of speech sounds. For example, they look at which sounds in any given language could be considered as groups of variants of a basic sound type; they examine the inventories of consonants and vowels of a language and compare these with those of other languages, or across dialects of a single language; they look at patterns of changes to the sounds of a language (for example, historical changes, or those that happen when an ending is added to a word). Most importantly, phonologists are less interested in how sounds are produced or transmitted by speakers; they are primarily concerned with how sounds are used in a language.

This distinction, however, doesn't mean that phonologists can do without phonetics. Drawing up descriptions of patterns of use of speech sounds clearly depends on accurate phonetic data. We can give an example of this. As we've just noted, one of the concerns of phonology is to examine which sounds of a language can be grouped together as variants of a basic sound type. Suppose we have a language where phoneticians have identified the following sounds: [l] and [ɫ]* (so-called clear-l and dark-l). Further, suppose that in looking at the patterns of usage of these sounds phonologists determine that the clear-l is always found before vowels, and the dark-l always after vowels. As these sounds are phonetically very similar, a phonologist can conclude that they are in fact positional variants of a single *l* unit. However, if the phonetic data were imprecise (for example, the person transcribing the language couldn't hear the difference between the two *l* sounds),

---

* Readers who need to access current phonetic symbols for normal and disordered speech should consult the charts in the appendix at the end of the book.

then we could not make this analysis. Indeed, if we acquire new and more precise transcriptions, we may find that the language has a third *l* variant (e.g., [l̥]: a voiceless clear-l), which is found following [p] and [k] and preceding vowels (where neither of the first two variants can occur). In other words, a phonological analysis is only as good as the phonetic data on which it is based. Too often, unfortunately, phonological theories are tested on second- or even thirdhand phonetic data (i.e., data obtained from published material rather than the author's own transcriptions). In these cases, it can be difficult to know the nature of the data being used: Are the data detailed phonetic transcriptions, or material that has already been subjected to some kind of analysis or simplification?

THE AIM OF PHONOLOGY

As we have just noted, phonologists attempt to describe patterns in the use of speech sounds in a given language or language variety or, indeed, in a given speaker (including speakers with speech disorders). This overall aim can, however, be achieved in different ways, and in this book we will examine many of the different approaches to phonological analysis that have been proposed over many years of research into the area. However, over and above these different approaches, we can distinguish two differing aims to any phonological analysis. First, the phonologist may wish to draw up the most comprehensive, and yet also the most economical, description of the phonetic data provided. In other words, the phonological description covers all the data available, and covers these data in the simplest way possible. This is indeed the aim of scientific endeavors everywhere: to be comprehensive and to prefer the most straightforward account of data over any more complex account. In phonology, such accounts may provide us with very satisfying descriptions of the phonetic data, but they do not necessarily tell us much about how speakers themselves organize their speech sounds.

In recent times, phonologists who are interested in psycholinguistics have turned from focusing purely on descriptively satisfying accounts of speech data, to concentrate more on what we may call psycholinguistically valid accounts. In other words, they have looked for theoretical models that might account for how speakers organize the phonology of their language internally, in the brain. Such accounts do not necessarily have to keep to the principles of maximum economy of description if this does not reflect the likely psycholinguistic organization of speakers' phonologies.

We can illustrate this difference of approach by considering a currently popular approach to phonological description, optimality theory (see Chapter 11). To simplify its theoretical apparatus, this approach requires a component that scans an *infinite* number of possible pronunciations for any given form (e.g., a word). Positing this principle allows the theory to avoid stating which forms are scanned and which are not. From a psycholinguistic viewpoint, however, such a requirement is clearly impossible. If speakers really scanned an infinite number of possible pronunciations, they would never get beyond scanning, and so never say anything!

The primary purpose of this book is to examine phonology in relation to clinical speech data: to examine which approaches to phonological theory may be most insightful for the analysis and diagnosis of speech disorders, and might feed best into remedial intervention. As we will see, mainly descriptive models (especially those relying on highly abstract units) are not always helpful to the clinician. As we might expect, models that attempt to provide an image of how phonology might be organized in the brain are often more directly helpful.

CLINICAL PHONOLOGY

The term *clinical phonology* refers to the relation between phonological theory and disordered speech data. Clinical phonology emerged as a field of study in the 1970s (see Grunwell, 1977, 1985, 1987), and in its early form it was primarily an endeavor to see what insights from phonological models could profitably be applied to speech data collected by speech-language pathologists to aid, as we noted earlier, in analysis, diagnosis, and remediation. More recently (as with other areas of clinical linguistics), scholars have developed a two-way relation: As well as examining how phonological theory can throw light on clinical data, we can also use clinical data to test the applicability of the numerous models of phonology that have been proposed over the last 40 years or so.

Whereas theoretical phonology uses data from normally produced natural language, clinical phonology tests its assumptions on data derived from the speech-language pathology clinic. Clients who present with speech problems do not all, however, have phonological problems, and traditionally the field has divided such examples into *articulatory* and *phonological* disorders. Such a distinction is applied to what the client produces; in other words, if a client uses the wrong phonological unit from the target language, this is typically deemed to be a phonological error; if a wrong variant of the unit is used, or if a sound from outside the language altogether is employed, this is deemed to be an articulatory (or phonetic) error. This usage ignores, however, the psycholinguistic aspects of speech production. In other words, we might ask whether the client was aiming to say the correct sound, but some problem with activating the relevant speech production routine intervened. On the other hand, the client may have an incorrectly stored unit neurologically, and so may "correctly" have produced the wrong target sound. We return later to this problem of classifying error types in disordered speech.

BASIC PHONOLOGICAL CONSTRUCTS

The main purpose of this chapter is to introduce some of the basic notions of phonological theory. It will take, to some extent, a historical perspective, and many readers may have already encountered some of these ideas. However, it is useful to go over them again, as much in the next few chapters builds on these basic constructs.

Phonemes

The earliest kind of analysis in modern phonology (i.e., from the development of this field of study in modern linguistics in the early part of the 20th century) was phonemic analysis. It had been clear to linguists working with the pronunciation systems of different languages that the main function of sound systems in language was to contrast one word with another, and that analyses of sound systems should overtly demonstrate this. Taking English as an example, we see that the two words *pin* and *bin* are contrasted with each other solely by the choice of the initial sound: The other sounds in these words are identical. The same can be said for *pat* and *bat*, *pride* and *bride*, *rip* and *rib*, and *napping* and *nabbing*. In other words, /p/ and /b/ are contrastive sounds in English. By comparing many other *minimal pairs* (pairs of words that differ in only one sound in the same position) we can discover other contrastive sounds. So, in English, the pairs *tin* and *din*, *cot* and *got*, *pin* and *tin*, *pin* and *kin*, *got* and *dot*, *cot* and *pot*, and so forth will allow us to establish that the language has six contrastive plosive consonants: /p, t, k, b, d, g/. These contrastive sound units are termed *phonemes*. The phoneme can be defined as the smallest sound unit capable of changing word meanings in a specific language.

However, not all sound differences are contrastive. Taking another example from English, we find the pronunciation [pʰ] at the beginning of the word *pot*, but [p˭] at the beginning of the word *spot* (denoting aspirated and unaspirated voiceless bilabial plosives, respectively). We do not find any minimal pairs, however. In fact, there are no words in English that start with an unaspirated [p˭], nor are there any where an aspirated [pʰ] occurs after /s/. Indeed, if we swap the pronunciations around, saying [p˭ɑt] and [spʰɑt], the result sounds odd, but doesn't give us a pair of different English words. It turns out that these sounds are variants of the /p/ phoneme, variants that are in complementary distribution (that is, where you find one variant you cannot get the other, and vice versa). Variants of a phoneme are called *allophones*, and allophones in complementary distribution can be thought of as context-dependent variants.

Not all allophones are context-dependent. In some cases they are context-free, in that the choice of using one variant over another appears to be a matter of personal preference, perhaps reflecting some stylistic distinction. In English we get such free variant allophones, for example, in word final fortis plosives. A word such as *cap* can be pronounced with either a final [pʰ] or a final [p̚] (aspirated or unreleased; in some dialects other forms also may be possible). The choice of one over the other does not make a new word (i.e., these are not minimal pairs), and speakers may well use one allophone at one moment and the other later in the same utterance.

Phonemic analysis sought to provide an inventory of the consonant and vowel phonemes of a language or dialect (the phonologial *system*), and for each phoneme to list the allophones, their phonetic contexts of use, and to note whether they were in complementary distribution or in free variation. To get an idea of how such an analysis was undertaken, consider the data sets in Exercises 1.1 and 1.2, and undertake the phonemic analysis tasks specified.

EXERCISE 1.1

Analyze the following data, and list as many vocalic segments that show contrastive function as you can (treat diphthongs as single units). The data show normal orthography, phonetic transcription, and the meanings in English.

a. Welsh

haedd	[hɑɨð]	reach; merit
tai	[taɪ]	houses
haul	[haɨl]	sun
tau	[taɨ]	thine
hael	[haɨl]	liberal, generous
taw	[tau]	that
llaes	[ɬaɪs]	loose
tei	[təɪ]	(neck)tie
hawdd	[hauð]	easy
tew	[tɛu]	fat
hail	[haɪl]	feast
llais	[ɬaɪs]	voice
haidd	[haɪð]	barley
tae	[tɑɨ]	would be (3s)

Analyze the following data, and list as many consonant segments that show contrastive function as you can. The data show normal orthography, phonetic transcription, and the meanings in English.

b) French

quelle	[kɛl]	which (fem)
lu	[ly]	have read
mettent	[mɛt]	(they) put
chu	[ʃy]	have fallen
tel	[tɛl]	such (masc)
sept	[sɛt]	seven
pelle	[pɛl]	shovel
rue	[ʁy]	road
faites	[fɛt]	(you) make/do (pl)
tu	[ty]	you, thou
celles	[sɛl]	those (fem, pl)
nette	[nɛt]	clean (fem)
belle	[bɛl]	beautiful (fem)
du	[dy]	of the (masc)

EXERCISE 1.2

Analyze the following data, and list as many allophones in complementary distribution as you can find, assigning them to their relevant phonemes. The data show normal orthography, phonetic transcription, and the meanings in English.

a. German

Examine the distribution of syllable initial aspirated and unaspirated voiceless plosives.

Port	[pʰɔɐt]	port
Skandal	[sk⁼anˈdaːl]	scandal
Taube	[ˈtʰaʊbə]	pigeon
Spiel	[ʃp⁼il]	game
Skizze	[ˈsk⁼ɪtsə]	sketch
Topf	[tʰɔp͡f]	pot
kennen	[ˈkʰɛnən]	to know
Sport	[ʃp⁼ ɔɐt]	sport
Stück	[ʃt⁼ʏk]	piece
Tier	[tʰiɐ]	animal
Pilz	[pʰɪl͡ts]	mushroom
still	[ʃt⁼ɪl]	silent
Pudel	[ˈpʰudl̩]	poodle
Stier	[ʃt⁼iɐ]	bull
spät	[ʃp⁼ɛːt]	late
kaufen	[ˈkʰaʊfən]	to buy

b. Spanish

Examine the distribution of voiced plosives and fricatives.

vino	['bino]	wine
algo	['alɣo]	something
goma	['goma]	rubber
haber	[a'βer]	to have
alba	['alβa]	dawn
tengo	['teŋgo]	I have
lodo	['loðo]	mud
lago	['laɣo]	lake
arde	['arðe]	burns
ambos	['ambos]	both
doy	[doj]	I give
ando	['ando]	I walk
toldo	['tolðo]	awning

Phonemic analysis was the first phonological approach used with clinical speech data. There are, however, two ways of applying any type of phonological theory to such data: One is to analyze the material as a phonology in its own right; the other is to use the theory to provide a contrastive analysis between the clinical data and the target pronunciation patterns. For example, we could describe a client as having a fricative system of seven phonemes, /f, v, s, z, ʃ, ʒ, h/, or assuming the target system is Standard English, we could note that this client lacks two target phonemes, /θ, ð/, replacing them with /f, v/. In Exercise 1.3, attempt first an analysis of the phonemes of the speaker as a system in its own right. Then do a phonemic contrastive analysis comparing the client with Standard English.

EXERCISE 1.3

Analyze the phonemic system of this client (the data provided cover only the plosive and nasal consonants), whose target language is English. Then contrast this with the relevant parts of the target system.

coat	[doʊd]
down	[daʊn]
mob	[mɑb]
beak	[bid]
gap	[dæb]
pen	[bɛn]
nag	[næd]
pang	[bæn]
tap	[dæb]
mud	[mʌd]
dumb	[dʌm]
toad	[doʊd]

Phonemic analyses of disordered speech prompted a traditional and long-lasting set of categories still encountered in descriptions of clinical speech data. These are deletion of a phoneme, substitution of one phoneme for another, distortion of a phoneme, and addition of a phoneme. At first glance these may seem like reasonable categories, but there are problems with them.

- Deletion: Is the phoneme deleted from every position in the word? How do we characterize selective deletion (e.g., a consonant deleted only when in a cluster)? How can we characterize the difference between the deletion of a common sound and that of an uncommon sound, as this clearly has implications for intelligibility?
- Substitution: Again, does the substitution occur at every possible place in phonological structure, or is it restricted to certain contexts? How can we characterize the difference between substitutions that seem to occur often in child speech development and in clinical data, and those that are extremely rare?
- Distortion: What exactly is this term meant to encompass? Among possible distortions we are presumably meant to include the choice of the wrong allophone of a phoneme (e.g., when we find [spʰɑt] instead of [sp˭ɑt] for *spot*), and the choice of a sound from outside the target system altogether (e.g., [jɛɬ] instead of [jɛs] for *yes*). Clearly, there is potentially quite a difference between these two types: The first shows at least a control of aspects of the target phonology, while the second may well reflect a motor problem, or a major disruption to the target phonology.
- Addition: This is perhaps the least controversial of the categories, but like the others, it does not distinguish between expected and unexpected additions, and it does not specify the context of an addition. For example, the addition of a schwa between two members of a consonant cluster occurs frequently in normal speech development and in clinical data (e.g., *blue* pronounced as [bəˈlu]). However, the addition of a consonant to the beginning of an /ɹ/ initial word, or the addition of an /l/ to a vowel final word are both unusual (e.g., *rue* pronounced as [fɹul], as reported in Ball et al., 2004).

So, while these terms may have some use as a brief shorthand account of a client's phonological behavior, we really need to go beyond categories as limited as this. Some scholars (e.g., Grunwell, 1987) have worked to expand phonemic analysis of clinical data into a contrastive analysis that combines both system and structure. To do this, charts may be drawn up that allow the clinician to compare target and realization at different positions within the word, and in clusters as opposed to singletons. Charts 1.1 and 1.2, for example, show the word initial and word final realizations of singleton consonants (i.e., excluding target clusters) of a seriously unintelligible child whose target language was General American English (the charts are derived from work by Pamela Grunwell, for example, Grunwell, 1985, 1987). The charts show not only the different realizations of target sounds at the different places within the word, but also the fact that there is a considerable amount of variability in her productions. (For another example, see Müller et al., 2006.)

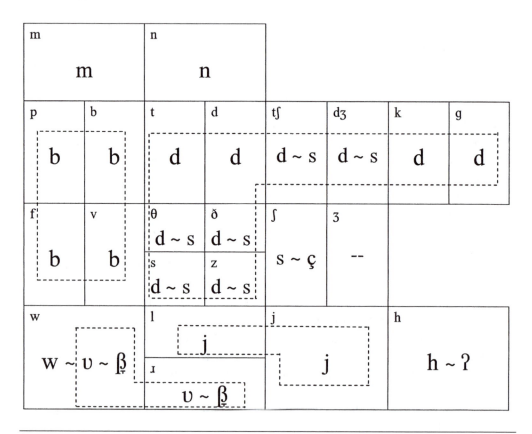

Chart 1.1 Syllable initial (English). Target sounds are shown by the symbol at the top left of each box; realizations are shown in the center of each box. -- means no examples recorded. ~ is used between variant realizations. Dotted lines connect identical realizations for different targets.

Syllable Structure

So far we have mainly been considering segmental phonology, that is, how to characterize the inventory of individual consonant and vowel segments. (The notion of *segment* is in itself not unproblematic, and we will return to discuss this point later in the book.) Of course, speech consists of more than just a system of sounds; as we noted earlier, we also have to take into account how these sounds structure together to make syllables and words (the phonological *structure*). Most simply, we can characterize syllables in terms of consonant and vowel slots. So, in English, for example, we can have syllables that consist solely of a vowel: *I, owe, ow*, and so on. These we can denote by V, for vowel. Then we have syllables that have an initial consonant followed by a vowel: *tie, go, bough*. These are CV syllables. English can also have VC syllables: *I'd, owes, out*. There are also CVC syllable shapes: *tied, goes*, and *bout*.

But this is not the whole picture. English allows consonant clusters. This means that the initial position in an English syllable may be filled by one C, two Cs, or even three Cs. As examples, we have *team, steam*, and *stream*, or *pay, play*, and *splay*. Further, in the final position of an English syllable we can have a singleton consonant, or two, three, or four consonants. To illustrate this we can consider *tech, Tex, text*, and *texts*, or *sick, six*,

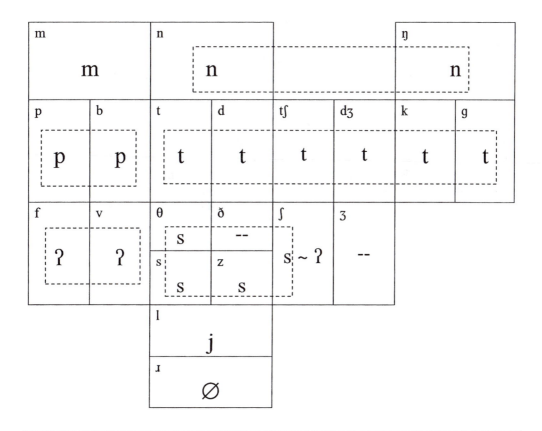

Chart 1.2 Syllable final (English). Target sounds are shown by the symbol at the top left of each box; realizations are shown in the center of each box. ∅ means deletion; -- means no examples recorded. ~ is used between variant realizations. Dotted lines connect identical realizations for different targets.

sixth, and *sixths*. Of course, there are constraints on which consonants can appear in the initial and final position in the syllable, and in specific slots in clusters; not every English consonant can appear in every position (these constraints are called the *phonotactic constraints* of the language, and we return to this topic below). Nevertheless, a handy shorthand to capture English syllable structure is $C^{0-3}VC^{0-4}$.

It should be noted that these structural characteristics of English will not be shared necessarily by other languages, just as the systemic characteristics (i.e., the inventory of vowels and consonants) may well not be. So, Hawaiian, for example, allows only V and CV*, and while Chinese allows V, CV, and CVC, only two consonants are permitted in syllable final position. Some languages allow certain clusters but not necessarily all those found in English. For example, Spanish only allows /s/ plus plosive to occur across a syllable boundary (which technically means they don't count as clusters). So where English has *Spain*, Spanish has *Es.paña* (where the period marks the syllable boundary). There are also languages that have clusters not found in English. Hebrew, for example, has initial /bn-/ clusters, and Georgian has /d͡zl-/ and /t͡ʃrd-/.

So far, we have been treating syllables as if they were flat. By this we mean that we have been treating the initial C slot and the final C slot as being of equal status as the medial V slot (often termed the *syllable nucleus*). However, most phonologists believe that this

---

* Although the V unit may be a short vowel, a long vowel, or a diphthong, and may be symbolized as V(V).

is incorrect; they propose that there is in fact a hierarchical relationship between the syllable elements. Evidence for this comes, for example, from rhyming. When we rhyme two syllables it is both the vowel and final consonant(s) that we need to make the same. For example, *hat* rhymes with *cat* but not with *coat*. On the other hand, when we alliterate, we need only ensure that the initial consonants are the same; the following vowel does not enter into alliteration. So *cat*, *coat*, *keep*, and *cough* all alliterate.

Syllables are generally therefore shown as hierarchical trees, with the vowel nucleus and following consonant (if any) constituting a unit called the *rime* (or *rhyme*), and the initial consonant (if any) being termed the *onset*. The rime itself is deemed to consist of the *nucleus*, and if there is a terminating consonant, this is called the *coda*. We can see examples of syllable trees for the following English words (Figures 1.1 to 1.4, where σ stands for syllable, O for onset, R for rime, N for nucleus, C for coda, and ∅ for empty slot):

goes

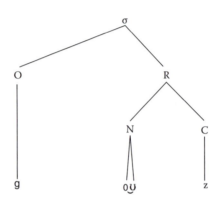

Figure 1.1 Syllable diagram of *goes*.

go

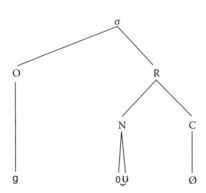

Figure 1.2 Syllable diagram of *go*.

owes

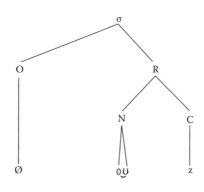

Figure 1.3 Syllable diagram of *owes*.

owe

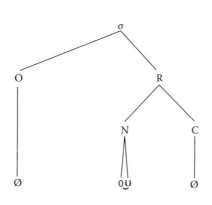

Figure 1.4 Syllable diagram of *owe*.

Clusters can also be shown (Figure 1.5):

sculpts

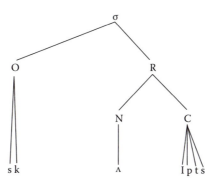

Figure 1.5 Syllable diagram of *sculpts*.

Words of more than one syllable can also be diagrammed, as in Figures 1.6 and 1.7:

undone

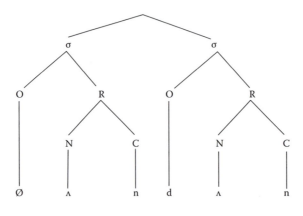

Figure 1.6 Syllable diagram of *undone*.

implying

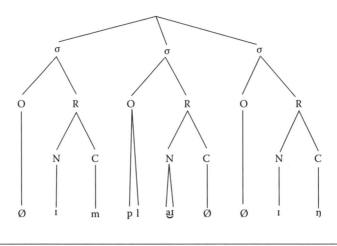

Figure 1.7 Syllable diagram of *implying*.

It is not always clear to speakers of English, however, exactly where syllable boundaries occur. In a word such as *writing* there may be debate as to whether the first syllable ends with /t/, or if that sound is the onset to the second syllable. Some scholars believe the best way around this problem is to count the relevant consonant as being both the coda of syllable one and the onset of syllable two (this has been termed *ambisyllabicity*). We show such a solution in Figure 1.8:

writing

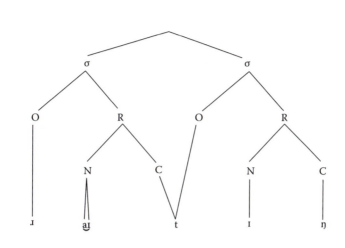

Figure 1.8 Syllable diagram of *writing*.

EXERCISE 1.4

Draw syllable trees for the words listed below. In polysyllables, assign medial consonants to one syllable or the other (i.e., don't use the ambisyllabicity solution). What guidelines can you use to help you decide where syllable boundaries occur?

street
restrict
racetrack
restroom
extract

The syllable diagrams in Exercise 1.4 can also be used to characterize the structural possibilities of clients with phonological disorders. For example, if we chart the syllable structure of the following data (the target accent is General American), we can understand the patterns of realization of word medial target /s/:

Word	Target	Realization
dismiss	/dɪsˈmɪs/	[dɪˈmɪ]
decide	/dəˈsaɪd/	[dəˈɬaɪd]
misapply	/mɪsəˈplaɪ/	[mɪ.əˈplaɪ]
research	/ɹiˈsɝtʃ/	[ɹiˈɬɝt]

Syllable structure diagrams of these words clearly demonstrate that /s/ is deleted when a syllable coda, but realized as [ɬ] when a syllable onset. See whether you can discover the pattern for /ɹ/ realization in Exercise 1.5.

EXERCISE 1.5

Using syllable trees for the following clinical data; see whether you can discover the patterns of usage this client's realizations of /ɹ/. Target accent: British RP (= *received pronunciation*; a nonregional standard).

red	[ɥɛd]
word	[wɜd]
rain	[ɥeɪn]
bark	[bɑk]
mirror	['mɪʊə]
row	[ɥoʊ]
water	['wɒtə]
orange	['ɒʊɪndʒ]
your	[jɔə]
read	[ɥid]
year	[jɪə]
rib	[ɥɪb]
core	[kɔə]
ring	[ɥɪŋ]
pure	[pjʊə]
poor	[pɔ]
therapy	['θɛʊəpi]
robin	['ɥɒbɪn]
shirt	[ʃɜt]
doctor	['dɒktə]
operation	[ɒpə'veɪʃn̩]
hair	[hɛə]
torn	[tɔn]
father	['fɑðə]
rat	[ɥæt]
mister	['mɪstə]

Phonotactics

The *-tactics* part of this term is cognate with *tactile*, and so refers to the study of which sounds can "touch" each other in a language. As we noted earlier, the structural description of the phonology of a language describes syllable shapes and cluster types. The phonotactics gives the detailed constraints about which consonants and vowels can fill the CV slots identified in the structural description. Most commonly such phonotactic constraints are posited for consonant clusters. For example, a full set of phonotactic possibilities for word initial three-consonant clusters in British English could be stated as follows:

$$p \quad + \quad ɹ, l, j$$
$$s \quad + \quad t \quad + \quad ɹ, j$$
$$k \quad + \quad ɹ, l, j, w$$

Such phonotactic layouts allow us to draw some conclusions about structural types. So, for these clusters, we can state that the first element is always /s/, the second is a fortis plosive, and the third is an approximant. (Gimson, 1989, notes that there is one exception: The bird name *smew* /smju/ allows the bilabial nasal instead of a fortis plosive.)

However, phonotactic constraints refer not only to clusters. A fully detailed phonotactic description will note precisely which consonant-vowel combinations occur in the language (and in which syllable structure positions). So, for example, Gimson (1989) tells us that in British English syllable initial /p, t, k/ are followed by all the vowel phonemes of the language, whereas several vowel phonemes do not occur before syllable final /p, t, k/ (i.e., /ʊ/, /ɔɪ/, and /aʊ/ do not occur before /p/, and the centering diphthongs /ɪə/, /ɛə/, and /ʊə/ do not occur before /p/, /t/, or /k/).

A knowledge of these combinations is useful in clinical phonology. When planning assessment and intervention, it is helpful to have some idea of the *functional load* of a sound (i.e., how commonly it occurs, thus contributing to the function of a phoneme, which is to contrast words). We may well need to prioritize assessment and treatment to sounds with relatively high functional loads. Part of the functional load is derived from simple statistics of how frequently a sound occurs in natural speech (see, for example, the tables in Ball and Müller, 2005, pp. 127–128). But partly it is derived from the phonotactic slots a sound can occur in. Take, for example, the sound /v/. It is 12th out of 24 consonants in terms of frequency (British English). Furthermore, it has 2 blank vowel slots following it (out of 20) in CV- position (there are no /vʊ-/ or /vʊə-/ forms), and 8 blank slots preceding it in -VC position (these are /ʊ, ə, ɔ, ɔɪ, aʊ, ɪə, ɛə, ʊə/). Added to this, it occurs in no initial consonant clusters, and just a few final ones. Compare /v/ with /t/: /t/ is the second most frequently occurring consonant; it has no blank vowel slots following it, and only the centering diphthongs are missing before it in final -VC position. Further, /t/ occurs in CC- and CCC- clusters initially (and is followed by many different vowels in most of these), and in -CC, -CCC, and -CCCC clusters finally (and again in many of these instances can be preceded by a large range of vowels). Such knowledge allows us to rank /t/ considerably ahead of /v/ in importance phonologically.

Returning to clusters, tables of cluster-vowel combinations are also useful in drawing up assessment tasks. Some assessments argue that representative cluster types are all that is needed: for two consonant initial clusters, one of the /s/ + plosive type, one of the plosive + approximant type, one of the fricative + approximant type, and so on. However, an examination of the phonotactics shows that /sp-, st-, sk-, sm- sn-, sl-/ have few empty vowel slots following them, whereas most of the other two consonant cluster types have several or many empty vowel slots. It would make sense, therefore, to have examples of most of the /s/ cluster types, and representatives of the other types (choosing those with the fewest empty vowel slots, e.g., /fɹ-/ over /θɹ-/).

CONCLUSION

In this chapter we have set the scene for the description of the development of phonological theory over the last 50 years or so, and the application of these developments to the analysis and remediation of disordered speech. You will need to bear in mind the distinction between phonetics and phonology as you work through the text: Remember that many models of phonology allow a considerable degree of abstraction in their characterization of speech organization, and that this may well have implications for how such models can be applied in the clinic.

FURTHER READING

The classic account of phoneme theory can be found in Daniel Jones (1976), although Jones had worked on phoneme theory much earlier than this publication. Other early texts in linguistics also cover phonemes in some detail, for example, Bloomfield (1933), Gleason (1956), and Hockett (1958). The hierarchical model of the syllable espoused by many phonologists is described in most current textbooks in phonology; see, for example, Carr (1993), Roca (1994), Davenport and Hannahs (1998), and Gussmann (2002). Gimson (1989) and the new edition by Cruttenden (2001) are good sources for information on the phonology of English.

SOURCES

The Spanish data are from Ian Mackenzie (University of Newcastle); the remaining data are from the authors.

REVIEW QUESTIONS AND STUDY TOPICS

Review Questions

1. Briefly describe the difference between *phonetics* and *phonology*.
2. What is *clinical phonology*?
3. Define the *phoneme*, and describe what *minimal pairs* are.
4. Define the *allophone*, and describe what *complementary distribution* and *free variation* are.
5. What problems have been encountered with the terms *deletion*, *substitution*, *distortion*, and *addition* in clinical phonology?
6. What are the components usually posited in a hierarchical model of the syllable? What evidence might we use to support such a model?
7. What is the difference between phonological *system* and *structure*? Explain how a clinical phonologist can use the notion of *phonotactics*.
8. What is the *functional load* of a sound, and how do we calculate it?

Study Topics and Projects

1. Use a good recording of a disordered phonology client from your clinic (or make a new recording of a suitable case with permission from your clinical supervisor), and undertake as detailed a transcription as you can. You will need a recording that contains about 200 words of spontaneous speech (rather than a limited articulation test). Then do a phonemic analysis in terms of the client's own phonology, identifying the client's phonemes and allophones as far as possible. Follow this with a contrastive analysis of the client's speech with the target system using the contrastive analysis charts described in the chapter.

2. Using the data from the previous project, list all the syllable shapes (including consonant clusters) that the client uses. Suggest some ways in which missing syllable shapes might be addressed in therapy.

2

SONORITY THEORY

INTRODUCTION

In this chapter we return to considering the syllable. We have seen how the syllable can be characterized as having a hierarchical structure of onset and rime, with the rime further divided into nucleus and coda. We have also seen how the onset, nucleus, and coda units can be simple or complex. In Chapter 8 we will look at the metrical weight of syllables and the CV skeleton; for our purposes in this chapter, however, we will need to work only with the basic hierarchical structure.

Syllables in different languages obviously will show different arrangements of segments in the differing syllable positions. There are languages where the coda position is always empty, and others where just a very few consonants are allowed into that position. Some languages allow no, or very few, complex onsets and codas; some may have no complex nuclei. Further, the fact that languages differ in their inventories of consonants and vowels is bound to lead to different syllable types. Nevertheless, despite these differences, phonologists have discovered that there are certain similar tendencies in syllable structure. For example, the nucleus is always filled by a vowel, or by a vowel-like segment. Furthermore, it appears that across languages there is also a discernible pattern holding between the onset and the nucleus, and in complex onsets and codas it seems there are preferred strings of consonants.

In this chapter, we are going to explore an account of these patterns, an approach that has often been applied in recent years to explain some of the patterns we find in disordered speech.

SONORITY

Phoneticians have long been able to measure the acoustic and aerodynamic characteristics of individual speech sounds. When this is done, it becomes apparent that different sounds have different average amplitudes, intensity, and amount of airflow. From these, we can derive a measure called *sonority*, which might be thought of as the amount of sound let out during the production of a segment (Roca, 1994, p. 152). Sonority cannot be correlated directly with instrumental measures, because numerical values for intensity and so forth depend not only on the inherent qualities of the sound, but also on the influence of the neighboring sounds, and the overall loudness and so on that the speaker happens to adopt at any one time. Further, some phonologists prefer to equate sonority with an articulatory parameter: the size and openness of the vocal tract during the production of the sound in question. Phonologists' sonority levels are, therefore, an idealized entity.

As each individual sound segment in any given language has a sonority ranking in respect to all the other segments, it is possible to produce a sonority scale of all the consonants and vowels concerned. However, in using sonority to account for the patterns we find in syllables, it becomes more useful to produce a scale of groups of sounds. It should be noted that not all phonologists agree as to how to produce these groupings, and some subsequent analyses may well be affected by the particular groupings established. Vowels are deemed to be the most sonorous group of sounds, but within the vowel group, low vowels are more sonorous than high vowels. Likewise, plosives are considered the least sonorous sounds, but fortis, voiceless plosives are less sonorous than voiced, lenis ones. Here we will show a hybrid listing, where broad groups of sounds may also have subgroupings within them. We list our groups from most to least sonorous:

- Vowels
  - Low vowels
  - High vowels

- Glides
- Liquids
- Nasals
- Fricatives
  - Voiced fricatives
  - Voiceless fricatives

- Plosives
  - Voiced plosives
  - Voiceless plosives

(Affricates are usually not given a separate category in sonority scales, and they may well be better considered phonologically as complex segments occupying two slots in syllable structure.)

This list can be further enhanced by assigning sonority values to the various categories. Following Roca (1994), we assign a value of 1 to the least sonorous group (plosives), 2 to fricatives, 3 to nasals, 4 to liquids, 5 to glides, and 6 to vowels (for the moment we will not number the subcategories). Using this numbering system we may begin to see patterns in syllable onset-rime patterns, and in consonant cluster patterns in onset and coda positions. For example, in English we find many CV- words of the following type: *pat, bat, two, do, cap, gap*, where the onset is 1; somewhat fewer overall of the type *fat, vat, thin, then, sue, zoo, shoe*, where the onset is 2; and it seems fewer still for levels 3 onsets, such as *my* and *nigh*, and again for level 4 onsets, in words such as *late* and *rate*; and the fewest for level 5 onsets, in words such as *wet* and *yet*. In fact, there is cross-linguistic support for the notion that a maximum sonority distance between the onset consonant and the nucleus (level 6) is preferred.

How do the values attached to our sonority scale operate in consonant clusters? Undertake Exercise 2.1, and attempt to work this out.

EXERCISE 2.1

Work out the sonority values for the following onset and coda consonant clusters of English (assume a rhotic accent of English). What pattern do you find?

Onset	Coda
trap	help
brush	task
play	hand
muse	delve
dwell	part
twice	aft
drain	harm
claim	lamp
green	malt
quick	turf

One of the ways we can show sonority values of syllable constituents is through syllable diagrams. These can be of two sorts: First, a bar chart where the height of the bars reflects the sonority values; second, we can adapt traditional syllable tree diagrams by adding a value beneath each segment. Figures 2.1 and 2.2 illustrate these approaches with the English word *draft*, which has both an onset and a coda cluster.

What these diagrams suggest, and what we hope you found from Exercise 2.1, is that there is a sequencing of sonority values in clusters, and that this consists of the lowest sonority value being at the syllable edges (or furthest from the nucleus, if you prefer), with higher values further in. If we recall the tendency in simple onsets to prefer lower sonority values in onsets, then we can construct a *sonority sequencing principle* (SSP) for syllables.

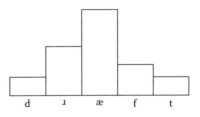

Figure 2.1 Bar chart sonority diagram.

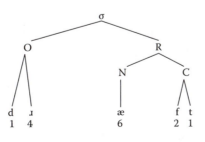

Figure 2.2 Syllable tree sonority diagram.

Roca (1994) proposed the following wording: "The sonority profile of the syllable must slope outwards from the peak," where *peak* means the syllable nucleus. This principle accounts for the consonant cluster patterns we have found and, indeed, for the fact that sonority values for simple onsets and codas will (of course) be lower than the value for the syllable nucleus. A stronger version of the SSP, as proposed by Clements (1990), states that syllables maximally rise in sonority from the onset to the nucleus, and this would account for the preferences in syllable initial shape noted earlier in this section.

Interestingly, Clements (1990) also notes that syllable codas do not share this preference for a sharp change in sonority, and claims that there is a greater preference for codas that fall less sharply. In syllables with an empty coda slot, of course, there is no fall at all in sonority level. One reason that has been hypothesized for the tendency in many languages to have a less sharp fall in sonority at the coda position is to enable the initial segment of the following syllable or word to be lower in sonority than the final segment of the previous syllable or word. In this view, a word like *entice* /ɛn.ˈtaɪs/ would be preferred over one like *excite* /ɛk.ˈsaɪt/ (where /./ represents the syllable boundary).

We will now return to consider some more consonant clusters of English. Undertake Exercise 2.2, and see what impact the results have for the SSP.

EXERCISE 2.2

Work out the sonority values for the following onset and coda consonant clusters of English. What pattern do you find in terms of the SSP?

Onset	Coda
stop	cats
scrape	ox
splash	dogs
scar	width
spin	hides
strike	eighth
spread	helps
squeak	six
sphere	act

The results of this exercise point to one of the problems with the sonority sequencing principle: It does not appear to account for a considerable number of the onset and coda clusters found in English (and indeed in many other languages). The problem is that the clusters show either a dip in sonority rather than a steady rise or fall or, as in the final two examples of Exercise 2.2, a level plateau rather than a rise or fall. Some of these plateau forms may be explicable within sonority theory. Recall that we said each individual vowel and consonant had a sonority level, and that we grouped sounds together for convenience. Ladefoged (1993) notes that the labiodental fricatives have a somewhat higher sonority level than the alveolar in English, and so the word *sphere* does in fact demonstrate a slight rise from the /s/ to the /f/. The situation is not so clear for words like *act* and *apt*. The voiceless plosives are shown by Ladefoged as being identical in sonority terms. However, at least one definition of sonority notes that degree of stricture relates closely to sonority values; for this reason, low vowels (with an open mouth position) are more sonorous than high vowels. If we examine the release stage of plosives, it is possible to claim that velar plosives have less sonority than alveolar, and alveolar less than bilabial. Under this view, *apt* shows a fall in sonority through the coda cluster; however, *act* now shows a rise. We turn next to consider how to account for the exceptions to the SSP that we have encountered.

EXCEPTIONS TO THE SONORITY SEQUENCING PRINCIPLE

There are several ways in which we can tackle the violations we've noted of the SSP. First, we can consider what we term a *metatheoretical* approach. Here, we simply note that the SSP is merely a tendency, and different languages may well provide counterexamples to it. This approach essentially allows us to ignore the fact that English /sp-, st-, sk-/ clusters, for example, do not adhere to the SSP. Interestingly, many phonologists have not been happy to support this suggestion, and partly, this may be due to the fact that some of them feel that sonority is a built-in part of our mental phonology, and as such, exceptions should not be possible.

A second approach we might term a *metaphonological* account. This explanation requires us to reconsider the sonority scale. As we noted, many different sonority scales have been proposed over the years, and in some of these proposals all obstruents are grouped together in the lowest sonority category (see, for example, Clements 1990). If this is done, the dip in sonority is /s/ + stop clusters initially, and stop + /s/ clusters finally disappears. Admittedly, the sonority patterns are now in plateau rather than a rise (initially) or fall (finally), but that only requires the SSP to be modified to admit both level and sloping sonority profiles. The problem with a solution of this kind is that the collapse of the separate categories of stops and fricatives will obscure some generalizations that had been possible under the separate classification; for example, that in English coda clusters of fricative + stop (e.g., *past*, *left*, *breathed*) did meet the SSP. Also, if we can collapse all obstruents into one category, what would stop us from collapsing all sonorants into another? If we only have two sonority categories, then the whole concept tells us very little about preferred patterns of syllable structure.

Third, there is a *phonetic* explanation. Phoneticians have found it difficult to devise a set of measures that adequately account for the differences in sonority posited by phonologists. Nevertheless, phonetics has shown that acoustic values of sounds uttered in one context may alter in another. So, as we can measure intensity, duration, and frequency aspects of an /s/ in a word like *sop*, and as we can measure these aspects in the sound /t/ as in *top*, so we can discover whether any of these alter when these sounds appear in the word *stop*.* We do know that /t/ in *stop* differs in several ways from the /t/ in *top*. For example, in *top* /t/ is aspirated [tʰ], and in *stop* it is unaspirated [t˭]. It is at least arguable that this difference results in the /t/ in *stop* being somewhat more sonorous than the /t/ in *top*. It may well be the case that the /s/ in *stop* is somewhat less sonorous than the /s/ in *sop*. If this is the case, then these /s/ + stop clusters may well have at the least equal sonority values, even if they don't display the rise predicted by the SSP. A phonetic account, therefore, claims that the precise sonority value of any sound is dependent upon the context of that sound, and that apparent breaches of the SSP can be explained by the movement up and down

---

* Ladefoged (1993) discusses the notion of prominence as a measure that accounts for context in working out comparative values of loudness, rather than sonority. He acknowledges, however, that we do not have an agreed way of measuring prominence.

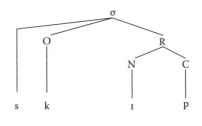

Figure 2.3 Syllable tree for adjunct /s/ clusters.

the sonority scale of the sound sequences in question. The problem with this account is that, as we have yet to devise a universally agreed set of phonetic parameters that define sonority, we are unable to prove or disprove that such context-bound sonority adjustments actually do occur.

Finally, we can consider a *phonological* account of these /s/ clusters. As noted by Gierut (1999), several researchers have suggested that these /s/ + stop onset combinations (and presumably also the stop + /s/ coda combinations) are not, in fact, true clusters, but what have been termed *adjuncts* or *appendices*. Adapting one of Gierut's diagrams, we can see how a word such as *skip* would be syllabified under this approach in Figure 2.3.

Gussmann (2002) describes both *extrasyllabic* segments and *appendices*, but the distinction between these units need not detain us here. It is certainly the case, however, that if we remove from the basic syllable all those segments that would cause a breach in the SSP (including dips and plateaus), then such breaches are avoided. But what evidence to support the notion of adjunct segments has been proposed? Clements (1990) outlines supporting examples from a wide range of languages. Here we will consider just a few examples. First, patterns of normal acquisition of two consonant onset clusters in English suggest that children often go through a stage where the clusters are broken up by the addition of a vowel. In most clusters this is done through the insertion of an epenthetic schwa between the first and second consonant, for example, *blue* [bə'lu], *clean* [kə'lin]. In the /s/ + stop clusters, however, the vowel may instead be added before the first consonant, to create a syllable boundary within the target cluster: *stop* [əs.'tɑp], *skip* [əs.'kɪp]. (In fact, this ties in with some theorists' views that the adjunct /s/ in these clusters might be considered as the coda of a nucleus-free preceding syllable.) Harris (1994) also proffers some evidence from the occurrence of /-ju/ combinations in most varieties of English. These do not occur following onset clusters that meet the SSP, so */pɹju-/, */klju/, but they do after /s/ + stop clusters in just those cases where you can find them after stops, for example, /pju/ ~ /spju/ (*pew* ~ *spew*). This suggests, then, that the initial /s/ is not part of a cluster, as all other cluster types ban the use of /-ju/.

While the use of the adjunct or appendix does get around the problem with the SSP, it can be criticized as an abstract device. In other words, the removal of /s/ from the normal syllable structure of onset-rime in the case of /s/ + stop initial clusters (and similar changes with final clusters that break the SSP) might be thought of as self-justifying: Syllable onsets have to obey the SSP; /s/ + stop does not obey the SSP; therefore, the /s/ cannot be in the syllable. Clearly, if the SSP is only a tendency, then adjunct-based proposals could be thought of as nonsolutions to a nonproblem. If sonority is hardwired into our mental language capacity, then it is difficult to argue that it is only a tendency; we return later in the chapter to a discussion of the neurolinguistic justification (or otherwise) of sonority.

EXERCISE 2.3

Identify the adjunct segments in the following English words, assuming a model of the syllable where SSP-breaking segments are extrasyllabic (including dips and plateaux).

spray
texts
strong
lacked
scrape
sculpts
sixths
split

We next turn our attention to data from normal and disordered phonological acquisition to find support for the notion of sonority, the SSP, and to the differing solutions to the problem of exceptions to the SSP.

SONORITY AND CLINICAL PHONOLOGY

There have been numerous studies of disordered speech that have appealed to the notion of sonority. In some of these sonority has been used to account for the results, in others the data have been used to test some aspect of the SSP (for example), and yet others have examined the claim that sonority is neurologically hardwired. Also, many of the studies have dealt with phonological development and disorder in children; however, there are some that have been concerned with adult acquired disorders. We only have space to look at some of these, but other studies are listed in the further reading section at the end of the chapter.

Child Speech

Ohala (1999) provides an interesting example of a study of normal phonological development, in this case concentrating on consonant clusters. The aim of the investigation was to see whether normal cluster development met Clements's (1990) claim that syllables show a marked rise in sonority from onset to nucleus, but that syllables end with a minimal (or no) decline in sonority. Ohala's experiments involved children between 1;1 (one year, one month) and 3;2 producing nonwords designed with initial or final consonant clusters. One set were all legal clusters of English, whereas a second set had non-English clusters, but ones that followed the predictions of the SSP. As children at this age regularly reduce clusters to a single consonant, Ohala wished to see whether the consonant predicted by the SSP would indeed be the one that was used. For example, an onset cluster of /pl-/ should reduce to /p/, while a coda cluster of /-lp/ should reduce to /l/. Ohala's results demonstrated that these children did indeed normally follow the SSP in their cluster reductions of nonsense syllables, and that they treated onset and coda clusters differently (i.e., according to the SSP). The results were strongest for the English-like clusters, and the non-English types were often resyllabified into two syllables.

Gierut (1999) also investigated cluster production, but in this case only two member onset clusters were examined, and the subjects were children with delayed phonological acquisition. Gierut was particularly interested in any potential differences between what she terms true clusters (i.e., English onset clusters not starting with /s/) and adjunct sequences (i.e., /sp-/, /st-/, and /sk-/). The theoretical focus of the study was the relative markedness* of onset clusters. Clements (1990) discusses markedness in the context of consonant clusters, and Gierut points out that even if the two consonants in the cluster follow the SSP, the greater the sonority difference between them, the less marked the cluster is. Under this assumption, a cluster like /pl-/ is less marked than a cluster like /fl-/. She notes that a /bl-/ cluster is intermediate between /pl-/ and /fl-/ (see above for the distinction between voiced and voiceless plosives and fricatives in the sonority hierarchy). Gierut found that with her subjects who were being taught clusters, the ability to produce marked clusters implied they could also produce unmarked ones, but that acquiring unmarked clusters did not imply they could produce marked ones. Gierut was especially interested in whether the adjunct sequences of English would behave similarly to the marked or unmarked clusters. The second experiment reported in this paper demonstrated that /sp-/, /st-/, and /sk-/ actually behave like unmarked clusters even though they violate the SSP. This can, of course, be taken as further evidence that they are not in fact true clusters and so, in that respect, do not in fact violate the SSP.

Many studies of clusters in acquisition and disordered speech seem to encounter only cluster reduction to one of the target consonants (or, of course, some kind of cluster production). However, the reduction of a cluster to a nontarget consonant is quite common in both normal and delayed/disordered phonological acquisition. In Exercise 2.4 we will examine how this might interact with sonority.

EXERCISE 2.4

Examine the following target clusters and their realization by a child presenting with disordered phonology. How does the realization of each cluster compare to the target in terms of the sonority profile? What phonetic reasons can you posit for the realizations used by this child?

Item	Target	Realization
swim	/swɪm/	[fɪm]
snail	/sneɪl/	[n̥eɪl]
slow	/sloʊ/	[ɬoʊ]
smile	/smaɪl/	[m̥aɪl]
slight	/slaɪt/	[ɬaɪt]
sweet	/swit/	[fit]
snow	/snoʊ/	[n̥oʊ]
smoke	/smoʊk/	[m̥oʊk]

Wyllie-Smith, McLeod, and Ball (2006) did, in fact, have examples of reduction to nontarget consonant in their data, some of which could be explained phonetically in the same way as the data in Exercise 2.4. The results of the experiments reported in this study (one on children with typical phonological acquisition, and one on subjects with disordered phonology) showed that whereas the cluster reductions to one

---

* Marked segments or segment sequences are those deemed to be less natural than unmarked ones. See Chapter 3.

target consonant generally followed the SSP (with a notable exception for /s/ + stop clusters in the typically developing children), the reductions to nontarget consonants did not. The authors conclude that although sonority is a valuable concept in clinical phonology, it may not account for all patterns of cluster reduction evident in children's speech.

Adult Speech

Romani and Calabrese (1998) applied the insights from sonority theory to account for the patterns of syllabification they found in an Italian male in his early 40s, who presented with aphasia typical of the Broca's type. The authors tape-recorded a large amount of data from this subject, and analyzed his errors in terms of the SSP. They looked not only at clusters, but at simple onsets and codas, and at the vocalic nucleus as well. In most cases, nontarget realizations by the client were in the direction of making syllables fit better into the predictions of the SSP. For example, with vowels the client is most accurate with the most sonorous /a/ vowel, as would be predicted by the SSP; with complex onsets the client makes no errors with /s/ + obstruent clusters and this, again, might be taken as evidence for their special status. There are some exceptions to the SSP in these data; for example, the client usually replaces /rj-/ clusters with singleton /j-/, rather than /r/, as would be predicted by the SSP.

The question raised by work of this kind with neurologically impaired speakers is that of the status of sonority. Clements (1990), for example, claims that sonority is not a surface phonological phenomenon, but holds at deeper levels of representation (though he is not specific as to whether he meant theoretical depth or psycho-/neurolinguistic depth). Other researchers have claimed that sonority is indeed hardwired neurologically, for example, Sussman (1984), supported by Christman (1992a, 1992b) in her work on jargon aphasia. This claim is based on the fact that even after severe injury to specific parts of the brain, the SSP is still operational as it shapes the phonological aspects of the restricted output of the client. Code and Ball (1994) were interested in this aspect in their study of nonlexical speech automatisms in English and German aphasic speakers. The vast majority of the speech automatisms demonstrated preferences for the syllable shapes predicted by the SSP, and interestingly, what few clusters did occur followed the SSP in that no /s/ + stop clusters for English or /ʃ/ + stop clusters for German were used.

These results might also suggest that sonority survives damage to the language production areas of the left hemisphere because it is hardwired throughout that hemisphere. However, as Code and Ball (1994) point out, studies of left hemispherectomy patients show that in their surviving speech, phonotactic constraints (such as those derived from the SSP) are not violated either. This must mean either that sonority is hardwired diffusely across both hemispheres (or possibly subcortically) or that sonority is in fact not a hardwired component of the language system in the brain.

Support for the latter view comes from Ohala (1990), who suggests that sonority is not an integral part of phonological processing, but only an artifact of speech production. Such an argument implies that what we analyze as sonority has no mental reality, but is an inevitable by-product of neurophysiological and mechanico-inertial constraints. To this we might wish to add that these constraints are bolstered by the perceptual aspects of sonority. We assume that syllables with sharply differentiated onsets and nuclei (in sonority terms) may well be more salient perceptually, so there would be little reason for speakers to try and overcome the speech production constraints. The fact that it is possible to overcome them, however, may well explain some of the exceptions to the SSP that we have been considering—a feature more difficult to account for if we assume sonority is hardwired. Indeed, it may well be that the /s/ + stop clusters that have been the focus of analysis problems for sonority theory could be explained more easily via Ohala's (1990) view than through appeals to devices such as adjunct segments.

FURTHER READING

Many textbooks on phonology discuss sonority. In addition to Clements (1990), Steriade (1982) and Giegerich (1992) supply important theoretical discussion. Other references within these sources to earlier discussion of sonority may also be useful.

Clinical studies that have used sonority (other than those referred to in the chapter) include Baker (2000), Chin (1996), Gierut (1998), Gierut and Champion (2001), and Goozee, Purcell, and Baker (2001) (all dealing with child data); Yavaş (2000), Yavaş and Core (2001), and Yavaş and Gogate (1999) (on phonemic awareness); and Béland et al. (1990), Buckingham (1986, 1990), and Christman (1994), who discuss aphasia. See also Mehmet Yavaş's guest-edited issue of the *Journal of Multilingual Communication Disorders* (4: 3), on the acquisition of s clusters.

REVIEW QUESTIONS AND STUDY TOPICS

Review Questions

1. Give two ways in which *sonority* has been defined.
2. Which sound type is the least sonorous, and which the most sonorous?
3. What does the sonority sequencing principle predict for syllable shapes?
4. How have phonologists attempted to get around breaches of the SSP in certain cluster types?
5. What evidence is there from normal and clinical phonology to support the notion that /s/ + stop clusters differ from "true" clusters?
6. Describe some of the findings relating to sonority in studies of child phonology.
7. Describe some of the findings relating to sonority in studies of adult acquired disorders.
8. Describe some of the arguments that have been used both for and against the idea that sonority is hardwired into the brain.

Study Topics and Projects

1. Review some of the sonority studies listed in the "Further Reading" section, plus any others you can find. Then write a paper on the application of sonority theory to clinical speech data.
2. Review the target consonant cluster usage of as many speech clients from your clinic as you can. Note their realizations of the clusters, and see whether these follow the SSP. Attempt an explanation of your findings in terms of the sonority hierarchy and the SSP.

3
DISTINCTIVE FEATURES

INTRODUCTION

The analysis of speech into phonemes does provide some important insights into phonological organization, but it became clear that certain characteristics of phonologies are not accounted for. Taking an example from English, we can look at what happens when we add regular plural endings to nouns. Orthographically, regular plural is marked by adding an *s*, but in phonological terms this *s* represents two different pronunciations. If *s* is added to a noun that ends with a voiceless consonant, it is pronounced /s/; if it is added to a noun that ends in a voiced consonant or a vowel, it is pronounced /z/. (If the noun ends in /s, z, tʃ, dʒ/, an ending of /ɪz/ is added, but this does not affect our argument.) A phonemic approach to phonology only allows us to note the fact that two different phonemes are employed, and to note the context of their occurrence. There is nothing inherent in the theory that allows any explanation of the choice. There is no overt metric that allows us to record that the two phonemes concerned are phonetically similar, and therefore, there's nothing to say that a choice between /s/ and /z/ is any more likely than one between /s/ and /b/.

However, if we allow phonological units smaller than the phoneme, then some of these problems can be overcome. Let us suppose that phonemes consist of a set of phonological features, and that one of these features is [±voice] (by which we mean a feature that can be [+voice], i.e., voiced, or [−voice], i.e., voiceless). Now, when we examine the regular plural formation process in English, we see that the choice of /s/ or /z/ is directly related to the value of the [voice] feature. When a word ends in a sound that has the [+voice] value of the feature, the choice is /z/, which also has the [+voice] value; when a word ends in a consonant that has the [−voice] value, then plural is formed with /s/ that also has the [−voice] value. This approach not only shows the reason behind the choice of plural form, but also shows the close relationship between /s/ and /z/, as all their phonological features are identical apart from [voice].

FEATURE SYSTEMS

The development of phonological feature systems is usually credited to Trubetzkoy and the Prague School of Linguistics in the 1930s, especially Trubetzkoy (1939/1969).

Trubetzkoy was interested in characterizing those phonetic distinctions in language that were used to contrast different sound units. However, he did not just wish to draw up a list of such features, he wanted to see how the features worked within specific languages. For example, in some languages sounds are in *bilateral* oppositions; for example, /k/ and /g/ in English are in just such an opposition, as they are oral velar stops (differing by one feature), and no other English sounds are oral velar stops. In languages such as Hindi, /k/ and /g/ are in *multilateral* opposition, as there are other oral velar stops (/kʰ/ and /gʱ/). Trubetzkoy also describes *proportional* and *isolated* oppositions. For example, English has proportional oppositions between its fortis and lenis stops; there are three sets: /p ~ b/, /t ~ d/, /k ~ g/. On the other hand, the /l ~ ɹ/ distinction is isolated, as there are no other pairs of sounds that share sets of the features of these two.

Trubetzkoy (1939) was also interested in classes of features in terms of the types and content of the feature values. For example, features can have a single value (the content of the feature is either present or absent) or two values (a plus value has one realization, a minus value has a different one) or be multivalued (there can be a range of realizations along a cline). Trubetzkoy termed these *privative, equipollent*, and *gradual*, respectively, and currently the terms *unary, binary*, and *multivalued* are also used.

An example of a privative opposition is the distinction between nasal and nonnasal sounds. Nasal consonants and vowels have the nasal feature; other sounds do not.* The equipollent, or binary, distinction would seem to be the preferred way of characterizing the contrast between consonant places of articulation. In other words, a place such as velar is not defined as being simply the lack of the place labial, or alveolar. The various places are discrete articulator locations, but are equivalent among themselves. Finally, vowel height or anteriority seems a good candidate for gradual oppositions of multivalued features. This is because the tongue positions are not discrete as with consonant place, but are situated along a continuum.

Interestingly, although Trubetzkoy proposed these three categories of features, researchers who developed phonological distinctive features from the 1950s onward usually restricted themselves to using just one or, at most, two types. Arguments from the need for theoretical simplicity have been used to explain this. So, Jakobson, Fant, and Halle (1952) and Chomsky and Halle (1968) restricted themselves to binary equipollent features (though some of these do seem to be privative; see below). Ladefoged (1971) drew up a mixed system of binary and multivalued features. More recent work in feature theory, described in Chapter 5, uses a mix of binary and unary features, while proponents of dependency phonology, government phonology (see Chapter 13), and related theories use only unary, privative features. For the remainder of this chapter we will be examining the SPE feature system described by Chomsky and Halle (1968).

SPE DISTINCTIVE FEATURES

We will illustrate the concept of *distinctive features* through the set of features proposed by Noam Chomsky and Morris Halle in their book *The Sound Pattern of English* (SPE) (1968). We make the point that these features are *phonological* (not phonetic), and that is why they were termed *distinctive*. To illustrate this we can consider the features proposed to describe tongue height in vowels. Two features only are used: [±high] and

---

* As we will see below, Chomsky and Halle (1968) class [nasal] as an equipollent binary feature by giving an articulatory configuration to both the plus value (velum lowered) and the minus value (velum raised).

[±low]. As this feature system uses only binary values for all the features (that is, the plus value and the minus value), there are three possible tongue heights captured: [+high, –low], [–high, –low], and [–high, +low] ([+high, +low] is ruled out as physiologically impossible). This compares to traditional phonetic labels used to describe the vowel space where we usually get four degrees of tongue height (close, half-close, half-open, open), together with a large number of possible modifications to these (e.g., raised above half-close, lowered below fully close, between half-close and close, etc.).

Why do the phonological, distinctive features provide us with fewer vowel height categories than traditional labels? The reason provided is that languages do not contrast phonologically vowels at more than three degrees of height (if you like, they don't have more than three vowel phonemes that are distinguished solely by height). We can look at English for an example. In the front of the vowel system we have four vowels: /i, ɪ, ɛ, æ/.* Straight away it looks as if we have a counterexample. However, the vowel /ɪ/ is notably retracted from the front compared to the other three, and is notably laxer. Therefore, a feature to do with tenseness/laxness would help distinguish /ɪ/ from /i/; height, then, can be retained to distinguish just /i, ɛ, æ/.†

The SPE distinctive features had the following characteristics:

- They were all binary and equipollent.
- They were all phonological.‡
- The aim was for them to be linguistically universal.
- They could be used to set up natural classes of sounds.
- They were based primarily on articulatory criteria, although some acoustic information was also provided.

The names of the various features, their definitions, and examples of their use are given in the following paragraphs. You should study the definitions closely before attempting the exercises.

Chomsky and Halle (1968) divided their binary feature system into four groupings: major class features, cavity features, manner of articulation features, and source features. (A fifth grouping of prosodic features is ignored, partly because they were not fully worked out in SPE, and partly because phonologists no longer treat prosodic phenomena as being features of particular segments, as explained in Chapters 7 and 8.)

In their original formulation, Chomsky and Halle proposed three binary major class features: [±sonorant], [±vocalic], and [±consonantal]. Full definitions of these are available in Chomsky and Halle (1968), but we can note here that obstruents (plosives, fricatives, and affricates) are [–sonorant], whereas liquids, glides, nasals, and vowels are [+sonorant]. The plus value of [vocalic] encompasses vowels and voiced liquids. Other sounds are [–vocalic]. Finally, [+consonantal] sounds include liquids, nasals, and obstruents, whereas vowels and glides are [–consonantal]. In their final chapter, the authors suggest that the vocalic feature might profitably be replaced by [±syllabic]. This feature would allow syllabic nasals and liquids to be distinguished from nonsyllabic

---

* We treat /eɪ/ as a diphthong, and so it does not fall into this group of front monophthongs.
† There are some languages (such as Dutch) where it seems as if there are four distinctive degrees of vowel height with no other features that can be appealed to. Therefore, this supposition of the SPE feature system may well not be appropriate.
‡ By this we mean that feature matrices are designed to capture phonological contrasts between phonemes, not to describe all the fine phonetic detail associated with a segment.

ones. We show this later formulation in Table 3.1. In this and the following chapter, we will assume this formulation for major class features.

SPE's cavity features are mainly to do with what would traditionally be termed place of articulation. The first two of these are [±coronal] and [±anterior]. Coronal sounds are those made with the tip and blade of the tongue, thus dental, alveolar, postalveolar (or palato-alveolar), and retroflex (including r-colored vowels); other places of articulation are [–coronal]. Anterior sounds are labials, dentals, and alveolars, all others are [–anterior]. Chomsky and Halle (1968) note that the next three cavity features relate to the position of the tongue body (thus prefiguring developments in feature hierarchies, described in Chapter 5). The three features are [±high], [±low], and [±back]. When used with vowels, they can characterize a wide range of values, as in Table 3.2.

The features can also be applied to consonants. High consonants are postalveolars, palatals, and velars; the remainder are [–high]. Low consonants are pharyngeals and glottals; the remainder are [–low]. Finally, back consonants are velars, uvulars, and pharyngeals (but not glottals), and labial-velars (such as [w]). Other consonants are [–back]. In this system, too, secondary articulations are marked by the use of one or more of these features. Palatalized consonants become [+high], velarized ones become [+back], and pharyngealized ones become [+low]. While distinctive features in this approach are claimed to be equipollent (see above), these three features do seem to be better characterized as privative in that, for example, [–high] is simply not high, rather than a specific other tongue position. Table 3.3 shows some of the consonant places with these three features, and the features of anteriority and coronality described earlier.

The feature [±round] is used to denote lip-rounding. Lip-rounded vowels, of course, are [+round], as are labial-velar and labial-palatal glides, and labialized consonants. Others are [–round]. It should be noted that [±round] is not the same as a labial feature, and bilabial and labiodental sounds are normally [–round], unless they have secondary lip-rounding. SPE does not have a labial feature, though one was introduced into later versions of distinctive features (see Chapter 5).

Table 3.1 SPE Major Class Features

	Sonorant	Syllabic	Consonantal
Vowels	+	+	–
Syllabic liquids	+	+	+
Syllabic nasals	+	+	+
Nonsyllabic liquids	+	–	+
Nonsyllabic nasals	+	–	+
Glides	+	–	–
Obstruents	–	–	+

Table 3.2 SPE [±High], [±Low], and [±Back] Features

	i	e	a	ɑ	o	u
High	+	–	–	–	–	+
Low	–	–	+	+	–	–
Back	–	–	–	+	+	+

Table 3.3 SPE Place Features Compared to Traditional Labels

	Labial	Alveolar	Postalveolar	Palatal	Velar	Uvular	Pharyngeal
Anterior	+	+	–	–	–	–	–
Coronal	–	+	+	–	–	–	–
High	–	–	+	+	+	–	–
Low	–	–	–	–	–	–	+
Back	–	–	–	–	+	+	+

The next cavity feature listed in SPE is [±distributed]. Distributed sounds are those with tongue blade articulation across a fairly long constriction (such as postalveolar fricatives), whereas [–distributed] sounds are produced with tongue tip articulation (for example, alveolars and retroflex sounds). For English, this distinction allows the separation of the dental fricatives from the alveolar ones, although the feature [±strident] can also do this (see below), and the distributed feature has often been ignored in descriptions of English. [±covered] is a feature that refers to the narrowing of the pharynx used in the production of some sounds in certain languages of West Africa. It appears that one of the main phonetic effects is a movement forward of the tongue root; for this reason, the feature soon came to be called [advanced tongue root], or [ATR] for short. [ATR] has been used to describe some of the tense-lax vowel differences in English (e.g., /i/~/ɪ/, /u/~/ʊ/) by some phonologists, though see the feature [tense] discussed below.

The final two features in this grouping are [±nasal] and [±lateral]. As the names suggest, nasal consonants, and nasalized consonants and vowels are [+nasal], and lateral approximants and fricatives (and indeed affricates) are [+lateral].

The first feature listed in the manner of articulation section by Chomsky and Halle (1968) is [±continuant]. Noncontinuant sounds are plosives, nasals (because the definition of continuancy refers to airflow through the oral cavity), affricates, and nonpulmonic stops such as clicks, ejectives, and implosives. All other sounds are [+continuant].* The authors then turn their attention to release features, in particular the difference between instantaneous release in plosives and delayed release in affricates. To capture this difference, SPE has the feature [±delayed release], normally abbreviated to [±del rel]. At this point, Chomsky and Halle describe potential suction and pressure features needed to describe implosives, clicks, and ejectives, but do not fully characterize a set of binary features. The final feature in this category is [±tense]. For vowels, this captures the difference between tense and lax vowel pairs such as English /i/~/ɪ/ and /u/~/ʊ/. For consonants, fortis (usually voiceless) sounds are [+tense], and lenis (usually voiced) sounds are [–tense]. This distinction is, of course, also carried by the voicing contrast (discussed shortly), and the tense feature was eventually restricted to vowels. The two features [suction] and [ejection] are needed to describe clicks and implosives ([+suction]) and ejectives ([+ejection]).

Table 3.4 shows how a range of English sounds can be characterized according to manner of articulation features.

The final category we will describe is source features. The main feature of interest is [±voice]. As we might expect, voiced sounds are [+voice] and voiceless ones are

---

* Chomsky and Halle (1968, p. 318) note there is some debate concerning liquids. They feel trilled-r is [+continuant], but tapped/flapped-r probably is not. Lateral approximants are normally thought of as [+continuant], but in some language varieties may behave as if they are [–continuant].

Table 3.4 SPE Manner Features

	t	ʃ	tʃ	d	ʒ	dʒ
Continuant	–	+	–	–	+	–
Del rel	–	–	+	–	–	+
Tense	+	+	+	–	–	–

[–voice]. However, Chomsky and Halle (1968) point out that there is a relation between voicing and stop release, in that both aspirated and unaspirated fortis plosives can be made, and in some languages (such as Hindi) this distinction is contrastive. If a language requires the distinction to be made, the aspirated stops will be shown using the feature values [–voice, +tense], while unaspirated fortis stops will be [–voice, –tense]. A [±heightened subglottal pressure] feature is also discussed, needed to characterize certain release types occurring with aspiration, especially the voiced aspirated stops found in languages such as Hindi, where the stops are [–tense], but [+heightened subglottal pressure].

The final source feature is [±strident]. It is listed here, as the noisiness of the airflow (which is the defining characteristic of the plus value of this feature) is deemed to be part of the sound source. In later descriptions, the feature is usually classed with other manner features. For English, this feature is most commonly employed to distinguish the dental from the alveolar fricatives, and to provide a natural class of /f, v, s, z, ʃ, ʒ/. So, whereas the feature [±distributed] could also contrast the dental and alveolar fricatives, it would set up the natural classes of /f, v, s, z/ as opposed to /θ, ð, ʃ, ʒ/. Interestingly, from the phonetic point of view, the traditional label *sibilant*, if used as a binary feature, would have established two classes of sibilants /s, z, ʃ, ʒ/ and nonsibilants /f, v, θ, ð/. In clinical phonology, it is arguable that the two classes established by the sibilance distinction make more sense than either of the class groupings established through the use of [distributed] and [strident]. The reason for this is that fricative simplifications in normally developing and disordered child speech often result in postalveolar fricatives being realized as alveolars, and dental fricatives being realized as labiodentals. The term *stridency deletion* encountered in some clinical phonological literature (e.g., Hodson & Paden, 1991) utilizes a feature that is ill-suited to capture either the phonetic characteristics or the clinical characteristics of the front fricatives in English.

EXERCISE 3.1

Draw up distinctive feature matrices for the systems and part systems of the following languages:

a. Hindi

Part of the consonant system

/p, t̪, ʈ, k, pʰ, t̪ʰ, tʰ, kʰ, b, d̪, ɖ, g, bʱ, d̪ʱ, ɖʱ, gʱ/

b. Turkish

Part of the vowel system (all considered tense here)

/i, y, u, ɯ, e, ø, o/

c. **Russian**
Part of the fricative system

/f, fʲ, v, vʲ, s, sʲ, z, zʲ, ʃ, ʒ, x, xʲ/ (assume /xʲ/ is [ç])

DISTINCTIVE FEATURES AND CLINICAL DATA

Distinctive features have also been used in the analysis of disordered speech. Indeed, for a time it was thought that counting features might tell us something about the severity of a specific inaccurate realization. It has also been suggested that in therapy we should train features rather than phonemes. Let us see how these points might be exemplified. If a child realizes target /p/ as [b], /t/ as [d], /k/ as [g], /f/ as [v], /θ/ as [ð], /s/ as [z], /ʃ/ as [ʒ], and /tʃ/ as [dʒ], then we would have to say that there are eight phoneme errors. (In fact, we could argue that there are 16 errors, as the child's [b] sound is now inaccurate phonologically as it contains both target /p/ and /b/, and so on.) A distinctive feature approach will tell us that there are not eight errors, but just one: All [−voice] consonants are realized as [+voice].

So, counting incorrect features tells us that this case is a one-feature error. The fronting of target velars to alveolars (/k, g, ŋ/ to [t, d, n]) comes out as a four-feature error; realizing target fricatives as plosives involves at least two errors, and fronting postalveolar fricatives to alveolar (/ʃ, ʒ/ to [s, z]) also involves two features. Counting can be less than insightful, however. Taking the last example, distinctive feature counting gives us two errors for the change postalveolar to alveolar (a common childhood speech error), but also two errors for a change alveolar to postalveolar (much less common). Further, a commonly occurring speech problem in English, the realization of target /ɹ/ as [w], involves at least five changes,[*] and this high number seems at odds with the frequency of the change and the phonetic similarity of the sounds.

Problems also arise if we try to apply distinctive features to therapy. A feature such as [voice] is relatively noncontroversial. However, other features are less obviously useful to intervention. For example, the feature [strident] divides the fricatives and affricates into two groups in a phonetically counterintuitive way (but one that is useful for the needs of a strictly binary approach to phonological description), and so may well not be useful in working with clients with fricative problems. Further, if a client experiences problems producing the central vowels /ə, ʌ/, but not the front or back vowels, the SPE distinctive feature system would characterize this as a problem with the feature value [+back]. This is because there is only [±back] to characterize the vowel anteriority parameter. Central vowels in English are [+back], and are distinguished from other back vowels by being unrounded (so, [−round]). Trying to use this for therapy would result in training back vowels, but as we've noted already, these are not disordered in this instance. Finally, we have to remember that the features are not phonetic, and the labels have emerged from a particular theoretical viewpoint rather than being designed for remediation in the clinic.

To experience some of the insights and the pitfalls of this approach, attempt Exercise 3.2.

---

[*] Under some approaches this number increases to seven; we discuss in Chapter 4 how it is possible to set aside some features that cannot apply to particular segments.

EXERCISE 3.2

Reexamine the clinical data from Exercise 1.3. Draw up a list of distinctive features (and their positive and negative values) used by the client for this set of consonants. Draw up a list of distinctive feature values of the target set not used correctly by the client. What problems do you encounter in making this analysis?

MARKEDNESS

Earlier we noted that when we count up features changes, we cannot distinguish between likely and unlikely ones. For example, the change from [−strident] to [+strident] in anterior fricatives (giving /θ, ð/ to [s, z]) is often reported in the phonological acquisition and disorder literature, whereas the opposite ([+strident] to [−strident]) is much less frequent.* Nevertheless, the use of binary distinctive features does not allow us any means of showing this difference. To deal with this problem, Chomsky and Halle (1968) reintroduced the notion of *markedness* that had been developed by Trubetzkoy (1939).

Markedness theory derives from the notion that in phonology certain aspects are more common, or natural, than others. These aspects are deemed to be *unmarked* (or unremarkable). Aspects that are not unmarked are termed *marked*. So far we have used the neutral expression *aspects*, but what exactly could be marked and unmarked? In terms of distinctive features, markedness theory dealt with combinations of features, and we will examine here how markedness was described in SPE. For example, some combinations are deemed to be physiologically impossible, and so marked. Among these absolute prohibitions (Roca, 1994) are vowel feature combinations such as [+high, +low], as the tongue cannot be simultaneously above and below the mid-part of the vowel area. Interestingly, as Roca (1994) notes, it has also been claimed that a combination of [−coronal, + lateral] is impossible. This would rule out velar laterals. However, as Ladefoged (1971), among others, has described languages with velar laterals, it would appear that this combination is not in fact an absolute prohibition, but belongs rather to a larger group of universal tendencies.[†]

There are a large number of universal tendencies described in SPE, but we need consider only a few as illustrations of this category of markedness conventions. There is a universal tendency for sonorants to be [+voice] and for obstruents to be [−voice]; there is also a universal tendency for back, nonlow vowels to be [+round] and for low vowels to be [−round]. A final group of unmarked versus marked feature combinations derives from language-specific tendencies. For example, language-specific phonotactic conventions can be captured through markedness. In Mandarin Chinese syllable codas can only be /n/ or /ŋ/; for this language, then, there is an absolute prohibition on coda consonants being [−nasal]. In German (and many other related languages) there is a language-specific prohibition on coda obstruents being [+voice]. We can also consider how some of the universal tendencies noted earlier may be mandatory in some languages. Thus, the tendency for back, nonlow vowels to be [+round] is compulsory in English, but not in Scots Gaelic, which has a set of back unrounded vowels as well as back rounded ones.

---

* The realization of /s, z/ as [θ, ð] can occur in acquisition and disordered speech, but is normally a phonetic-level error, rather than a phonological merger.

[†] We will not follow here the argument described in Levin (1988a, cited in Roca, 1994) that velar laterals are velar phonetically but not phonologically.

Interestingly, these universal tendencies can be used to illustrate universal implicational hierarchies. For example, if voiced obstruents are more marked than voiceless ones, it will turn out that a language that has voiced obstruents always also has voiceless ones, whereas finding voiceless obstruents in any given language does not necessarily imply that it will have voiced ones as well. Conversely, a language with voiceless sonorants always has voiced sonorants, but the presence of voiced sonorants in a language does not imply that any voiceless ones are also to be found.* Finally, a language like Turkish, with its back rounded vowels, also has back unrounded ones, whereas the existence of back rounded vowels in English certainly does not imply that any back unrounded ones are to be found.

Markedness Conventions

These ideas on markedness were incorporated in SPE into the theoretical formalism of generative phonology. We saw earlier that distinctive feature matrices can be used to specify the feature values of each vowel and consonant in the phonological system of a particular language. In (1) we show the feature matrices of /u/ and /p/ in English. In these we have filled in the values for all the features listed (some features have been omitted as not relevant to the segment in question). However, if we bring markedness into play, we need only fill in the values for those features (for a specific segment) that are contrary to the expected value as suggested by the set of markedness conventions. For example, we have already seen how obstruents have a universal tendency to be voiceless; therefore, we do not need to specify [–voice] for /p/. We have seen how back, nonlow vowels tend to be [+round] (and in English, have to be so); therefore, we do not need to specify [+round] for /u/. We can show the feature matrices for the same two segments in (2) with the unmarked features shown by *u*.[†]

(1)

/u/	/p/
+son	-son
-cons	+cons
+syll	-syll
-cor	-cor
-ant	+ant
+high	-high
-low	-low
+back	-back
+round	-nasal
-nasal	-lat
+cont	-cont
-ATR	-voice
+voice	-strident

---

* In these instances we are restricting ourselves to phonological (or contrastive) existence of certain sound types; allophonic use may well occur.
† Different sets of features and markedness conventions have been proposed at different times, and other combinations of +/–/u values could be listed for these two segments.

(2)

/u/

$$\begin{bmatrix} u\text{son} \\ -\text{cons} \\ +\text{syll} \\ u\text{cor} \\ u\text{ant} \\ +\text{high} \\ -\text{low} \\ +\text{back} \\ u\text{round} \\ u\text{nasal} \\ u\text{cont} \\ u\text{ATR} \\ u\text{voice} \end{bmatrix}$$

/p/

$$\begin{bmatrix} -\text{son} \\ +\text{cons} \\ u\text{syll} \\ -\text{cor} \\ +\text{ant} \\ -\text{high} \\ u\text{low} \\ -\text{back} \\ u\text{nasal} \\ u\text{lat} \\ -\text{cont} \\ u\text{voice} \\ u\text{strident} \end{bmatrix}$$

If we look first at /u/ we can see that the value of [sonorant] is predictable from the value of [syllabic]: All syllabic segments must also be sonorants. Nonconsonantal sonorants (i.e., vowels) are all [–coronal] and [–anterior], so these features can be given as *u*. As we saw earlier, nonlow, back vowels are usually round, so the [round] feature, too, can be marked as *u*. By markedness conventions, vowels are usually oral and voiced, and are always continuant so, again, these three features can be given as *u*. Finally, the advanced tongue root feature is by default assumed to be negative, so can be listed simply as *u*.

Turning to /p/, we can see that a segment that is [–sonorant] (i.e., an obstruent) and [+consonantal] has to be also [–syllabic], so this last feature need only be specified as *u*. All obstruents are [–low], and here again we can simply use the unmarked notation. Further, nasals and laterals are sonorants, so we need not give a ± value to these features, as we already know the segment is not a sonorant. The voice feature is marked *u*, because /p/, being voiceless, fits the default setting for obstruents. The final feature, [strident], is left unmarked, because only continuant sounds can be [+strident], and we know that this segment is not a continuant.

Markedness conventions are shown in SPE as rewrite rules (similar to other generative phonological rules; see Chapter 4). For example, the universal prohibition on [+high, +low] vowels is given in (3).

(3)

$$[+\text{low}] \quad \rightarrow \quad [-\text{high}]$$
$$[+\text{high}] \quad \rightarrow \quad [-\text{low}]$$

In other words, if a segment is [+low] it must have the feature value [–high], and if it is [+high] it must also have the feature value [–low]. The tendency for obstruents to be voiceless and sonorants to be voiced can be seen in conventions (4) and (5).

(4)

$$[u\text{voice}] \quad \rightarrow \quad [-\text{voice}] \text{ / } \begin{bmatrix} \underline{} \\ -\text{son} \end{bmatrix}$$

(5)

$$[u\text{voice}] \quad \rightarrow \quad [+\text{voice}] / \quad \begin{bmatrix} \underline{\quad\quad} \\ +\text{son} \end{bmatrix}$$

Finally, the tendency for nonlow, back vowels to be rounded is given in (6).

(6)

$$[u\text{round}] \quad \rightarrow \quad [+\text{round}] \quad \begin{bmatrix} \underline{\quad\quad} \\ +\text{back} \\ -\text{low} \end{bmatrix}$$

In fact, as there is also a tendency for front vowels to be unrounded, we can combine that convention with the back vowel one, using the alpha notation (described in more detail in Chapter 4), which can be read to mean "either + or –," to give (7).

(7)

$$[u\text{round}] \quad \rightarrow \quad [\alpha\text{round}] / \quad \begin{bmatrix} \underline{\quad\quad} \\ \alpha\text{back} \\ -\text{low} \end{bmatrix}$$

Clinical Utility of Markedness

We have seen how markedness conventions have gone some way toward dealing with the problem we identified in the introduction of which feature changes in disordered speech are to some extent expected (or, if you will, more natural) and which are unusual. We might also claim that markedness helps to some extent in identifying which features are dependent on which others (for example, we saw above that the value of [strident] depends crucially on the value of [continuant]). Can this idea be applied to clinical data?

In (8), we consider two sets of possible data from clients assessed in the speech clinic. The first case shows the following target realizations:

(8)

i)	/b/	→	[p]
	/d/	→	[t]
	/g/	→	[k]
ii)	/ɪ/	→	[i]
	/ʊ/	→	[u]
	/æ/	→	[ɑ]

These data can be represented by the following feature changes (using SPE features), where (9) describes the realizations in (8i) above, and (10) describe those in (8ii):

(9)

$$[\text{+voice}] \quad \rightarrow \quad [\text{-voice}] / \quad \left[\begin{array}{c} \underline{} \\ \text{+cons} \\ \text{-cont} \end{array} \right]$$

(10)

$$[\text{-tense}] \quad \rightarrow \quad [\text{+tense}] / \quad \left[\begin{array}{c} \underline{} \\ \text{-cons} \\ \text{+syll} \end{array} \right]$$

Both sets of realization rules mirror, in fact, markedness conventions as proposed in SPE. We have already encountered the convention whereby obstruents (in this case plosives) are unmarked when voiceless (9); we see in (10) the convention whereby vowels are unmarked when tense rather than lax. (In fact, the change /æ/ → [ɑ] might also be thought of as backing of a low vowel, and this is an SPE markedness convention as well.)

The second case is different, and we have the realization in (11):

(11)

i)   /tʃ/   →   [ʃ]

      /dʒ/   →   [ʒ]

ii)   /p/   →   [f]

      /t/   →   [s]

      /k/   →   [x]

These data can be described with the following feature changes, where (12) describes the realization in (11i), and (13) describes those in (11ii).

(12)

$$[\text{+del rel}] \quad \rightarrow \quad [\text{-del rel}] / \quad \left[\begin{array}{c} \underline{} \\ \text{+cons} \\ \text{+high} \\ \text{-ant} \\ \text{+cor} \end{array} \right]$$

(13)

$$[\text{-cont}] \quad \rightarrow \quad [\text{+cont}] / \quad \left[\begin{array}{c} \underline{} \\ \text{+cons} \\ \text{-voice} \end{array} \right]$$

Both sets of realization rules in this case actually breach markedness coventions; in other words, the changes go from an unmarked form to a marked one. In the case of (12), SPE markedness conventions note that affricates are the unmarked consonants at the palato-alveolar position (or postalveolar, as is the current usual label), whereas the change in (13) goes against the convention that plosives are the unmarked consonants at all places other than palato-alveolar.

These examples show that markedness allows us to move beyond a simple statement of the number of distinctive features that are in error (two in each case above), to a more nuanced statement of both the number of feature changes and the direction of markedness changes. So, case 1 shows two feature changes both in the direction of unmarked from marked, whereas case 2 illustrates the opposite: two features moving to marked from unmarked. Case 2, therefore, might be considered less natural, more unusual, or at least a greater error than case 1.

However, markedness conventions do not account for all changes commonly occurring in clinical data. For example, the realization of target /ɹ/ as [w] is not covered by the SPE conventions, and neither is the realization of target velars as alveolars, while dental/alveolars seem to be among the least marked segments according to SPE, and so are labials; thus, there would be no difference if the realization of target velars were alveolars or labials. Further, some commonly occurring clinical examples (such as the voicing of target word initial voiceless obstruents) run counter to the markedness conventions.

EXERCISE 3.3

SPE gives examples of feature matrices fully specified for ± values of all features, and specified for marked and unmarked values. These latter matrices also give complexity values to each segment based on how many marked features are used. Using this information, work out the overall complexity of the following two vowel systems that might be encountered in the clinic for the target English system. (Use only the features [low, high, back, round].)

   i. [i e æ ɑ o u]
  ii. [i e ɛ ɑ ɔ u]

EXERCISE 3.4

Using the markedness conventions we have discussed, and those available in SPE, examine the following two sets of data, note which set of changes is less marked, and explain why.

Set 1. /p, t, tʃ, k/ realized as [b, d, dʒ, g]; /f, θ, s, ʃ/ realized as [v, ð, z, ʒ]
Set 2. /p, t, k/ realized as [m̥, n̥, ŋ̊]; /b, d, g/ realized as [m, n, ŋ]

FURTHER READING

Hyman (1975) discusses the history of feature systems, and describes developments from Trubetzkoy on. Early versions of distinctive feature theory are explored in Jakobson, Fant, and Halle (1952) and Jakobson and Halle (1956), and the version described in this chapter comes from Chomsky and Halle (1968). Ladefoged (1971) describes a multivalued feature system. Markedness derives from work by Trubeztkoy (1939), and Chomsky and Halle (1968) describe its use in terms of their feature system.

Grunwell (1987) devotes a chapter to the clinical use of distinctive features, and also describes some assessment procedure based on the theory. Recent work that uses phonological features within a broader phonological framework will be referred to in later chapters. Markedness has also been applied to analyses of disordered speech. A recent example is Miccio (2002, p. 227) who notes, "Principles of markedness are also used to determine treatment targets. A nonstimulable fricative, for example, is given preference over a nonstimulable stop because the presence of fricatives enhances the learnability of stops." Miccio also notes that Elbert and Gierut's (1986) handbook and Gierut's (2001) article also refer to markedness in clinical decision making.

SOURCES

Languages referred to in the discussion of SPE are mostly from that source. The Hindi, Turkish, and Russian data are derived from the *Handbook of the IPA*; the remaining data are from the authors.

REVIEW QUESTIONS AND STUDY TOPICS

Review Questions

1. Describe the difference between privative, equipollent, and gradual oppositions.
2. List four criteria of Chomsky and Halle's distinctive feature system.
3. What were the main groupings of SPE features called?
4. What was the main reason why the [vocalic] feature was replaced by the [syllabic] feature?
5. List some of the advantages and disadvantages of using distinctive features to analyze clinical data.
6. What does the term *markedness* mean?
7. What are implicational universals?
8. How can markedness be used to analyze clinical data?

Study Topics and Projects

1. Review the proposals for feature systems of Jakobson, Fant, and Halle (1952), Jakobson and Halle (1956), and Ladefoged (1971). Summarize the pros and cons in your view of these two systems and the SPE system described in this chapter.
2. Review the target consonant or vowel usage of any two phonology clients from your clinic. List the features that the clients use incorrectly, and attempt a contrastive assessment of error severity in terms of markedness.

4

EARLY GENERATIVE PHONOLOGY

INTRODUCTION

Although many of the approaches to phonology outlined in this book can be thought of as falling within the broad heading of *generative phonology* (for example, lexical, autosegmental, and metrical phonology), the earliest full exposition of the model came in Chomsky and Halle's (1968) *Sound Pattern of English* (SPE). It is this early generative model that we explore in this chapter, together with ways in which it can be applied to disordered speech data. The use of the term *generative* is taken to mean a formal system that can describe (or *generate*) all and only the phonologically acceptable forms of a language.

LEVELS OF REPRESENTATION

As we saw in the discussion of the phoneme in Chapter 1, many approaches to phonology envisage at least two distinct levels of representation. In the case of phoneme theory, these two levels consist of the phoneme and the allophones that make up the phoneme. Generative phonology builds on this insight of an abstract organizational level existing apart from a more concrete realizational level. Indeed, the terms used to denote these levels clearly show their origin in phoneme theory: the *systematic phonemic level* and the *systematic phonetic level*.

Because allophonic variation (excluding free variation due to stylistic considerations) is predictable, it is theoretically redundant to list such variation in the lexicon.* So, at the systematic phonemic level of representation, allophonic variation is omitted. However, speakers do have to use the correct allophones in order to sound natural, and the phonology therefore has to supply this information somewhere: at the systematic phonetic level. How do we derive the surface pronunciation (the systematic phonetic level of representation) from the underlying systematic phonemic level? We can illustrate this by showing how generative phonology would describe the process whereby vowels become nasalized before nasal consonants in English. Although English (unlike French and Portuguese, among others) does not have nasalized vowel phonemes, a certain amount

---

* Generative models of language assume there is a lexicon containing the lexical items of the language together with grammatical (including phonological) information about each item. Most psycholinguistic models of language also assume that individual speakers have mental lexicons. It is not always clear that theoretical phonologists adequately distinguish between the lexicon as a theoretical construct and the lexicon as a mental reality.

of nasalization does occur when vowels are in the context of a following nasal consonant. This is because the velum starts lowering to make the nasal consonant during the production of the preceding vowel (the velum cannot lower instantaneously, and so needs a certain amount of time to get into position for the nasal consonant). This results in vowel phonemes having a nasalized allophone in this context only. Generative phonology shows this process through the use of phonological rules (see below for more details), to link the two levels of representation. The input to the rule (in front of the arrow) is the underlying level (systematic phonemic); the output (after the arrow) is the realization (systematic phonetic).* Rules use distinctive features (see Chapter 3) rather than phoneme symbols, and the context that a rule applies in is shown after the output following a slash line. In (1), let's see how this looks for the vowel nasalization rule:

(1)

$$\begin{bmatrix} +\text{syll} \\ -\text{cons} \end{bmatrix} \rightarrow \begin{bmatrix} +\text{nasal} \end{bmatrix} / \underline{\quad\quad} \begin{bmatrix} +\text{cons} \\ +\text{nasal} \end{bmatrix}$$

One difference between generative and traditional phonemic approaches to phonological representation is that generative rules extend from simple allophonic variation to the area traditionally termed *morphophonemics*. Morphophonemics, as the name suggests, is the intersection between phonology and morphology. To illustrate this intersection we can consider regular plural suffixes in English. There are three phonological forms for this regular suffix: /-s/, /-z/, and /-ɪz/. Examples of their use can be seen in (2):

(2)

        cat+s /kæts/   dog+s /dɑgz/   horse+s /hɔɹsɪz/

Extrapolating from these examples, we can state that the /-s/ plural is added to stems ending in a voiceless consonant (/s/ of course is voiceless); /-z/ is added to stems ending in a voiced consonant (/z/ of course is voiced); and /-ɪz/ is added to stems ending in sibilant consonants to avoid a cluster of two sibilants that are perceptually and articulatorily unsatisfactory (the sibilants in question are /s, z, ʃ, z, tʃ, dʒ/).

In extending generative phonology into morphophonemics, we may well be faced with the choice of which form is the underlying one. (Of course, even with allophonic variation it is not always clear which variant should be considered the underlying form, but normally, as in the case of vowel nasalization, one variant is clearly the most commonly occurring one.) Taking our example of plural suffixes (which, by the way, is identical in its variants to the possessive s and to the third person singular present tense suffix on verbs) one could argue for any of the three forms. This is because—as we will see in more detail later—generative phonological rules can change feature values (e.g., from voiced to voiceless or vice versa) and can add in or delete segments (e.g., the /ɪ/ vowel in the /-ɪz/ suffix). In making decisions in cases like this, phonologists use a simplicity metric: The solution that is most economical is to be preferred over less economical ones. So, if we take /-ɪz/ as the base form, we need a rule that deletes /ɪ/ after all sounds except the sibilant consonants we listed earlier; taking /-z/ as the base we need an /ɪ/ insertion rule after only those six sibilant consonants. Therefore, the /ɪ/ insertion rule is simpler, as it occurs in fewer contexts than the /ɪ/ deletion rule. Further, if we take

---

* As we will see, many derivations require several rules, and only the final output, therefore, will be the systematic phonetic level.

/-s/ as the base form, then voicing to /-z/ is required in all contexts apart from following /p, t, k, f, θ/ (and the sibilant contexts of course). On the other hand, with /-z/ as the base, devoicing is only needed after following final /p, t, k, f, θ/, again, a much simpler context. These arguments strongly suggest that an underlying form of /-z/ for the plural suffix is the best motivated. It should be noted at this point that the rules describing the variants of the plural suffix (and possessive suffix) are limited to these morphophonological contexts, and that this has to be made explicit in the description.* It is quite possible for English words to end with voiced sounds followed by /s/—*mess, prince, pulse*—though we do not find voiceless final consonants followed by /z/ or sibilants followed by /s/ or /z/.

WHY HAVE TWO LEVELS OF REPRESENTATION?

As we have seen, much of modern phonology has assumed that there are two levels of representation: the more abstract underlying phonemic level and the more concrete surface phonetic (or allophonic) level. The motivation for this has been simplicity, both in theoretical terms (we don't have to list similar allophonic variation for classes of sounds—just the set of phonological rules that apply to all the sounds in the class) and partly on the grounds of psycholinguistic simplicity (two levels suggests a simpler mechanism for the production of sounds by the speaker). We look here at these and other arguments in more detail.

The simplicity, or economy, argument can be illustrated as follows. In English, /p, t, k/ are all unaspirated prevocalically when following /s/; otherwise, they are aspirated in prevocalic position. Rather than list three phonemes, each with (for this case) two allophones, we can reduce the description to a rule that de-aspirates voiceless plosives when following /s/. In terms of the number of units required to express a wide range of phonological processes, a two-level approach usually is more simple than if we listed in the lexicon every sound with all context-dependent variants. However, it is more debatable as to whether this simplicity can be justified psycholinguistically. As Gussenhoven and Jacobs (1998) note, arguments that the brain simply couldn't store all the information if we had a single level of representation are probably not valid (see also Bybee's, 2001, arguments for the ability of the brain to store redundant information, described in Chapter 14). Gussenhoven and Jacobs (1998) note, instead, arguments from processing speed that suggest that it would be more time-consuming to have to retrieve a fully specified phonological representation than to retrieve more economical representations. That, however, would appear to ignore the extra time needed to fully specify the representations through the rule system to produce pronounceable phonetic units, and to ignore (as Bybee, 2001, points out) the fact the commonly produced segments or strings of segments are likely to be stored whole (and fully specified), and therefore to be speedily accessible.

Perhaps a more powerful argument comes from the generative phonology's application to morphophonemic alternations as well as allophonic variation, which we noted earlier. At the systematic phonetic level of representation it appears that English has three different (regular) plural suffixes, as we saw earlier: /-s/, /-z/, and /-ɪz/. It is only if we have a systematic phonemic level (together with a phonological rule component) that the unity of the regular plural suffix can be seen.

A third argument noted by Gussenhoven and Jacobs (1998) concerns the fact that there are phonological generalizations in a language or dialect that can be captured at

---

* This is done by using a special symbol that represents a morpheme boundary in the phonological rule (e.g., the symbol +), so we know that this form only applies to morphological suffixes.

the underlying level of representation but not at the surface level. We can illustrate this with an example from Welsh. Negative forms of the verb in standard literary Welsh require a preposed negative particle, which in main clauses is either *ni* or *nid*. Let us consider the following examples in (3):

(3)

(i)	ni soniodd e amdano	He didn't mention it
(ii)	ni phostiodd e'r cerdyn	He didn't post the card
(iii)	nid atebodd e	He didn't answer
(iv)	ni adawodd e hi	He didn't leave her

If we were to consider the first three of these sentences only, we might assume that the *ni* form occurred before consonants, while the *nid* form occurred before vowels. Indeed, all consonant initial verb forms occur with preceding *ni*, and many vowel initial ones occur with preceding *nid*. However, as the fourth example shows, some vowel initial verb forms do occur with *ni* (note that this is not stylistic variation). The situation becomes clearer once we know that the *ni* negative triggers a phonological process that affects the following consonant (i.e., the initial consonant of the following word). This process is traditionally called the mixed mutation and turns voiceless plosives into voiceless fricatives, and voiced plosives into voiced fricatives (except /g/, which deletes), and /m/ into /v/. This results in /g-/ initial verbs ending up as vowel initial ones in most cases. The rule that adds *d* to *ni* is applied before this mutation process, so formerly /g-/ initial verbs do not receive the *nid* form. Let's see how this works in (4):

(4)

Underlying	ni soniodd	ni postiodd	ni atebodd	ni gadawodd
d-insertion	(n.a.)	(n.a.)	nid atebodd	(n.a.)
Mixed mutation	No change	ni phostiodd	No change	ni adawodd
Surface	ni soniodd	ni phostiodd	nid atebodd	ni adawodd

This example shows that the underlying level of representation illustrates the generalization that *ni* occurs before consonants and *nid* before vowels—a generalization that is not available at the surface level.

EXERCISE 4.1

What problems arise if you try to describe the regular past tense suffix of English using only one level of representation?

What are the variants of the regular past tense suffix in English? Which of these variants would be the best choice as the underlying form, and why?

GENERATIVE PHONOLOGICAL RULES

As we have noted above, generative phonology makes use of rules as descriptive devices. It is important that we do not consider phonological rules as prescriptive devices telling us how we ought to pronounce things; this is not the meaning of the term *rule* as used in formal grammar. Rather, rules are formalized ways of describing the changes that take place between the underlying and surface forms of phonological representation. Rules can change feature values (as we saw in the nasalization example earlier); they can delete segments; they can add segments (as in the Welsh example in (3) and (4)); and they can change the order of segments. We will see examples of all these rule types in this section of the chapter. We will also examine the importance in many instances of rule ordering (as, for example, with the Welsh negatives) and the use of the *elsewhere condition*.

Before we look at types of rules, we need to recall the format of rules in generative phonology. Rules consist of an input (often called the *structural description* (SD)) and an output (the *structural change* (SC)). The input and output are generally expressed in terms of feature matrices (see Chapter 3) that contain those features needed to specify the segment or segment class under consideration, and how the relevant features change in a specific process. Finally, many rules are context dependent, and so rules usually have a context expressed—again in the form of a feature matrix, often with other necessary information identifying the position within a word where the rule applies and whether it is a morphophonemic rule. The SD and SC do not always represent the underlying and surface realizations, as some derivations require several rules to apply; therefore, the SD and SC could be intervening steps in such a derivation. So, remember that SD and SC do not need to represent realizations that actually occur in a language, and this abstractness of underlying representations has been criticized in some models of phonology (for example, government phonology as described in Chapter 13). In rule layouts, SD and SC are linked by an arrow; the context is shown by a diagonal slash line. In the context, if we need to show the position of the matrix being changed, we do this with an underline (rather than repeat the whole matrix from the input to the rule). Finally, we should note that word boundaries are shown by the use of #, and morphological boundaries by +.

Feature-Changing Rules

Rule (1) above is an example of a feature-changing rule. We show a slightly more complex example in (5). This rule expresses that alveolar stops (plosives and nasals) in English become postalveolar when preceding the postalveolar /ɹ/ (e.g., *train, dream, unrest*).

(5)

$$
\begin{bmatrix} +cons \\ -cont \\ +ant \\ +cor \\ -high \end{bmatrix} \rightarrow \begin{bmatrix} -ant \\ +high \end{bmatrix} / \underline{\hspace{2cm}} \begin{bmatrix} +son \\ +cons \\ -ant \\ +cor \\ +high \end{bmatrix}
$$

In (5), the input matrix contains just enough features to identify the class of segments that is to undergo the rule, that is, noncontinuant alveolars. To the right of the arrow, the output shows the changed feature values (these do not always have to be included at the left of the arrow, because they may not be needed to describe just the class of segments undergoing the rule; see (3) above, where [–nasal] was not needed in the structural description*). The context states that this rule occurs when our class of segments (shown by the underline) is followed by another segment type: Here the final matrix contains just enough feature information to identify the postalveolar liquid: /r/. There is

---

* This means, of course, that nasal stops meet the SD, and so are entered into the rule. As they are [+nasal] anyway, the rule applies vacuously to them, and no changes take place.

no need to include syllable boundary in the context, as the examples show this occurs both after syllable boundaries and across syllable boundaries.

Both (3) and (5) need following contexts; some rules need preceding, or both preceding and following contexts. Let us reconsider the example referred to earlier of aspiration deletion in English plosives following /s/.[*] We need a rule that removes aspiration (we will use the feature [tense] for this, though some phonologists have used [aspirated], and more recently [spread glottis]). This applies only to voiceless plosives, which we can characterize by just the features [–consonantal, –continuant, –voice] (we do not need to specify [–nasal], as a range of redundancy rules exist that allow us to assume that noncontinuants are oral unless otherwise stated). The context requires the features for /s/, and the syllable boundary marker as this process occurs with syllable initial (though not necessarily word initial) /s/ clusters. Again, we need only specify a strident continuant (thus excluding all nonfricative continuants). We do not need to specify /s/, as the redundancy rules for English phonotactics only allow /s/ before the voiceless plosives.[†] Note in (6) that the context is a preceding one.

(6)

$$
\begin{bmatrix} +\text{cons} \\ -\text{cont} \\ -\text{voice} \end{bmatrix} \rightarrow \begin{bmatrix} -\text{tense} \end{bmatrix} / \quad \# \begin{bmatrix} +\text{cons} \\ +\text{cont} \\ +\text{strid} \end{bmatrix} \underline{\quad\quad}
$$

An example of a rule applying between two contexts can be seen in (7). In American English, intervocalic /t/ is typically flapped (but only when the preceding syllable is stressed). This does not occur when the /t/ is word final or word initial, so we need to specify the presence of a vowel both before and after the /t/. In this rule, we use the abbreviation V to stand for vowel, and an acute accent over the V to show stress.

(7)

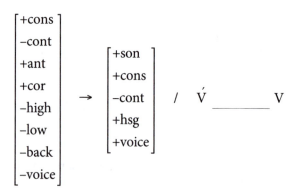

([hsg] = [heightened subglottal pressure]; this distinguishes trills from flaps.)

---

[*] We leave aside the argument here as to whether the aspirated or unaspirated variant of English voiceless plosives be deemed the underlying form, and assume it is the former.

[†] It is arguable that just [+consonantal] is needed, as no other consonants can occur before /p, t, k/ in clusters in English.

Some rules require more than one context. For example, the rule for dark-l usage in most varieties of English needs to show that this occurs when /l/ is syllable final, and when /l/ precedes a syllable final consonant; we can't just list it as when /l/ follows a vowel, because if the /l/ is syllable initial (as in *allow*), then a clear-l results. Rule (8) shows how we mark a syllable boundary (with the symbol σ) and use a brace to capture the two contexts:

(8)

$$\begin{bmatrix} +son \\ +cons \\ +lat \end{bmatrix} \rightarrow [+back] \ / \ \begin{cases} \underline{\hspace{1cm}} \sigma \\ \underline{\hspace{1cm}} C\sigma \end{cases}$$

EXERCISE 4.2

Write a phonological rule that expresses the allophonic pattern that, in English, obstruents become rounded when preceding a rounded vowel.

Segment Deleting, Inserting, and Rearranging Rules

Generative phonological rules need not only deal with changes to feature values, but they can delete whole segments (i.e., an entire feature matrix), create new segments (insert an entire feature matrix), or rearrange segments (transpose whole feature matrices). We can see examples of this in the following rules.

Segments may be deleted for various reasons, as a result of morphophonological processes, fast speech processes, or dialectal variation. Taking another example from Welsh, we can see that in the standard spoken form of the language final-/v/ is usually deleted. So we get forms like /ara/ *slow* and /kri/ *strong*. We know there is an underlying final /v/, as the comparative form of these adjectives is /aˈravax/ and /ˈkrəvax/, respectively, and the /v/ is not added to adjectives ending in other consonants, or to the majority of vowel final adjectives (compare /harð/-/ˈharðax/ *attractive* and /di/-/ˈdiax/ *black*). The rule in (9) shows how we display deleting rules (we use the phonetic symbol /v/ here as a shorthand for the full feature matrix):

(9)

$$/v/ \quad \rightarrow \quad \varnothing \qquad / \underline{\hspace{2cm}} \#$$

Here, Ø is the zero sign and represents the deletion of the feature matrix for /v/. We can reverse this notation to show segment insertion. In English, words like *prince, mince, sense,* and so on are often pronounced with a /t/ after the nasal and before the /s/. We can show this in the rule in (10), where again we use symbols as shorthand for full feature matrices:

(10)

$$\varnothing \quad \rightarrow \quad /t/ \qquad / \ /n/ \underline{\hspace{2cm}} /s/$$

Finally, we can consider examples of *metathesis*, that is, the switching around of segments. In various English dialects, forms such as *aks* and *waps* appear instead of standard *ask* and *wasp*. While these forms tend to be restricted to a subset of lexical items, we can illustrate the general principle with rule (11):

(11)

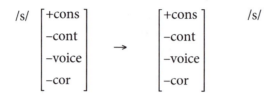

$$/s/ \begin{bmatrix} +cons \\ -cont \\ -voice \\ -cor \end{bmatrix} \rightarrow \begin{bmatrix} +cons \\ -cont \\ -voice \\ -cor \end{bmatrix} /s/$$

EXERCISE 4.3

Write a phonological rule that expresses the fast speech pattern that, in English, /t/ deletes when it is the second member of final three consonant clusters such as in *facts*, *kept quiet*, *opts*, and *looked back*.

Special Notational Devices

Generative phonology uses a series of special notational devices that allow rules to be simpler, or allow two or more subprocesses to be collapsed into a single rule. We will look at some of the more common special notations here, starting with the idea of variable feature values. In English, word final alveolar stops (plosives and nasals) will tend to assimilate to the place of articulation of the initial consonant of the following word (if the two words form a close syntactic bond). The changes are in two directions: alveolar to bilabial (if the following word starts with a bilabial) and alveolar to velar (if the following word starts with a velar. Clearly we can express this as two separate rules, as in (12) and (13):

(12)

$$\begin{bmatrix} +cons \\ -cont \\ +ant \\ +cor \end{bmatrix} \rightarrow [-cor] \ / \ \underline{\qquad} \# \begin{bmatrix} +cons \\ -cont \\ +ant \\ -cor \end{bmatrix}$$

(13)

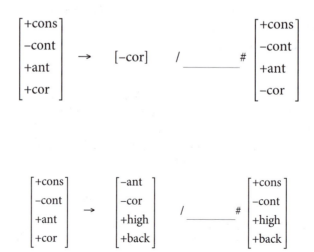

$$\begin{bmatrix} +cons \\ -cont \\ +ant \\ +cor \end{bmatrix} \rightarrow \begin{bmatrix} -ant \\ -cor \\ +high \\ +back \end{bmatrix} \ / \ \underline{\qquad} \# \begin{bmatrix} +cons \\ -cont \\ +high \\ +back \end{bmatrix}$$

However, it would be more economical if we could collapse these two rules into a single assimilation process. However, if we do this, we want to ensure that the [–high, –back] feature values of the input alveolars only change to [+high, +back] if the following word starts with a velar, but retain their minus values if the following word starts with a bilabial. The [coronal] feature needs to change to minus in both instances. We can adopt Greek lowercase letters to represent *either plus or minus*. So, if we have [α anterior] in both the rule and the context, we read this to mean that if we see [–anterior] in the context, change the input to [–anterior], but if we see [+anterior] in the context, do not change the input. Let's see how this might work in (14):

(14)

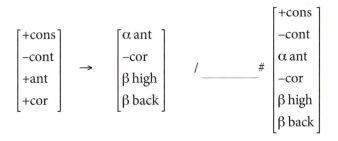

We use β for both [high] and [back] because these two features have minus values for both alveolar and bilabial, but both have plus features for velar; in other words, their values pattern together. In fact, in English, the values of [high] and [back] are predictable for bilabials, alveolars, and velars from the values for [anterior] and [coronal]; it is arguable, therefore, that this rule can be even simpler through the omission of the [high] and [back] features.

Parentheses are used to express portions of a rule that are optional, in that it applies both when that material is present and when it is not. We can return to our analysis of dark-l in English to illustrate this. Rule (8) can actually be made simpler; instead of listing two separate contexts, we can combine them into one, by showing that a syllable final consonant is optional. We do this in (15):

(15)

$$\begin{bmatrix} +son \\ +cons \\ +lat \end{bmatrix} \rightarrow [+back] \ / \ \underline{\hspace{2cm}} (C)\sigma$$

This can now be read as "/l/ is realized as the dark-l variant when before syllable final consonants, or syllable finally."

Angled brackets are the last special notational device we will consider. These, like the others, allow separate rules to be collapsed, but in this instance we can say "do X if Y is present, otherwise do Z." The X and Y portions are shown within angled brackets. We can illustrate this concept with the rule in (16), which shows the mixed mutation of Welsh (referred to earlier). Recall that in this mutation, word initial plosives become fricatives, but word initial /m/ becomes /v/. (Word initial /g/ actually deletes, but we assume that this is accomplished through a later rule that deletes the [ɣ] produced by this rule.) We use angled brackets to deal with the case of /m/:

(16)

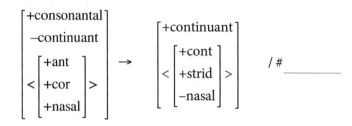

EXERCISE 4.4

Write a phonological rule that expresses the pattern in Turkish that high vowels in suffixes agree in terms of [back] and [round] with the preceding vowel (assume there is a consonant between the preceding vowel and the suffix vowel). Which special notational device did you use to express this rule?

RULE ORDERING

We have seen how generative phonology proposes that phonological description is accomplished by positing two levels of representation and a series of rules linking the underlying level to the surface level. One question that arises in an approach like this is whether the rules are ordered in some way, or whether we should consider that they all apply simultaneously. If we consider rules (14) and (15) (that is, the alveolar assimilation rule and the dark-l rule) we can see that there appears to be no reason whatsoever to prefer an order of application of (14) and (15) over (15) and (14), so we can assume there is no linear ordering needed for these two rules. However, if we return to the example of *ni(d)* negatives in Welsh discussed in (3) and (4) above, then it is clear that the /d/ insertion rule has to apply before the mixed mutation rule; if the ordering were the other way around, then we would get the *nid* form before verbs like *adawodd*.

Another aspect of rule ordering needs to be considered when there are two rules that can apply in the same context. For example, we have already discussed the rule for regular plurals in English, but what about irregular plurals? A form like *ox–oxen* requires a specific rule to add *-en* to the base form; such a rule will be marked to apply to *ox* only (the irregular plural *child–children* differs in that the suffix is *-ren* and there is a vowel change to the stem). However, the general rule could also be applied to *ox*. To avoid this, the rule must be drawn up with a formalism that specifically blocks it from applying to *ox* (and, of course, all other irregular plurals), or rule ordering has to apply the irregular rule before the regular one. Kiparsky (1973) proposed a way to avoid both ordering constraints on these types of rules, and a blocking formalism within the rules. Kiparsky proposed the *elsewhere condition*, which ensures that if two or more rules can apply to the same input, that with the most specific application (e.g., to *ox*) applies before the least specific (e.g., regular plural rule).

However, even with the elsewhere condition there will be many examples where rules do need to be ordered. An examination of various interactions between rules has resulted in the drawing up of a set of different forms of these interactions. We will conclude this section by examining these, in each case assuming we are dealing with just two rules. The first type is termed *feeding order*, and here the ouput of the first rule increases the number of contexts eligible to be input into the second rule. We can illustrate this interaction through the example from British English given by Gussenhoven and Jacobs (1998, p. 98). In British English fortis stops receive glottal reinforcement postvocalically and preconsonantally in syllable final clusters. We can see this in the examples in (17):

(17)

Underlying	Derived	
lʊkt	lʊˀkt	looked
kæts	kæˀts	cats
hɪnts	hɪnˀts	hints
kæmp ɡɹaʊnd	kæmˀp ɡɹaʊnd	campground

Another rule (fortis plosive insertion) is common in many varieties of English. Consider the data in (18):

(18)

Underlying	Derived
pɹɪns	pɹɪnts
lɛŋθ	lɛŋkθ
wɔmθ	wɔmpθ

Now, the output of (18) also undergoes the glottal reinforcement process, as seen in (19):

(19)

Underlying	Derived
pɹɪnts	pɹɪnˀts
lɛŋkθ	lɛŋˀkθ
wɔmpθ	wɔmˀpθ

Because the output of fortis plosive insertion feeds the glottal reinforcement process, we can say that these two rules are in a feeding relationship.

In some instances, all the input contexts to one rule are derived from a previous rule. We can return to Welsh for an example. The nasal mutation converts voiced and voiceless plosives to voiced and voiceless nasals. Voiceless nasals are only found as reflexes of this mutation rule. There is a later phonetic realization rule that shows that voiceless nasals are realized as clusters of nasal + /h/. Clearly, if the nasal mutation rule does not apply (it is only needed in a small number of contexts), then the voiceless nasal realization rule cannot be triggered. In this case there is total feeding of the second rule by the first.

Counterfeeding occurs when the output of the second rule would have fed the input to the first rule, if the rules had been ordered the other way around. We can give here the example of masculine and feminine adjectives in French. We assume that, underlyingly, feminine adjectives end in schwa (/-ə/) and masculine ones end in a consonant. To get to the surface realization, masculine adjectives undergo final consonant deletion while feminine ones undergo final schwa deletion. Let's see how this works in (20):

(20)

	Petit (garçon)	Petite (fille)
	pətit	pətitə
Final consonant deletion	t → Ø	n.a.
Final schwa deletion	n.a.	ə → Ø
	pəti	pətit

If we had ordered these two rules the other way around, then the feminine forms too would have undergone final consonant deletion (incorrectly, of course). So we can say that final schwa deletion counterfeeds final consonant deletion.

A *bleeding* relation holds between two rules if the application of the first rule removes some (or all) of the contexts required to input to a second rule. The English regular plural rule is often referred to as an example of this interaction. The /ɪ/ insertion rule applies before the devoicing rule (the rule that changes /-z/ to /-s/ after voiceless consonants). This means that nouns that end in /s, ʃ, tʃ/ in the singular cannot enter into the devoicing rule, as the /ɪ/ insertion rule has changed the suffix such that it no longer fits the input criteria for devoicing. Let us look at the ordering in (21):

(21)

	Dogs	Cats	Horses
	dɑg-z	kæt-z	hɔɹs-z
/ɪ/ insertion	n.a.	n.a.	ɪ
Devoicing	n.a.	s	n.a.
	dɑgz	kæts	hɔɹsɪz

Finally, we can consider *counterbleeding*. This applies when the second rule would have been in a bleeding relation with the first if they had been ordered the other way around. Kenstowicz (1994) gives an example from Icelandic. In a certain group of nouns, glides (for example, /j/) at the end of the stem are deleted if the suffix is zero, or a consonant, but retained if the suffix is vowel initial. The only exception is in the nominative singular, where the glide is deleted even though the suffix is vowel initial (/-ur/). This is accounted for by positing an underlying form of that suffix as /-r/, with an epenthetic vowel added later to avoid a combination of consonant followed by /r/. We can see the importance of rule ordering in (22):

(22)

	Nominative Singular	Gen sg	Dat pl
	lyfj-r	lyfj-s	lyfj-a
Glide deletion	lyf-r	lyf-s	n.a.
Vowel epenthesis	lyf-ur	n.a.	n.a.
	lyfur	lyfs	lyfja

If these rules had been ordered the other way around, then the vowel epenthesis rule would have supplied a vowel to the nominative singular before the glide deletion process had been undertaken, which would have led to the nominative singular not undergoing glide deletion (vowel epenthesis would have bled glide deletion). As this is not what happens in Icelandic, we can state that vowel epenthesis and glide deletion are in a counterbleeding relation.

EXERCISE 4.5

Rule ordering is required to account for some features of Canadian English. One pattern is the voicing of intervocalic /t/ (realized as [d]). The other pattern is Canadian raising, where the diphthongs /aɪ/ and /aʊ/ are realized as [ʌɪ] and [ʌʊ] when preceding voiceless consonants. Using rule columns (as in (20) and (21) above), show which order these rules must go in to account for the following forms: *write, writer, ride, rider*: [ɹʌɪt], [ɹʌɪdɚ], [ɹaɪd], [ɹaɪdɚ].

CLINICAL APPLICATIONS OF CLASSICAL GENERATIVE PHONOLOGY

One way in which we could apply the model of phonological representation sketched so far in this chapter would be to look at the speech output of a client with phonological disorder and note which phonological rules had been disrupted to produce the observed output, as opposed to the expected output. Such a disruption might involve an alteration to a rule, or the complete deletion of a rule. An example can be seen in a client with hearing impairment whose allophonic assimilation rule* is altered such that it only applies word internally, not across word boundaries; or a client with dysarthria whose allophonic assimilation rule is deleted altogether. However, in the largest disordered speech client group, children, the usual patterns of phonological disorder are often not amenable to this approach. This is because many of the patterns of speech disorder in this group are best described as loss of phonological segments from the speaker's inventory, or restriction of segments to a subset of the contexts found in normal speech. As it is often the case that the speakers have the full range of sounds perceptually, such patterns are best captured through the addition of rules that restrict the appearance of the relevant segments in the output phonology while assuming they are present in the underlying representation. When segments are lost, they may be replaced by zero (i.e., totally deleted), or they may be replaced by other segments in the inventory (neutralization), or by different segments altogether; in all these cases, additional rules are needed rather than changes to existing ones. Rules of this type, therefore, take the target pronunciation as an input and the client's realization as the output.

Grunwell (1987) illustrated the clinical application of the early generative model of phonology in detail, and here we will look at just a few rule types that account for commonly occurring disordered patterns. First, we can look at rules that describe systemic simplifications (i.e., simplifications to the client's phonological system). Among the common phonological patterns found in this category are the realization of target fricatives and affricates as stops, the realization of target velars as alveolars, and the realization of target /ɹ/ as [w]. As these patterns are systemwide (i.e., they apply irrespective of context), these rules are context-free, and the context part of the rule is used merely to expand the features of the input. We can illustrate them in (23) to (25).

---

* This is the rule that adjusts alveolars to dentals when they precede a dental, and to postalveolars when they precede postalveolars.

(23)

$$\left[+\text{cont}\right] \quad \rightarrow \quad \left[-\text{cont}\right] \quad / \quad \begin{bmatrix} -\text{son} \\ +\text{cons} \end{bmatrix}$$

(Fricatives and affricates realized as stops.)

(24)

$$\begin{bmatrix} -\text{ant} \\ -\text{cor} \\ +\text{high} \\ +\text{back} \end{bmatrix} \quad \rightarrow \quad \begin{bmatrix} +\text{ant} \\ +\text{cor} \\ -\text{high} \\ -\text{back} \end{bmatrix} \quad / \quad \begin{bmatrix} +\text{cons} \\ -\text{cont} \end{bmatrix}$$

(Velars realized as alveolars.)

(25)

$$\begin{bmatrix} +\text{cons} \\ +\text{cor} \\ -\text{high} \\ -\text{back} \end{bmatrix} \quad \rightarrow \quad \begin{bmatrix} -\text{cons} \\ -\text{cor} \\ +\text{high} \\ +\text{back} \end{bmatrix} \quad / \quad \begin{bmatrix} +\text{son} \\ -\text{ant} \\ -\text{lat} \end{bmatrix}$$

(Target [ɹ] realized as [w].)

Another process that effects a systemic simplification is where syllable initial obstruents are realized as voiced only, and syllable final ones as voiceless only. This can be expressed in the rule in (26):

(26)

$$\begin{bmatrix} +\text{cons} \\ -\text{cont} \end{bmatrix} \quad \rightarrow \quad \begin{cases} [+\text{voice}] \; / \; \sigma \; \underline{\hspace{1cm}} \\ [-\text{voice}] \; / \underline{\hspace{1cm}} \; \sigma \end{cases}$$

In some instances this pattern is restricted to voiceless realizations at the end of syllables (or less commonly voiced realizations at the beginning of syllables). In such cases, the pattern does not effect systemic simplifications, but structural ones (as the voicing contrast is still available, albeit in limited positions in phonological structure). Other structural simplifications include the deletion of word final consonants and the simplification of consonant clusters. The first of these can be expressed in the simple rule in (27):

(27)

$$[+\text{cons}] \quad \rightarrow \quad \emptyset \; / \underline{\hspace{2cm}} \; \#$$

In English, consonant cluster simplifications are of various types. First, we need to consider whether the cluster is syllable initial or syllable final. For each position we need to know whether the target cluster was of two or three consonants (and in final position, some four-consonant cluster types are also found). Finally, we need to note what patterns of simplification occur. In syllable initial position a common pattern is for two-consonant cluster targets of the stop + approximant type to simplify to the stop (e.g., /bl-/ targets realized as [b-]). Two-consonant cluster targets of the /s/ + stop type typically simplify to the following stop (explanations for these patterns in terms of sonority theory are dealt with in Chapter 2). These two patterns can be shown in the two rules in (28) and (29) (where we use /s/ as a shorthand for the full feature specification):

(28)

$$\begin{bmatrix} +son \\ +cons \end{bmatrix} \rightarrow \emptyset \ / \ \# \begin{bmatrix} +cons \\ -cont \end{bmatrix} \underline{\hspace{2cm}}$$

(29)

$$/s/ \rightarrow \emptyset \ / \ \# \underline{\hspace{2cm}} \begin{bmatrix} +cons \\ -cont \end{bmatrix}$$

Another fairly common pattern with initial clusters consisting of /s/ plus a following nasal is for a coalescence of the two target consonants into a voiceless nasal.* We can express this coalescence as shown in (30):

(30)

$$\begin{bmatrix} +cons \\ +cont \\ +ant \\ +cor \\ +strid \\ -voice \end{bmatrix} \begin{bmatrix} +cons \\ -cont \\ +nasal \\ \alpha \ cor \end{bmatrix} \rightarrow \begin{bmatrix} +cons \\ -cont \\ +nasal \\ \alpha \ cor \\ -voice \end{bmatrix}$$

The special notations described earlier in the chapter may also be found in rules describing disordered patterns. So, for example, Grunwell (1987) describes a case where, in /s/ + stop clusters, the realization of /s/ was determined by the place of articulation of the following stop. So, /sp-/ and /sm-/ were realized as [fp-] and [fm-], /st-/ and /sn-/ as [θt-] and [θn-], and /sk-/ as [çk-]. These three place changes can be expressed in a single rule through the use of the Greek letter convention, as shown in (31):

(31)

$$\begin{bmatrix} +cons \\ -son \\ +cont \end{bmatrix} \rightarrow \begin{bmatrix} \alpha \ ant \\ \beta \ cor \\ \gamma \ high \end{bmatrix} / \ \# \underline{\hspace{2cm}} \begin{bmatrix} \alpha \ ant \\ \beta \ cor \\ \gamma \ high \end{bmatrix}$$

---

* Other coalescences may also occur, for example, /sl-/ realized as [ɬ], and /sw-/ realized as [ʍ]. The rules in these cases will be somewhat different (see Grunwell, 1987, p. 185).

Grunwell (1987) also provides an illustration of the use of the angled bracket notation with disordered data. She refers to a case where target /s/ and /z/ are realized as [t] and [d], respectively, and where target /ʃ/ is also realized as [t] (we assume that target /ʒ/ would be realized as [d] if the data had provided examples of this rare target). The change of /s, z/ to [t, d] does not require any place feature value changes, but the post-alveolar /ʃ/ to [t] does require the change of [−anterior] to [+anterior]. The rule in (32) shows how we can combine these requirements.

(32)

$$
\begin{bmatrix}
+\text{cons} \\
+\text{cor} \\
+\text{cont} \\
+\text{strid} \\
< -\text{ant} >
\end{bmatrix}
\rightarrow
\begin{bmatrix}
-\text{cont} \\
-\text{strid} \\
< +\text{ant} >
\end{bmatrix}
$$

Finally, we can consider examples where rule ordering plays a part in the description of disordered phonology. Grunwell (1987) refers to a case where a child realized target /t, d/ as the affricates [tʃ, dʒ]. He also realized target /k, g/ as [t, d]; however, these instances of [t, d] did not undergo the rule of affricativization. Therefore, the affricate rule has to be ordered before the velar to alveolar rule, as shown in (33).

(33)

	two	cup
	tu	kʌp
Affricativization	tʃ	n.a.
Velar to alveolar	n.a.	t
	tʃu	tʌp

Clinical Studies Using Classical Generative Phonology

There have been few clinical studies using the classical approach to generative phonology as outlined in this chapter. This is mainly because the developments in the theory as outlined in the following chapters (especially Chapters 5–8) occurred soon after clinical phonologists had turned their attention to the theoretical approaches launched by Chomsky and Halle (1968). Nevertheless, Compton (1970, 1975, 1976) published a set of papers using the generative framework to describe the substitution patterns noted in disordered speech, and later, with a colleague, produced a generative assessment tool (Compton & Hutton, 1976). Grunwell (1987) points out the limitations of both the papers and the assessment. In fact, the worked example in her own chapter on generative phonology is arguably one of the better applications of the theory to clinical data. Interestingly, by the early 1980s researchers had already turned to the application of autosegmental versions of theoretical phonology (see also Chapter 7), and Spencer (1984) explicitly rejects the model of phonology presented in this chapter.

EXERCISE 4.6

Write the set of rules to account for the following disordered data, using the target form as the input. Note whether any of the rules need to be ordered. Target accent is General American.

Client LW. Age 6:9. Narrow Transcription.

pin	[p'in]	ten	[t'ɛn]
bin	[pʰin]	den	[tʰɛn]
cot	[k'ɑt]	pea	[p'i]
spin	[pɪn]	Stan	[tæn]
got	[kʰɑt]	bee	[pʰi]
skin	[kɪn]	spoon	[pun]

CONCLUSION

The early version of generative phonology was a major step forward in the formal description of both allophonic and morphophonemic alternations in the sound systems of natural language. As we noted earlier, however, there exists in this and later versions of the theory a tension as to whether it is aiming merely at theoretical simplicity and economy, or whether it is also attempting to model psycholinguistic organization. The latter approach would, of course, be of special interest to the clinical phonologist. However, as we have seen, in reality the clinical use of the theory has been as a set of formalized statements linking target with realization. The classical generative approach does not provide much insight into the client's psycholinguistic ability, for example, as to whether a particular pattern is motivated by motor or organizational considerations.* We return to this tension in more detail in Chapter 15.

FURTHER READING

Many introductions to phonology describe the earlier forms of generative phonology, and readers may wish to consult Carr (1993), Kenstowicz (1994), Spencer (1996), Gussenhoven and Jacobs (1998), and Roca and Johnson (1999). However, the best way to get a good view of the theory is to examine Chomsky and Halle (1968).

Clinical applications of generative phonology are explored in Grunwell (1987). She also lists a set of studies on normal and disordered phonological development, noting that Smith (1973) and Braine (1974) write rules that deal with the child's phonology as a system in its own right. Apart from the Compton articles referred to earlier, Oller (1973) and Lorentz (1976) adopted the generative model in their studies. Ingram (1997) provides a very useful guide to the application of generative phonology to disordered data, but goes beyond the early version discussed in this chapter and explores some later developments with feature specification.

---

* A good example is the velar to alveolar changes noted earlier. These would appear to be purely phonological (i.e., organizational), but research in Gibbon (1990) shows that a motor explanation is better motivated in most cases.

SOURCES

The Welsh, English, and disordered data are from the authors. Other data are referenced in the text.

REVIEW QUESTIONS AND STUDY TOPICS

Review Questions

1. Briefly describe the reasons for positing two levels of representation in phonology.
2. What is the difference between allophonic and morphophonemic alternation?
3. Describe the format of generative rules.
4. What are the actions that generative phonological rules can do?
5. What are the special notational devices used in rules?
6. Why must some phonological rules be applied in a specific order?
7. What is the *elsewhere condition*, and what does it do?
8. What is the difference between the way phonologists understand the *input* to rules and the way clinical phonologists use the same idea when describing disordered speech?

Study Topics and Projects

1. Using the data you recorded for the study topics of Chapter 1, write a set of generative rules to account for your data. Note where rule ordering may be needed, and if any rule sets are feeding or bleeding.
2. Using research resources, investigate the debate in the phonology of the late 1960s and 1970s about how abstract or concrete phonology should be.

5

DEVELOPMENTS WITH FEATURES

INTRODUCTION

In Chapter 3 we introduced the notion of distinctive features. We described the development of distinctive feature theory, and the system drawn up by Chomsky and Halle (1968). However, as we might expect, phonologists have developed the theory over the years since *The Sound Pattern of English* (SPE) was published. They have considered the number and description of features to deal with the range of phonological systems encountered in the languages of the world, and they have researched some of the problems encountered with using a system of binary features, especially where there were no hierarchical relations between the features.

In terms of clinical usage also, there are problems with distinctive features. For example, a simple counting of feature errors doesn't distinguish between independent feature errors and errors on features that are dependent in some way on another feature value. An instance of this is the fact that [+strident] can only co-occur with [+continuant], so if the [+continuant] feature is in error (i.e., realized as [−continuant]), then [strident] is automatically converted to its minus value as well.

Further, we can note that some changes of segment realizations encountered in the acquisition and disorder literatures seem to require a large number of distinctive feature changes, whereas others do not, and that this difference does not always seem phonetically justified. For example, a less commonly encountered segment change in developmental or disordered phonology, such as /l/ to [ɹ], involves just two features ([+anterior] to [−anterior], and [+lateral] to [−lateral]), whereas the commonly encountered change of /ɹ/ to [w] involves five features: [+consonantal] to [−consonantal] in the major class features, [+coronal] to [−coronal], [−high] to [+high], [−back] to [+back], and [−round] to [+round].

In this chapter we will look at some of the ways in which researchers working within the paradigm of generative phonology have attempted to address these problems. First, we turn our attention to developments in the number and description of features.

Table 5.1 Four-Way Plosive System of Hindi

	/p/	/pʰ/	/b/	/bɦ/
Voice	–	–	+	+
Spread glottis	–	+	–	+
	Voiceless unaspirated	Voiceless aspirated	Voiced unaspirated	Voiced aspirated

Table 5.2 Stops of Xhosa

	/pʰ/	/p'/	/b/	/ɓ/
Voice	–	–	+	+
Spread glottis	+	–	–	–
Constricted glottis	–	+	–	+
	Voiceless aspirated	Voiceless ejective	Voiced unaspirated	Voiced implosive

A CURRENT VERSION OF DISTINCTIVE FEATURES

Phonologists during the 1970s (e.g., Hyman, 1975) and the 1980s (e.g., Halle & Clements, 1983; Sagey, 1986) proposed changes to the set of features described in SPE. The account given here is derived mainly from the synthesis of these proposals given in Gussenhoven and Jacobs (1998) and Roca and Johnson (1999). Features are now divided into four main categories: *major class*, *laryngeal*, *manner*, and *place*.

Major class features include [±consonantal], [±sonorant], and [±approximant]. In SPE the feature [±syllabic] was used instead of [±approximant] (the two terms express the same phonetic distinction). However, because in modern nonlinear approaches to phonology (see Chapters 7 and 8) the property of syllabicity is expressed in a different way, the feature label has been changed in recent times.* The features [±consonantal] and [±sonorant] have the same definitions as in SPE.

Laryngeal features in SPE centered around [±voice]. However, it is clear that a range of phonetic phenomena derives from laryngeal activity, and in later models of distinctive features this is recognized through the provision of more laryngeal features. These phonetic phenomena include aspiration, and glottalic ingressive and egressive airstream mechanisms. SPE had tried to deal with these through features such as [±tense] and [±checked], but these features were not clearly linked to laryngeal activity. The first of these new features is [±spread glottis]: The plus value includes aspirated plosives and glottal fricatives; the minus value is used for all other sounds. To see how this feature interacts with the voice feature, we can consider the four-way plosive systems of north Indian languages (such as Hindi), shown in Table 5.1.

The second of the new features is [±constricted glottis]. The plus value includes laryngealized vowels and consonants (i.e., those spoken with creaky voice), preglottalized or glottally reinforced stops, and ejectives and implosives. We can see how these features interact in Table 5.2, using data from Xhosa.

Manner features according to Gussenhoven and Jacobs (1998) consist of the three features [±continuant], [±nasal], and [±lateral], with definitions as in SPE. Other researchers

---

* Many recent works do retain the traditional [±syllabic] label, however.

Table 5.3 Manner Features of Selected English Consonants

	/t/	/n/	/l/	/θ/	/s/
Continuant	–	–	+	+	+
Nasal	–	+	–	–	–
Lateral	–	–	+	–	–
Strident	–	–	–	–	+

(such as Roca and Johnson, 1999) also include [±strident] under the manner features. Gussenhoven and Jacobs (1998), however, list it under the place feature [Coronal], as they suggest that it only applies to coronal fricatives and affricates. It is arguable, however, that this feature can be used to distinguish velar from uvular fricatives, or bilabial from labiodental ones, in which case, [±strident] must remain independent of a specific place label. SPE also utilized the [±delayed release] (usually abbreviated to [±del rel]) feature to distinguish affricates from fricatives and plosives; however, nonlinear phonology (see Chapters 7 and 8) treats affricates in a way similar to that of diphthongs and long vowels, that is, as occupying two timing slots. In treatments like this, each part of the affricate has its own set of features (i.e., a plosive set for slot 1 and a fricative set for slot 2), and so the [del rel] feature is no longer required. Table 5.3 shows manner features applied to some English consonants.

The most important changes to feature theory have occurred with place features. The requirement for strict binarity of features here has been relaxed in an attempt to capture the relations that exist between place features. So, for example, because the feature [±anterior] only proved distinctive for consonants that were also [+coronal], it makes sense to consider [±anterior] as a subfeature of coronal sounds. Likewise, as the features [±high], [±low], and [±back] only co-occur with sounds that are also [+dorsal], these features came to be deemed subservient to the dorsal characteristic. Finally, the feature [+round] could only co-occur with labial sounds (recall that not all labially produced sounds have to have lip-rounding).

To account for these feature hierarchies (which we return to in more detail below in the section on feature geometry), several unary place features are now found in current versions of distinctive feature theory, each having one or more binary subfeatures. Unary features, of course, lack plus and minus values, and are normally written in small capitals. The first of these is [LABIAL], which is found with all sounds that are pronounced with the lips (e.g., [p, f, m, o, u]). These segments may also have lip-rounding, in which case they are [+round] ([p^W, m^W, o, u]), or lack lip-rounding, in which case they are [–round] ([p, f, m]).

The feature [CORONAL] has two agreed dependent features (and the disputed stridency feature we discussed above). [+anterior] consonants are those articulated at the dental and alveolar positions, and [–anterior] consonants are those articulated at the postalveolar, palatal, and retroflex positions. Note that in this arrangement, values of anterior no longer need to be given (indeed, cannot be given) for sounds that do not have the [CORONAL] feature, and in the same way, the feature [±round] cannot be assigned to sounds that are not also LABIAL.* The other dependent feature is [±distributed]. [+distributed] sounds for English include the laminal (tongue blade) postalveolar fricatives and the dental fricatives.

---

* Labialized velars, for example, are accounted for by positing two places of articulation for the segment, albeit linked to only one timing slot.

Alveolar stops and fricatives in English (mainly apical or tongue tip articulations) are [–distributed], as are retroflex consonants. This feature has also been suggested as a means of distinguishing bilabial from labiodental fricatives in those few languages where they are contrasted. As we noted earlier, [±strident] may also be used for this purpose, and would avoid the need to extract [±distributed] from its hierarchical position beneath [CORONAL]. Unlike Gussenhoven and Jacobs (1998), we follow here Roca and Johnson's (1999) position allocating [±strident] to the independent manner features.

The feature [DORSAL] covers consonants and vowels articulated with the body of the tongue. For consonants, this covers the velars and uvulars. The binary features [±high], [±low], and [±back] are found under this unary feature. As well as their use with vowels (which we saw in Chapter 3), it needs to be remembered that two of these features are also used with consonants. [+high] consonants include fronted velars and velars; [+back] covers velar and uvular consonants. As its name suggests, [+low] does not cover any dorsal consonants (although in SPE, glottals and pharyngeals were [+low]). In the current account, the [±tense] feature is also restricted to vowels; [+tense] applies to a vowel such as the more peripheral English /i/ in *seat*, while [–tense] applies to a vowel like the more centralized English /ɪ/ in *sit*.

Gussenhoven and Jacobs (1998) treat [±advanced tongue root] and [±retracted tongue root] as dependent features of [DORSAL]; however, Roca and Johnson (1999) believe that the final unary feature—[RADICAL]—can apply to vowels as well as [DORSAL] can, and list these features as dependent on [RADICAL]. [±ATR] and [±RTR] apply only to vowels and are used in certain languages where the tongue body position is similar between certain pairs of contrastive vowel segments (so [±high], [±low], and [±back] cannot be used to distinguish them), but the advancement or retraction of the tongue root appears to be the most important distinguishing characteristic phonetically. Some researchers (such as Roca and Johnson) believe that the English tense-lax distinction can be adequately captured via the use of [±ATR], and do not include the feature [±tense] in their inventory. [RADICAL], when applied to consonants, covers glottals and pharyngeals.

In Table 5.4 we show some English vowels and consonants, with their place features marked. Note how the use of unary and dependent features alters the shape of this chart

Table 5.4 Place Features of Selected English Sounds

		/u/	/ʊ/	/ɑ/	/p/	/s/	/ʃ/	/k/	[ʔ]
LABIAL		√	√		√				
	round	+	+		–				
CORONAL						√	√		
	anterior					+	–		
	distributed					–	+		
DORSAL		√	√	√				√	
	high	+	+	–				+	
	low	–	–	+				–	
	back	+	+	+				+	
	tense	+	–	+				–	
RADICAL									√
	ATR								–
	RTR								–

compared to tables in Chapter 3, where the original strict binarity of SPE resulted in values being filled in for all features. Check marks are used to note when a unary feature applies to a particular sound.

EXERCISE 5.1

Using the changes to feature systems described in this chapter, draw up distinctive feature matrices for the part systems of the following languages, which we first saw in Chapter 3.

a. Hindi

Part of the consonant system:
/p, t̪, ʈ, k, pʰ, t̪ʰ, ʈʰ, kʰ, b, d̪, ɖ, g, bʱ, d̪ʱ, ɖʱ, gʱ/

b. Turkish

Part of the vowel system (all considered tense here):
/i, y, u, ɯ, e, ø, o/

c. Russian

Part of the fricative system
/f, fʲ, v, vʲ, s, sʲ, z, zʲ, ʃ, ʒ, x, xʲ/ (assume /xʲ/ is [ç])

The changes in features we have just described do have some implications for the analysis of clinical data via distinctive features. For example, the commonly encountered process of the realization of target velars as alveolars (e.g., /k/ → [t], /g/ → [d]) needed four binary feature changes in classic SPE features (involving [anterior], [coronal], [high], and [back]). While four binary feature changes are still needed, these features are dependent on changes to only two unary place features: [DORSAL] is turned off, and [CORONAL] is turned on. This captures the notion that moving from velar to alveolar is a simple movement from back tongue to front tongue (whatever the precise phonetic formulations needed to characterize the actual realization of these two basic tongue positions).

However, the problem of [±strident] referred to above is not solved in the current view of features. This is because it remains a feature independent of any other. The proposal noted above of assigning it as a dependent feature of [CORONAL] might go some way toward solving the problem, but we have noted before that this feature is better thought of as a dependent feature of [±continuant], in that when that feature is set to minus, then stridency must also be set to minus. One solution, therefore, might be to allow manner features as well as place features to be unary, and establish a unary [CONTINUANT]. Alternatively, we might wish to omit [±strident] from our list of features (phonetically, the division of fricatives into [+strident] and [−strident] is not well motivated either acoustically or articulatorily) and find some other means of distinguishing between the anterior fricatives.

FEATURE GEOMETRY

We saw in the preceding section that research into distinctive features suggests that certain features are subordinate to certain others (indeed, this very notion is foreshadowed in SPE). A first attempt to formalize the idea that features exist in a hierarchy was made

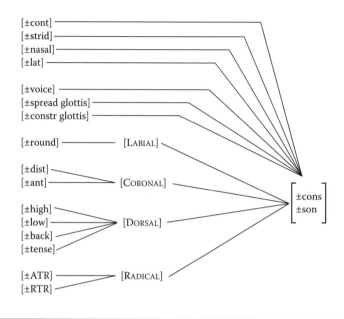

Figure 5.1 Feature geometry tree. (Adapted from Roca & Johnson, 1999, p. 524).

by Clements (1985). It is clear, for example, that features that apply only to consonants should somehow be separate from those applying only to vowels. However, the precise number of feature levels, and therefore intermediate categories, has been a matter of considerable debate since Clements's first proposal. (Indeed, as we saw above, the number of features and their labels has also been subject to debate.) We include here an adaptation of a recent version of the feature tree (that of Roca & Johnson, 1999, p. 524), but readers are urged to consult other accounts and the justification for them as noted in the further reading suggestions at the end of this chapter.

Many feature trees place intermediate labels (*place*, *laryngeal*, and sometimes *manner*) between the root node of [±cons, ±son] and the features to the left. However, as these are mere labels (as opposed to phonological features), they are perhaps best omitted. It should be noted that in most feature trees that have been proposed since Clements (1985), at least some of the intermediate features (in the case of Figure 5.1, the intermediate-level place features) are monovalent (i.e., having just one value; see the discussion in Chapter 3 and earlier in this chapter). The debate on monovalent features as opposed to binary ones still continues, and we return to this issue in Chapter 13.

Feature geometry has usually been used in conjunction with autosegmental phonology (see Chapter 7) to express phonological relations in natural language. We won't go into the mechanisms of autosegmental phonology here, but can illustrate some of the strengths of the feature geometry approach through consideration of some clinical data. In Ball, Müller, and Damico (2003) a case is reported of a young female client with phonological disorder who used double onsets in certain repetition tasks. These double onsets included those where modeled initial nasals were repeated with the nasal as the first onset, immediately replaced by an oral consonant (/mu/ → [m: bu]), and those where a modeled fricative was replaced by a glottal stop in the second onset (/su/ → [s: ʔu]). In the first example, we can use feature geometry to show how the [nasal] is decoupled from the segment (redundant place features are omitted). Figure 5.2 represents the initial onset, and Figure 5.3 the second onset.

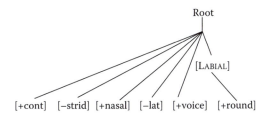

Figure 5.2 Initial onset with [nasal].

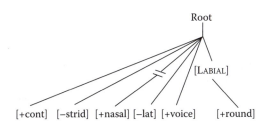

Figure 5.3 Second onset with decoupled [nasal].

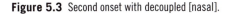

We can do the same with the fricative-glottal stop example. Here we again omit most redundant features. Figure 5.4 represents the initial onset with the fricative, and Figure 5.5 the second onset, where manner, place, and laryngeal features have been decoupled (we assume here that glottal stop is best characterized as a default consonant).

There have been several studies that have applied the insights of feature geometry to disordered phonology, and we include references to these in the "Further Reading" section. We will return to this area in later chapters, where the usefulness of a hierarchical approach to phonological features will be illustrated.

EXERCISE 5.2

The realization of target velar consonants as alveolars is often reported in the clinical literature. How would a feature geometry account of this error be superior to one where the analyst counted the total number of ± feature errors? Using the tree given in this chapter, see whether this velar to alveolar change can be described with just one place node being decoupled. If not, do you consider this is a strength or a weakness of our proposed feature geometry?

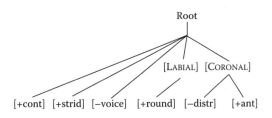

Figure 5.4 Initial onset with fricative.

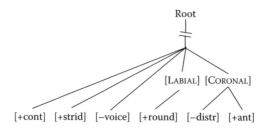

Figure 5.5 Second onset with glottal stop.

UNDERSPECIFICATION

The notion of having default entries in feature matrices, filled in later by markedness conventions (see Chapter 3), is closely related to another development in phonology: *underspecification*. This idea, rather than being based on the feature description of individual segments, was used in the description of lexical items where, in certain circumstances, the segments making up the word could be underspecified (i.e., the values for several features would be left blank), with the full specification given later through *redundancy rules*. As the input of these rules is blanks (rather than ± or *u/m*), they appear as shown in (1):

(1)

$$[\ ] \quad \rightarrow \quad [+\text{voice}] / \quad \left[\overline{} \atop +\text{son} \right]$$

Before we look at how underspecification works, we need to consider why phonologists might consider it a good idea. Generative linguists have always been concerned with what can be called the *economy principle*: In any scientific description, when all other factors are equal, we should prefer the most economic account out of all those accounts that adequately describe the data. As applied to feature descriptions in phonology, Archangeli (1984, p. 50; see also 1988) states in (2):

(2)   Feature minimization principle

A grammar is most highly valued when underlying representations include the minimal number of features necessary to make different the phonemes of the language.*

We can illustrate a general application of underspecification to a commonly occurring type of phonological disorder in children: *consonant harmony* (or *consonant assimilation*). Here we find that one consonant in a word (often the initial one) influences later consonants to agree with it in terms of place, and sometimes also manner and voicing. Examples include [dadi] or [gagi] for target /dagi/, [danti] for /daŋki/, and [mʌmpi] for /mʌŋki/. For such a case, then, we need only specify the place features for the initial consonant of a word (if we were providing a phonological description of the child's output), and the remaining consonants could be underspecified for place features. The correct values for these features would be filled in later, and in cases of harmony or assimilation,

---

* We return in Chapter 14 to examine whether ideas about descriptive economy are also psycholinguistically plausible.

this could be understood as being done through a spreading of the relevant value from the fully specified segment (this notion of spreading will be returned to in Chapter 7). Such assimilatory processes—including tone harmony in tone languages—are commonly found in languages where, for example, certain features of the vowel in a morphological suffix can be underspecified, as they are always dependent on (or spread from) the vowel of the root (see descriptions of Turkish vowel harmony in Roca and Johnson, 1999).

Underspecification can also be appealed to in order to account for apparent lexical exceptions to a phonological rule. Again, if we consider clinical examples, we can think of a change such as fricatives being realized as stops. In such a system, the true consonants can be underspecified for the feature [continuant], because there is a redundancy rule that states that all such consonants are by default [–continuant], as shown in (3):

(3)

$$[\ ] \quad \rightarrow \quad [\text{-cont}]\ /\quad \begin{bmatrix} \overline{} \\ +\text{cons} \\ -\text{son} \end{bmatrix}$$

However, it may be the case that a client (especially on the verge of moving further toward target realizations) may have a group of words where fricatives, rather than stops, are in fact used for target fricatives. This can be accounted for in underspecification theory by assuming that this group of words with fricatives are fully specified for [continuant], whereas the rest of the lexicon is underspecified.

Radical Underspecification

Some researchers pushed the idea of economy in phonological description to the limits, and proposed that segment inventories should be as underspecified as possible. As we saw earlier, the markedness conventions that attempt to express degrees of naturalness in feature combinations (and so, how "natural" particular segments are) allow us a first removal of fully specified features, but the result is not always as underspecified as it is possible to achieve—remembering that we only need the smallest set of fully specified features that would allow us to separate the segments in question into separate phonemes. If we consider a simple vowel system such as might be found in clients with vowel disorders (see Ball & Gibbon, 2002, for a full treatment of vowel disorders in children), we can see how we can produce radical underspecification.*

We start with a simple five-vowel system, /i, e, ɑ, o, u/, and will examine only the use of vowel-specific features. The matrix in (4) shows this five-vowel system fully specified for vowel features.

(4)

	i	e	ɑ	o	u
high	+	–	–	–	–
low	–	–	+	–	–
back	–	–	+	+	+
round	–	–	–	+	+
ATR	+	+	–	+	+

---

* We adapt the example from Roca and Johnson (1999) here, as it is suitable both for natural language and disordered phonology.

By applying the markedness conventions described in Chapter 3, we can reduce the number of specified features as shown in (5):

(5)

	i	e	ɑ	o	u
high	+	–		–	–
low		–	+	–	
back	–	–		+	+
round					
ATR					

This is possible if you recall the convention that vowels cannot be simultaneously [+high, +low], that low vowels are usually [+back], that nonlow back vowels are usually [+round] (and conversely that nonlow front vowels are usually [–round]), and that the default setting for ATR is minus.

However, radical underspecification can take this further if the vowel system is considered as a system and if we can identify a segment that can be maximally underspecified. Such a segment might be some kind of default segment, for example, in clinical data, the one inserted by the speaker between consonants in clusters that are as yet not part of the speaker's repertoire. Following the example of Roca and Johnson (1999, p. 514), we will select /i/ to be this maximally underspecified vowel. Once all feature values are stripped from this segment, all we need to distinguish the remaining vowels can be shown as in (6):

(6)

	i	e	ɑ	o	u
high		–		–	
low			+		
back				+	+
round					
ATR					

Clearly, at some stage in the phonological derivation we need to resupply the feature values for this vowel system. Apart from the redundancy rules, we need first to replace the values for our maximally underspecified segment. This is done through a *complement rule*, which supplies the exact ± values for the vowel features to specify /i/; from this, the remaining values for the other vowels can be obtained. So, one complement rule (together with the universal redundancy rules) can save some 20 feature specifications in this vowel system.

However, there are problems with radical underspecification, and we'll consider just one here (see Roca & Johnson, 1999; Roca, 1994; Kenstowicz, 1994, for more examples). We might consider a clinical case where choice of realization of certain consonant targets depends crucially on the value of a vowel feature: A good example might be the choice between labial and nonlabial consonants dependent on the value of the [round] feature in the preceding vowel. A radically underspecified vowel system such as in (6) does not allow us to "spread" the feature from the vowel to the consonant. Further, it also means that the underspecification of the consonants for features such as [anterior] is predicated on values of the feature [round] that do not exist at the underlying level. We can also mention here that the identification of a suitable segment to be maximally underspecified is not always straightforward, and considering the variability often encountered in disordered speech, this problem is also a relevant one for clinical phonology.

Contrast-Restricted Underspecification

Restricted or contrast-restricted underspecification attempts to get around the problems with radical underspecification. This approach allows full specification where necessary to avoid the pitfalls described in the literature. So, taking our hypothetical example, the value of [round] would be specified, but only when the vowel was followed by a consonant that was subject to the assimilatory process noted. In other words, word final vowels, or those followed by nonassimilating consonants, could still be unspecified for [round]. Problems have been encountered with this approach to underspecification; for example, the fuller specifications of some features appear as if they would block vowel harmony that does in fact spread across certain contexts in specific languages (see Roca & Johnson, 1999, pp. 534–537).

Underspecification builds on the insights of markedness, but is powered by the desire for descriptive economy. Clinically, it may go some way toward dealing with the difference between numbers of feature errors in commonly occurring clinical realizations, but its psycholinguistic validity—which must be of importance to clinical phonologists—remains to be justified.

EXERCISE 5.3

Assume part of a target vowel system is /ɪ, ɛ, æ, ɔ, ʊ/, which is changed in the case of a speech disordered client to [i, æ, ɑ, ɒ, u]. Assume that [ɑ] can be utilized as the maximally underspecified segment for this client. Use the feature [tense] rather than [ATR].

Draw up a fully specified matrix of the client's realization, an underspecified matrix using markedness conventions only, and a radically underspecifed matrix. Calculate the feature errors between the client's system and the target system using these three matrices. When calculating errors, count only changed values, not blanks. What differences do you find? Which of the calculations do you feel would be clinically most useful in describing the client's vowel problems and thinking about planning remediation for them?

FURTHER READING

An account of a recent version of distinctive features is given in Gussenhoven and Jacobs (1998). Underspecification and feature geometry are described in detail in Roca (1994), Kenstowicz (1994), and Roca and Johnson (1999). Underspecification can be traced from early work by Kiparsky (1973, 1982a, 1982b), through Steriade (1987) and Clements (1988) on contrast-restricted underspecification, to radical underspecification in Archangeli (1984, 1988). Feature geometry first appears in Clements (1985), with refinements discussed in Sagey (1986) and Halle (1992).

In clinical phonology, feature geometry is used in studies by Chin and Dinnsen (1991), Bernhardt and Gilbert (1992), Gierut, Cho, and Dinnsen (1993), and Heselwood (1997). Underspecification has featured in the work of Dinnsen and his colleagues, for example, Chin and Dinnsen (1992), Dinnsen (1996, 1997), and Dinnsen and Barlow (1998).

SOURCES

The Hindi, Turkish, and Russian are derived from the *Handbook of the IPA*; the remaining data are from the authors.

REVIEW QUESTIONS AND STUDY TOPICS

Review Questions

1. Describe the main changes in feature theory illustrated by the current view of distinctive features given in this chapter and the view given in Chapter 3.
2. How would you address the problem of the feature [±strident] described in this chapter?
3. Describe how the developments in feature theory noted in the first section of this chapter could aid in the analysis of disordered speech.
4. What are the motivations for ranking phonological distinctive features into hierachical tree structures?
5. How do underspecification redundancy rules differ from markedness conventions? Give examples of each to illustrate the different formalisms.
6. What underlying principle drives the move to underspecify phonological representations of lexical items? How relevant do you feel such a principle is to the psycholinguistic explanation of how phonological organization is actually operationalized by speakers?
7. How does radical underspecification differ from contrast-restricted underspecification?
8. What, if any, are the clinical uses for any of the models of underspecification described in this chapter?

Study Topics and Projects

1. Review some of the other proposals for feature trees described in the relevant literature listed in the "Further Reading" section. Briefly summarize the pros and cons for at least three different proposals.
2. Review the target consonant or vowel usage of at least four phonology clients from your clinic. Attempt an explanation of their realizations in terms of underspecification.

6

DEVELOPMENTS WITH DERIVATIONS
Lexical and Prosodic Phonology

CYCLICAL RULES

In Chapter 4 we saw that certain generative phonological rules have to be ordered if a particular derivation is to be successfully accomplished. In this chapter we are going to start by looking at some rules that need to be applied cyclically for a successful description of certain phonological processes within the generative phonological approach. First we need to consider different types of phonological rules.

One sort of generative phonological rule is found in what traditionally has been termed allophonic alternation. For example, the rule that describes the nasalization of vowels before nasal consonants is shown in (1):

(1)

$$[-\text{cons}] \quad \rightarrow \quad [+\text{nasal}] \quad / \quad \begin{bmatrix} +\text{cons} \\ +\text{nasal} \end{bmatrix}$$

This rule applies across all lexical items where the context is met; its output is an allophone of the relevant vowel (i.e., not one of the distinctive sound units of the language), and there is a clear phonetic motivation for the change described in the rule.

A second type of rule differs from this sort in all of these respects. Let us take an example from English. In a group of words in English ending in /-k/, this final /-k/ changes to /s/ when the affix *-ity* is added. Examples include *opaque ~ opacity, electric ~ electricity, specific ~ specificity*. This rule differs from the nasalization one given in (1) above in that the output to the change is another of the contrastive sound units of English (rather than an allophone), and that there is no immediate phonetic motivation for the change.* Some of these lexical rules also show exceptions, and for English this is best illustrated by considering patterns of stress assignment in trisyllabic words (which

---

* It is true that /s/ is more anterior than /k/, and that the influence of the initial /ɪ/ of the suffix might be appealed to in order to explain this anterior movement. However, there is no immediate reason why /k/ should move to /s/ rather than to /ʃ/ (cf. electrician) or to /tʃ/ (as has happened in other languages).

73

also allow us to look at other effects of the *-ity* suffix). The relevant rule is usually called trisyllabic laxing (TSL), and although its precise formulation is controversial, we will follow Kenstowicz (1994). TSL shortens a long vowel when it is followed by two syllables, the first of which is unaccented and the last of which is one of a group of specific derivational affixes (i.e., *-ity, -ify, -ual, -ize, -ous*). We can see the effects of vowel shortening in the examples in (2):

(2)

opaque	~	*opacity*	/eɪ/	~	/æ/
obscene	~	*obscenity*	/i/	~	/ɛ/
sublime	~	*sublimity*	/aɪ/	~	/ɪ/

(It should also be noted that the vowel quality changes in these examples. Some phonologists account for this by positing underlying forms of the unaffixed words with long versions of the vowels in the affixed form, together with a vowel shift rule applying after TSL that changes the vowels in unaffixed forms to the surface realization. Whether this is a useful assumption or not, it is not relevant to our discussion of TSL.)

This rule differs from rule (1) above. It applies only to words with suffixes (so trisyllabic words such as *apricot* do not undergo TSL), and even when suffixes are present, only certain suffixes trigger the rule (so, for example, *easily, slavery,* and *piloting* do not undergo TSL). In other words, it is lexically restricted. There are also ad hoc exceptions that meet all the characteristics needed to trigger TSL, but where the rule is not triggered (e.g., *obese ~ obesity*). It also lacks clear phonetic motivation (i.e., there is no natural explanation for TSL in terms of the articulatory system). Finally, the changes are not allophonic, as the short and long vowel forms are all contrastive items in the phonological system of the language. These rules are termed *derived environment rules*.

EXERCISE 6.1

Which of the following phonological rules of English are allophonic alternations, and which are derived environment rules? (We are using abbreviated rule formats here, but the meaning should be clear if you have read Chapter 4; V denotes vowel and C denotes consonant.)

    a. [pʰ, tʰ, kʰ] → [p⁼, t⁼, k⁼] / /s/ _____ (e.g., port → sport)
    b. ['σ σ]ₙₒᵤₙ → [σ'σ]ᵥₑᵣᵦ (e.g., 'object → ob'ject)
    c. V: → V· / _____ C_fortis (e.g., seed → seat)
    d. /t/ → /ʃ/ / _____ "ion" (e.g., deliberate → deliberation)

It turns out that some lexical rules (such as TSL) operate in a cyclical manner. As we have seen, TSL only applies when certain derivational morphological suffixes are applied to the stem. Kenstowicz (1994) illustrates these derived environment rules with an example from Finnish. In Finnish, there is a rule that changes underlying /t/ to surface [s] when preceding [i] in a suffix. When [t] precedes [i] within a morpheme, the rule does not apply (similar to the TSL rule above). Examples are given in (3), where the first example shows the change at a suffix boundary, and the second shows the change blocked morpheme internally:

(3)

    (i)   halut-a *to want*; halus-i *wanted*

    (ii)   tila *room*; äiti *mother*

(Kenstowicz, 1994, p. 201)

However, there are some Finnish words where morpheme internal [t] to [s] before [i] *does* take place. Consider the examples in (4):

(4)

    vesi *water* (cf. vete-nä, essive singular)

    käsi *hand* (cf. käte-nä, essive singular)

We know that in other forms (such as the essive singular forms given in parentheses) these items normally have morpheme internal [t]; why have these undergone the rule change when the items in (3ii) did not? The answer begins to appear when we consider that the essive singular forms end in [te], and that Finnish has a general rule that raises word final [e] to [i]. So, when we get the bare stem of these [te] final forms, the raising rule produces [ti], and this is subject to the [t] to [s] rule. The problem is, how can we order these rules to produce the surface realizations of Finnish? Rule ordering (as described in Chapter 4) cannot help us, because we need to order the [t] to [s] rule after the word final vowel raising rule, but at this point in the derivation there is nothing to stop [t] to [s] from applying to words like *tila* and *äiti*. If, on the other hand, we restrict [t] to [s] until after the addition of *-i* suffixes, then we can't account for the examples in (4). A possible solution of this dilemma by allowing rules to take into consideration the previous derivational history of the form in question is not encouraged, as it increases the class of possible grammars too much.

It was through problems like these that phonologists came up with the notion of *strict cyclicity*. This results in lexical rules that are restricted to derived environments being applied cyclically, that is, in stages, the stages being linked to morphological derivation within words. So, the set of ordered cyclical rules applies first to a monomorphemic stem, then the same set of rules is applied again when a particular affix is added, then again when another affix is attached to the new enlarged stem, and so on. Clearly only certain rules will be triggered in some cycles, as the contexts for some will be absent, but this cycle approach allows ordering restraints to be applied several times for certain derived environments. An example of English stress assignment illustrates how this approach works. The words *condensation* and *compensation*, being similar in phonological makeup, would be expected to have identical stress and vowel weakening patterns. However (in most varieties of English, at least), while the secondary-primary stress patterns are the same, *compensation* undergoes vowel weakening of its second syllable to schwa, while *condensation* does not: /ˌkɒmpənˈseɪʃn̩/ versus /ˌkɒndɛnˈseɪʃn̩/. Let's follow Kenstowicz's (1994, p. 204) reasoning as to how this difference can be explained through cyclic rules. The first cycle is the bare stem, and so stress is assigned to the bare stems of the two words (remember, these differ in structure: *condense* and *compensate*). In the second cycle, stress is assigned to the stem plus *-ation* affix. A later rule undertakes vowel weakening, but the output of the cyclical rules means that only *compensate* is a candidate for this process because it can only apply to syllables with neither primary nor secondary stress. A further later rule neutralizes stress differences, resulting in the identical stress pattern, but different vowel weakening patterns. We can see how this works in (5):

(5)

		First Cycle
[condense]	[compensate]	
con'dense	'compen,sate	Stress rule
		Second Cycle
[con'dense]ation	['compen,sate]ion	
con,dens'ation	,compen'sation	Stress rule
		Later Rules
——————	,compǝn'sation	Vowel reduction
,condens'ation	——————	Stress neutralization

To make cyclical rules work, a *strict cycle condition* (SCC) was drawn up that requires any cyclic rule to refer to information taken from an earlier cycle and that taken from the current cycle (Kenstowicz, 1994, p. 208). It is the SCC that allows us to account for the Finnish data we looked at earlier. The *halut+i* change to *halus–i* comes about because the rule uses information that bridges the boundary between the stem and the suffix (one of the conditions of the SCC). The *vete* to *vesi* change involves the vowel raising, which again uses information bridging the stem-suffix boundary, and the [t] to [s] change, which uses information from a rule operating on the current cycle (i.e., the raising rule)—another condition of the SCC. However, forms like *tila* satisfy neither of the SCC conditions, as they don't refer to stem-suffix boundaries, nor to any previous or current cycle rules. Therefore, in those cases, the [t] to [s] rule is blocked.

LEXICAL PHONOLOGY

Work in this area led some phonologists (mainly Kiparsky 1982a, 1985) to develop a theory of lexical phonology. In this approach, phonological rules are divided into two types: *lexical* and *postlexical* (this has already been foreshadowed in the distinction made above). Lexical rules were applied within the lexicon (i.e., the list of words of a language) in cycles, whereas postlexical rules applied noncyclically, outside the lexicon, after all lexical rules in their cycles had been applied.

The model is envisaged as consisting of links within the lexicon between *word formation rules* (WFRs), which are the morphological rules combining stems with affixes (or, in the case of compound words, stems with stems), and lexical phonological rules, organized in cycles (called *levels* or *strata*), the levels being delimited by the particular morphological processes they contain. We can see how the model operates diagrammatically in Figure 6.1.

This model shows clearly how lexical rules can refer to morphological structure, but not syntactic conditions, whereas postlexical rules cannot refer to morphological structure, but can refer to syntax (e.g., processes that can go across word boundaries). It also helps explain how lexical rules can have exceptions (these exceptions will be marked in the lexicon, while postlexical rules do not have exceptions—because they cannot access the lexicon).

One important condition imposed by Kiparsky is that the output of each level is a lexical item. It is also worth noting that all words are deemed to pass through

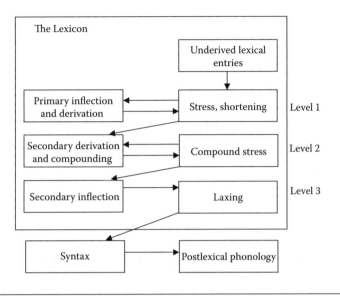

Figure 6.1 A model of lexical phonology. (Adapted from Kenstowicz, 1994, p. 215.)

all the levels of WFRs and their linked lexical rules, even if they have no affixes of any kind. So, a word like *cup* is passed through the system (with, of course, no phonological changes accruing), just as a word like *impossibilities*, with its prefix and derivational and inflectional suffixes. The requirement for the output of each level to be a lexical item accounts for why, for example, we have in English *inept* and not **unept*. As Kenstowicz (1994, p. 215) points out, the base form **ept* cannot pass from Level 1 (where the *in-* prefix is situated) across to Level 2 (where the *un-* prefix would be attached), as it would have to be a full lexical item when it leaves Level 1. So, *unhappy* is possible because the full lexical item *happy* can go from Level 1 to Level 2, but not **unept*. Finally, we can note that the addition of an affix (i.e., through a WFR) does not always have any phonological consequence. So, if we add the suffix *-er* to a stem such as *walk*, there is no phonological rule required for the resultant form *walker*.

As the model in Figure 6.1 shows, for English the main lexical phonological rules are concerned with stress assignment, vowel weakening, and related processes. We can take some examples and work them through the various levels.* Level 1 WFRs include primary inflections, and here we can see phonological lexical rules that are other than stress and weakening related. Irregular plurals such as *foot ~ feet* (which Kiparsky calls umlaut) and past tenses such as *ring ~ rang* (Kiparsky's ablaut) and *weep ~ wept* all require phonological changes. Primary derivations may also require vowel shortening changes: *deep ~ depth*; others may require stress changes: 'medicine ~ me'dicinal. Level 2 suffix WFRs usually do not have an effect on stress assignment: Compare Level 1 stress shift e'lectric ~ elec'tricity with Level 2 no-stress shift in 'kind ~ 'kindness. Level 3 WFRs include regular inflections such as plural, past tense, and so on, with the irregular forms being found in Level 1. (Some researchers, such as Katamba, 1989, have only two levels; others have four, such as Halle & Mohanan, 1985.) The levels have implications for the

---

* We do not have the space here to list all the morphological operations that occur at the different levels, but readers can consult any of the texts in the "Further Reading" section to follow up on this if they wish.

ordering of affixes: Level 1 affixes are nearest the root, Level 2 are beyond Level 1. So, we can have *authorit-arian-ism* but not *authorit-ism-arian*.

We can trace the progress of a multimorphemic word—*exporters*—through the levels. The underived lexical entry is **port*, which has the Level 1 prefix *ex-* added, followed by stress assignment to give 'ex₁port. Conversion from noun to verb results in a change in the stress pattern: ₁ex'port. This leaves Level 1 as a full lexical item and enters Level 2. In Level 2, the *-er* agentive ending is added, which has no phonological consequences. In Level 3 the plural inflectional suffix is added to give ₁ex'porters. This also has no phonological consequences, but if the third-person singular suffix had been added to ₁ex'port, then the rule converting the [z] ending to [s] following a voiceless consonant would have been triggered.

EXERCISE 6.2

Describe how the following English words pass through the three levels of lexical rules, noting which forms emerge from each level.

    a. unhappiness
    b. widths
    c. totalitarianism
    d. objecting
    e. adjuncts
    f. mice's

CLINICAL APPLICATION OF LEXICAL PHONOLOGY

The first major tenet of lexical phonology is that there is a division between lexical and postlexical phonological rules. The second is that lexical rules interact with WFRs in a set of different levels. Let us consider whether these views have any clinical implications. Oetting and Rice (1993) considered the application of lexical phonology to the analysis of plural acquisition in children with specific language impairment (SLI). Clearly, the notion of levels of lexical rules may well be useful in examining nonnormal acquisition of certain bound morphemes in SLI, and Oetting and Rice noted that studies of normal acquisition of regular and irregular plurals support the lexical phonology view that these belong to separate levels (Level 1 for irregular and Level 3 for regular in Kiparsky's (1982a) formulation). Their study of plural usage in SLI children also supported the separation of regular and irregular plurals into separate levels, and they concluded that their use by the SLI children is rule based, differing from the non-SLI children only in a frequency effect whereby their performance was superior on commonly pluralized nouns as compared to infrequently pluralized ones. Studies of other bound morphemes with SLI children would further test the value of the levels approach to lexical rules, and investigations of phonological problems within the lexical and postlexical domains would help support or cast doubt on the separation of these two types of rules as posited in lexical phonology. From a therapeutic viewpoint, this theory would suggest that children with morphological problems (as opposed to strictly phonological ones) would benefit from intervention dealing with the different levels separately.

PROSODIC PHONOLOGY*

We noted earlier that among other things, postlexical rules could interact with syntax and so accounted for phenomena such as juxtapositional assimilation in English. Naturally, a question that arose soon after the development of the lexical phonology paradigm was how this interaction was organized. At first sight, it might seem to make sense to use the same hierarchical structure that has been posited for syntactic organization (e.g., noun phrase, prepositional phrase, etc.). However, the assignment of stress patterns (i.e., rhythm) in English, at least, does not always coincide with syntactic boundaries. For example, Roca and Johnson (1999) note that stress retraction in noun phrases (a process to avoid too many stressed syllables close to each other) occurs in some noun phrases, but not all. We can see this when we compare (6i) and (6ii):

(6)

(i)	Japa'nese 'railways→ 'Japanese 'railways
(ii)	Japa'nese 'railways and 'motorways

(Adapted from Roca & Johnson, 1999, p. 472)

Prosodic phonology has developed a hierarchy of prosodic units within which postlexical rules can operate. Selkirk (1984) suggested the structure shown in Figure 6.2, which we will use in this chapter.

Common abbreviations for the levels are U (utterance), I (intonational phrase), Φ (phonological phrase), W or ω (word), and F (foot), or the ones used in Figure 6.2. We can now use the insights from this phonological hierarchy to explain the differences in the stress retraction behavior of the two noun phrase examples in (6). While they are both noun phrases, (6ii) is made up of two phonological phrases ([Japanese]$_{PhP}$ [railways and motorways]$_{PhP}$), but (6i) is made up of only one ([Japanese railways]$_{PhP}$). So, as the retraction rule only operates with a PhP, it can only change stress patterns in (6i).

Typical phonological processes at the U level would include the insertion of intrusive-r in those dialects that use it, or the flapping of intervocalic-t (again, in those dialects that do this). Examples adapted from Roca and Johnson (1999) include those shown in (7):

(7)

(i)	Don't sit on that sofa: it's broken (intrusive-r after *sofa*).
(ii)	Don't stand on that mat: it's damp (flapped-t after *mat*).

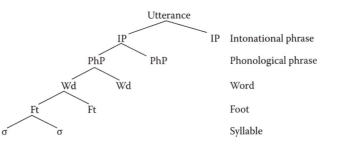

Figure 6.2 Hierarchy of prosodic units. (Adapted from Selkirk, 1984.)

* We are discussing here the approach of Nespor and Vogel (1986), and others in the same tradition, rather than the prosodic phonology of Firth and his followers, described in Chapter 9.

However, as Roca and Johnson point out, there has to be a semantic connection between the elements for these rules to operate. Therefore, the examples in (8) do not show intrusive-r or flapped-t:

(8)

>   (i)   Don't sit on that sofa! It's Mary.
>   (ii)   Don't stand on that mat! It's dinnertime.

We can assume that the U level also is the domain of operation for rules that regulate intonation across utterances. English, among other languages, has the feature of *declination*, where intonation patterns across an utterance gradually decline in pitch, clearly a U-level characteristic.

As the name suggests, the IP level is that at which intonation patterns (IPs) are assigned. It is important to remember that any collection of words may have a variety of intonation patterns placed over them, and that different numbers of such patterns can be associated with the same set of words. So, for example, the phrase *thank you very much* can be said with a pattern suggesting sincerity or a pattern suggesting sarcasm. The sentence *my uncle is coming to see me* can be said with a single intonation pattern or with two patterns, with a division after *uncle*, as shown in (9):

(9)

>   (i)   [My uncle is coming to see me.]$_{IP}$
>   (ii)   [My uncle]$_{IP}$ [is coming to see me.]$_{IP}$

The phonological phrase has already been referred to in the explanation of why stress retraction occurred with (6i) but not (6ii). Another example given by Gussenhoven and Jacobs (1998) shows that in English the syntactic rule known as *heavy NP shift* (whereby a direct object is moved to the end of a sentence) is only grammatical if the object consists of two PhPs even though the object may have a similar noun phrase (NP) structure. Examples are given in (10), where the second, starred, example is ungrammatical:

(10)

>   (i)   Al gave to John [that report]$_{PhP}$ [on George W.]$_{PhP}$
>   (ii)   *Al gave to John [that report on him.]$_{PhP}$

The phonological word does not always correspond to the lexical word. A good example is to consider compound words. For example, although English *teapot* is considered a single lexical word, phonologically it behaves like two phonological words in that it carries two main stresses: ['tea]$_W$ ['pot]$_W$. The foot unit is defined by the placement of stress: All the syllables between one stress and the next are grouped into a foot (languages differ as to whether these syllables should be calculated from left to right, i.e., beginning to end, or right to left, i.e., end to beginning). Spencer (1996) gives the example of the English word *compartmentalization*, which would be divided into feet as follows [compart]$_F$ [mentalize]$_F$ [ation]$_F$. There are not many totally convincing cases where the foot unit plays host to postlexical rules, however. Spencer (1996) describes a case of reduplication in the Australian language Diyari, where only the first foot of a word is reduplicated. It is possible that this unit might be appealed to in some instances of reduplication in disordered phonology. The final level we posited in Figure 6.2 is the syllable. Here, we are looking for phonological processes that affect syllables or parts of syllables. Spencer (1996) refers to work on Spanish, where apical nasals are realized as velar nasals in noninitial position. However, this change only occurs when the [n] is in the rime, and not when it is in the onset. For example, compare *kantan* → *ka[ŋ]ta[ŋ]* and *poner* → *po[n]er*. Again, this level would appear to be important in the explanation of some instances of disordered phonology.

EXERCISE 6.3

a. Analyze the following word into feet and syllables:

antidisestablishmentarianism

b. Analyze the following into phonological words and phrases:

Mary broke the Japanese teapot.

c. Undertake two different IP analyses of the following and explain any differences of meaning:

Thank you very much.

CLINICAL APPLICATIONS OF PROSODIC PHONOLOGY

Adi-Bensaid and Bat-El (2004) use the framework of prosodic phonology to examine the development of speech in a hearing-impaired child who had been fitted with a cochlear implant. The authors refer to the considerable body of literature that has examined the normal development of the prosodic word in a variety of different languages; the language involved in this case is Hebrew. Their investigation showed that the child followed the same path of acquisition of the prosodic word as normal children (the few exceptions were accounted for by considering the late onset of adequate auditory input). The authors find that the prosodic phonology framework "may have important implications for clinical use" (Adi-Bensaid & Bat-El, 2004, p. 201). They cite Fee (1997), who concluded that the prosodic stages identified in normative work could be used as an assessment metric, and as treatment goals in children with delayed phonological development. It would also be interesting to see the application of the model to acquired neurological disorders and to hearing impairment, where stress patterns may be disrupted. This would test the model's predictions about the application of different stress patterns at the different levels of analysis.

FURTHER READING

Kenstowicz (1994) is the phonology text that gives one of the clearest accounts of cyclical rules and lexical phonology, although Katamba (1989) also covers the topic. You may wish to consult the original formulations of the approach in Kiparsky's (1982a, 1985) articles. Prosodic phonology (the non-Firthian variety discussed in this chapter) is described in Spencer's (1996), Gussenhoven and Jacobs' (1998), and Roca and Johnson's (1999) texts, although again you may wish to consult a variety of original papers, for example, Selkirk (1984) and Nespor and Vogel (1986).

REVIEW QUESTIONS AND STUDY TOPICS

Review Questions

1. What is the difference between allophonic alternation and derived environment rules?
2. What is trisyllabic laxing?
3. Explain, with examples, the operation of the *strict cycle condition*.
4. What morphological operations and phonological rules take place in the three levels of lexical rules posited in Kiparksy's model of lexical phonology?
5. What types of processes are described in postlexical rules?
6. What structure of prosodic units is suggested in Selkirk's model of prosodic phonology?
7. Describe typical phonological processes that take place at any two of the units of prosodic phonology.
8. Explain and exemplify why the phonological word and the lexical word need not always be in agreement?

Study Topics and Projects

1. Read the original sources on either lexical phonology or prosodic phonology, then provide a detailed account of the theory, and suggestions on how the theory may throw light on various patterns of disordered speech and their remediation.
2. Choose a short passage of disordered speech and undertake an analysis using both lexical phonology and prosodic phonology. Do you find any ways in which these two approaches can be combined? What insights (if any) does the analysis shed on the disorder and on ways of planning intervention?

7

AUTOSEGMENTAL PHONOLOGY

INTRODUCTION

In Chapters 3 and 4 we introduced distinctive features and looked at generative phonological rules. Such rules were introduced in Chomsky and Halle's (1968) seminal work *The Sound Pattern of English* (SPE) and form the basis of standard generative phonology. In SPE the phonology of a language was regarded as a linear string of segments, each given a binary specification for a set of features. The features were unordered, nonoverlapping, and appeared in a feature matrix. Rules operate on these strings deriving surface forms from underlying specifications. Standard generative phonology was the dominant approach to phonology for much of the 1960s and 1970s, but was not without its problems. Due to the linear mapping of features to segments, there were many natural language phenomena that were not easily expressed. Most notably, perhaps, were tonal languages, which were given limited discussion in SPE. Subsequent attempts to handle tonal data using the SPE framework were generally considered inadequate. Inspired by this, Goldsmith (1976) introduced the model of autosegmental phonology. Initially formalized to address tonal phenomena in Igbo (a West African language), the theory had far-reaching applications in phonological theory.

Autosegmental phonology established the idea of *phonology with tiers*, where phonological representations comprise at least two tiers of segments. Segments appear on only one tier, and are connected using association lines. Importantly, segments on one tier do not necessarily have to be mapped one-to-one with those on another tier. This gives rise to phonological representations that permit a nonlinear mapping between features. For example, in English, when a nasal proceeds a plosive (such as /nt/ in *mint*, /mp/ in *limp*, or /ŋk/ in *sink*) the two segments necessarily have the same places of articulation. We might, then, choose to represent these sequences as having only one place of articulation feature, and claim that these two segments in fact share this feature. In doing so, we would be employing an autosegmental style representation. In this chapter we will explore the motivations for such representations, the way they are formalized, and the potential applications to clinical data.

AUTOSEGMENTAL REPRESENTATIONS: PHONOLOGY WITH TIERS

Much of Goldsmith's motivation for autosegmental phonology came from research into tone languages. Goldsmith realized that the absolute splicing hypothesis, the notion in mainstream phonology that speech can be divided phonologically into isolated segments, did not lend itself well to the study of tone. Specifically, Goldsmith observed that there was not always a one-to-one mapping of tones to vowels, and that, in fact, two tones could occupy one vowel, or that two vowels could be occupied by a single tone. The reason for this, Goldsmith claimed, was that speech consists of a series of *gestures*, each relating to different parts of the articulatory anatomy, which do not all necessarily start and finish at the same time (Goldsmith, 1990, p. 10).

Goldsmith proposed that phonological representations should be composed of multiple tiers of segments. The tiers correspond to the different gestures of speech and differ according to the features that are specified for the segments on them. For example, we may have a tonal tier, where segments are specified only for tone, and a second tier where segments are specified for all other features. This would yield representations such as those in (1).

(1)

$$
\begin{array}{cc}
\textit{baka} & \textit{bulu} \qquad \textit{segmental tier} \\
| & | \\
H & L \qquad\quad \textit{tonal tier}
\end{array}
$$

As you will see, the segments on the tonal tier are linked to the segments on the segmental tier via lines. These are called *association lines* and, along with the tiers and their segments, form the basic representational machinery of autosegmental phonology. An association line between two segments on two tiers means they are articulated simultaneously, or are *co-registered*. Crucially, segments on one tier do not need to be mapped one-for-one onto another tier. This means we have a total of three possible mapping relations, shown with tonal data from Mende (another language of West Africa) in (2), (3), and (4) (Goldsmith, 1976).

(2) **One-to-one association**

$$
\begin{array}{ccc}
\textit{fàndé} & X & X \\
|\;\; | & | & | \\
L\; H & \textit{Tone} & \textit{Tone}
\end{array}
$$

The representation in (2) is how tonal associations were traditionally conceived of, that is, of mapping directly onto single vowels. In (3) and (4), however, we see the idea of nonlinear linear representations exploited to the full. In (4) you can see three vowels, or syllables, that are all produced during the period of a single, low tone. We can say that the tone is *multiply associated*. In (3), on the other hand, a single syllable is produced during the period of two distinct tones.

(3)

Many-to-one association

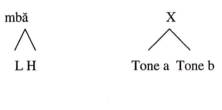

mbă   X

L H   Tone a Tone b

(4)

Multiple linking

kpàkàlì   X X

L   Tone

The representations in (2), (3), and (4) show the possible ways we can link segments on a tonal tier to those on a nontonal tier. Importantly, however, the same representations can and have been applied to a far greater range of the phonological processes found in natural language. This is not at all surprising, as researchers long before Goldsmith had argued that many phonetic features could not be assigned a scope of a single phonological segment. Harris (1944), for example, talked about "long components," and the theory of prosodic analysis (Firth, 1957) posited "prosodies" (see Chapter 9 for an introduction to prosodic analysis). In autosegmental phonology, however, the notion of phonological features varying in their domain was introduced to the mainstream. Particularly insightful have been accounts of nasal harmony (Goldsmith, 1976) and vowel harmony (Vergnaud, 1977). In (5), the harmonizing feature, nasality, appears on a separate tier and spreads independently of the features on the other tier.

(5)

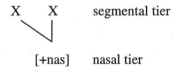

X X   segmental tier

[+nas] nasal tier

In the clinic, a commonly reported speech error is *consonant harmony*, where consonants in a word agree with one another for some or all of their respective distinctive features (usually, but not always, these are the place features). An example might be the production of [kæk] for the target *cat*, or [gɑg] for target *dog*. In both cases the features on the place tier are associated with both consonants. This is sketched in (6).

(6)

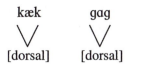

kæk gɑg   X X

[dorsal] [dorsal]   PLACE

The issue of whether the child has a correct underlying representation, with differing place features, and the harmony comes about via rule, or whether in fact the underlying representation itself has the one single place feature would be dependent on the individual case. In (6) the place feature [DORSAL] is associated with both consonants in the underlying representation itself. We discuss the issue of the nature of underlying representations more fully later in the chapter.

As the harmony processes show, autosegmental representations proved to be rather versatile in their applicability to phonological processes. Equally, so-called complex segments* (singleton segments that bear more than one specification for a single feature) such as affricates and prenasalized stops had previously been very difficult to account for using linear representations, but seemed better explained using this newly developing approach. In order to demonstrate such representations it is appropriate to introduce the notion of the *skeletal tier*. The skeletal tier is a means of representing the units of phonological timing. In its original form (McCarthy, 1979; Clements & Keyser, 1983) the skeletal tier manifested itself as a sequence of C and V slots (and was hence called the CV tier). This was simply intended to indicate whether an associated segment was consonantal (C) or vocalic (V). Since then, Kaye and Lowenstamm (1984) and Levin (1985), among others, recognized that the feature [+syllabic] already conveyed this fact, and so the units of the skeletal tier were to be stripped down to a simple timing slot, symbolized as **x**.

The skeletal tier serves as a point of attachment for the segmental tier. The independence of these two tiers can be easily demonstrated using the affricates of English, which comprise two featural groupings on the segmental tier, but which occupy only one point on the skeletal tier (in other words, they are quantitatively equivalent to a single segment, not a consonant cluster). In (7) representations of the affricate /tʃ/, the cluster /st/, and the singleton /t/ are shown.

(7)

You should note that using these autosegmental *graphs* as a means of phonological representation, be it for ordered or disordered speech, leaves us with a rather different idea as to what constitutes a phonological segment (from what you have read about in the preceding chapters of this book, for example). In autosegmental representations, segments are simply the minimal unit of organization on their respective tiers, and behave *autonomously* (hence the name *autosegment*). What emerges is a picture of phonology quite different from that found in SPE: one with several simultaneous tiers of segments, related to each other through association lines, but ordered independently. As a result, the term *nonlinear* is employed to describe this and some more recent approaches to phonological representation. Indeed, in the following chapter we describe a second exponent of the nonlinear approach to phonology, that of metrical phonology, which deals exclusively with stress and syllabification. We turn now, however, to look at how rules and derivations work in the autosegmental framework.

---

* Sometimes referred to as contour segments.

AUTOSEGMENTAL TRANSFORMATIONS: RULES AND CONSTRAINTS

Autosegmental phonology is nonlinear in its approach to representation, but is still derivational in nature. This means surface forms are derived from underlying forms via the application of rules. As in standard generative phonology, rules are formalized using a structural description of the environment in which they operate, and a description of the change that the rule brings about. You should be familiar with the basic rule notation used in SPE from Chapter 3, that of A→B/C_D, and so we now look at how rules are expressed in autosegmental phonology.

Rules in Autosegmental Phonology

An autosegmental rule indicates the environment where the rule occurs, and then some form of change. The change involves an association line being either added or removed (called *linking* and *delinking* in autosegmental terms). In (8), for example, we have a rule expressing the spreading of nasality from some nasal consonant to a preceding vowel. This is found in English in words like *can*, where the vowel is phonetically nasalized due to the following nasal consonant. As you can see in (8), the lower tier corresponds to a nasal gesture, while the segments on the top tier are specified as being ± consonantal.

(8)

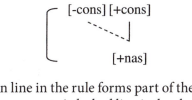

An unbroken association line in the rule forms part of the structural description and is to be read as already being present. A dashed line is the change and denotes spreading. In (6) above we said that the child's production of *cat* as [kæk] could actually be due to a rule rather than the child having an incorrect underlying representation. If this were the case, we could represent it in a way similar to that shown in (6). In (8) the consonant was already nasalized underlyingly, and the action of the rule is to spread this nasality to the vowel. Essentially, the features on the nasal tier are behaving autonomously to those features on the higher tier. We can contrast this rule with (9), an SPE style formalism of the same process.

(9)

$$\left[-\text{nas}\right] \rightarrow \left[+\text{nas}\right] / \underline{\hspace{1cm}} \begin{bmatrix} +\text{nas} \\ +\text{cons} \end{bmatrix}$$

There are a number of advantages with the autosegmental rule. First, it demonstrates clearly that there are not two [+nas] features which associate themselves with two adjacent segments, but rather that the same single feature applies to both segments. The vowel shares its specification for the nasal feature with the proceeding consonant. According to Goldsmith's gestural view of speech, this is both phonetically motivated and theoretically preferable. Second, due to the *constraints* of the theory (see below), the number of rules that can be expressed is considerably reduced.

An autosegmental rule can also delete an association line. Goldsmith (1990, p. 17) gives the example of a high tone shift rule in the Sukuma language of East Africa. In this language, there is a rule that, at a particular stage in derivation, shifts high tones one syllable to the right. The rule is formalized in (10).*

(10)

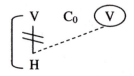

Here the broken association line represents deletion. The then unassociated high tone reassociates with the encircled vowel. A circle around a segment in autosegmental notation means that it is unassociated with a segment on the adjacent tier. Effectively this rule has delinked the high tone and associated it with the next unassociated tone-bearing unit in a single action.

This process demonstrates another dimension to autosegmental phonology that is of note, namely, *stability* (Goldsmith, 1990, p. 28). Stability is a property of autosegments, and means they remain present in a representation even if those segments with which they are associated on another tier are deleted via a rule. In (10), for example, the stability of the high tone is evident. Stability can also apply to slots of the skeletal tier, where the deletion of a root node can bring about an unassociated or bare x slot, as shown in (11).

(11)

In cases such as (11) a process called *compensatory lengthening* can occur, where the empty x slot is filled by a lengthening of the remaining vowel. This demonstrates the use of the skeletal tier to separate information regarding phonological timing from other aspects of the phonological representation, as shown in (12).

(12)

This is a process that has occurred in the history of English (Ewan & van der Hulst, 2001, p. 152; Harris, 1994, p. 34) involving words such as *night*, *right*, and *might*. Traditionally, the form /nɪxt/ was used, and is in fact retained by modern-day Scots. In English the velar fricative /x/ was lost, and the vowel /ɪ/ lengthened to /ɪː/, yielding a pre vowel-shift form of /nɪːt/[†]. The vowel-shift brought about the modern-day form of /naɪt/, as shown in (13).

---

* The two lines crossing the association line between V and H show that this association line is delinked (i.e., broken).

† This form can still be heard in some parts of rural England.

(13)

Bernhardt (1992b, p. 131) proposes a similar analysis of the process of coda deletion and subsequent vowel lengthening in child speech. The implication is that the child is lengthening the vowel to compensate for the loss of the consonant, and hence retaining the same length for the word. The representation in (14) is based on that proposed by Bernhardt.

(14)

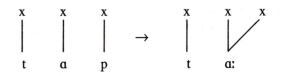

Rules such as those in (14) can quite easily show how surface forms can be generated from underlying representations in specific languages or cases, but autosegmental phonology also posits general conventions of the theory. These are universal across languages, and they constrain the theory from generating words that are simply impossible.* As a result, we can call them well-formedness constraints, or simply constraints. The most important of these for our concerns is the no-crossing constraint, which can be summarized as in (15):

(15)

No-crossing constraint: Lines associating segments on two tiers may not cross each other.

As we said above, this constraint is not language specific, but a constraint of the autosegmental theory of language. But how does it work? Let's take the rule in (5) above as an example. It states that nasality spreads from a nasal consonant to a preceding vowel in English. But given a word like *film*, why wouldn't the vowel here become nasalized? We know it doesn't, but there is nothing explicit in the rule that predicts this. To deal with this and many other similar examples, the no-crossing constraint was introduced. The idea was to constrain the *power* of the theory. A theory's power is a measure of how much it can generate. If, for example, I wanted to construct a theory detailing the characteristics of all the citizens of the United States, as opposed to any other country of the world, and my theory simply stated that citizens of the United States are human, then the theory is clearly too powerful. In other words, I need to reduce the possible outcomes that the theory can generate. If we return to the *film* example, we can see that the spreading of the feature [+nas] from the nasal consonant to the vowel would cross the association line between the nasal tier and the lateral on the higher tier, shown in (16).

---

* That is, they are outlawed by the general principles of universal grammar.

(16)

$$* \quad \text{[-cons] [+cons] [+cons]}$$

[-nas]   [+nas]

Due to the constraint, the spreading is not permitted by the theory and the rule is illegal (signified by *). You should notice that the constraint actually serves to block the rule from applying, rather than bringing about any change itself. This is the crucial difference between a rule and a constraint, and herein lies the ability of the constraint to limit the power of the theory. As discussed above, this reduction in power is considered an advantage of autosegmental phonology over its predecessors in the generative movement.

In clinical phonology the notion of power is a moot one. Because of the very nature of a disordered phonology, productions that violate the phonological rules of the language being acquired are possible. As a result, we require a means to represent them. With constraints like (15) we may often be forced to explain an error by stating that the constraint itself has been violated.

A second example of a constraint in autosegmental phonology is the obligatory contour principle (OCP) (see Leban, 1973). We will not discuss this in detail here for two reasons: (1) It has been applied predominantly to tonal phenomena only, and (2) it has been the subject of almost consistent debate. It can, however, be summarized as in (17) (adapted from Harris, 1994, p. 172):

(17)

Obligatory contour principle (OCP): At the segmental level, adjacent identical units are disfavored.

The principle states that morphological rules must not generate two consecutive, identical segments. Any such occurrences must subsequently be collapsed into a single segment associated with two slots on the skeletal tier. This supposedly accounts for such fake geminates as that occurring across the boundary of the form *unnerved*. This is shown in (18).

(18)

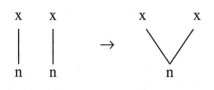

As you can see, constraints work quite differently from rules. Rather than bringing about change, they constrain the set of well-formed representations that are possible. In recent phonology, there has been a total abandonment of rules in favor of a complete reliance on constraints. Languages differ in how these constraints are ranked, with the highest ranked being the most critically abided by. This is optimality theory and is discussed in Chapter 11. Now, we turn to the idea that within an autosegmental framework, features can be shown to have hierarchical relations, and should be organized thus.

EXERCISE 7.1

Luganda, a language spoken in Uganda, features prenasalized consonants (Goldsmith, 1990). The segments [^{m}p ^{n}t ^{ŋ}k], for example, behave just like other singleton consonants in the language. What's more, when a nasal comes into contact with a stop, a prenasalized consonant is formed. This has the subsequent effect of lengthening the preceding vowel.

to see   ku laba   *to see me*   kuù ndaba

    Draw an autosegmental graph that captures this process.

THE GEOMETRY OF FEATURES IN AUTOSEGMENTAL PHONOLOGY

So far we have discussed the idea of phonological representations that posit segments specified for different features on numerous tiers (e.g., a nasal tier or a tonal tier). These segments are linked with association lines, signifying co-registration. The segments are autonomous and need not be paired one-to-one. These are the fundamentals of autosegmental phonology. But within the theory, we can talk about a geometry of the many phonological features. Rather than simply claiming that each distinctive feature occupies its own tier, we can go further and outline an organization of the features, where features are grouped into *feature classes*. Feature geometry (see Clements, 1985, for a detailed introduction) does just this and is particularly useful for explaining cases of assimilation.

Let's begin with a very commonly exhibited assimilation process: nasal place agreement. In many languages across the world, nasal consonants assimilate in place of articulation to the consonants that follow them. English, German, and Polish all demonstrate this phenomenon to a certain extent, and Exercise 7.2 requires you to consider some data from Spanish.

EXERCISE 7.2: SPANISH NASAL ASSIMILATION

What is the underlying form of the article *un*? Formulate an autosegmental rule capturing the process of place assimilation evident in this data.

[un topo]   *a mole*

[um pato]   *a duck*

[uŋ gato]   *a cat*

[un oso]   *a bear*

(From Clements, 2006)

There are two important points to consider here. First, although the nasal changes place, all its other features remain the same (it does not lose it nasality or become a fricative, for example). This provides evidence that all place features can be the target of a single phonological rule, and hence justifies grouping them together under some organizing node. We can call that node simply *place* and formulate the rule as in (19).

(19)

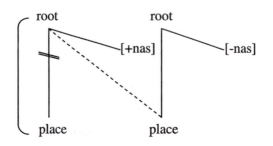

In (19) you can see that the place tier has spread to the preceding nasal, delinking its existing place specification, but the nasal tier has remained unchanged. We can say that the rule reads: Spread the place node from a consonant to a preceding nasal. This reflects the facts: The place characteristics of the nasal have assimilated, but it is still [+nasal]. What is also important here is the fact that the place tier immediately dominates the coronal, labial, and dorsal tiers, and we can express the entire assimilation process in a single rule. In (20) we represent the place tier and its dependents.

(20)

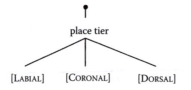

Clearly, the features that are dominated by the place node are in a *disjunctive* relationship. That is, some segment is going to be specified as being *one* of the three place categories, but not *all*. If some rule, as in (19), targets the place node, then all segments will be affected, regardless of their place. Following Sagey (1990), we can further identify features for the specific places themselves. The feature [±round] is only applicable to labial sounds, for example, while the feature [±anterior] is only applicable if a sound is coronal. Therefore, in (21) these features are dominated by the places they apply to, and only these places.

(21)

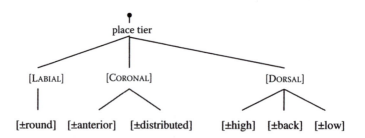

What we are starting to build is an organization of features. The question now is, what does the place node attach to? Well, we know that sometimes a rule affects some other features but not the place node. For example, in rule (5) above the feature [nasal] spreads its value from consonant to vowel. The feature [nasal], then, needs to be under a different node to place. Sometimes, however, both place and nasality can spread, meaning that some organizing node needs to dominate both of them. If both place and nasality spread, then the target of the rule can be this very node. This we can call the supralaryngeal node, shown in (22).

(22)

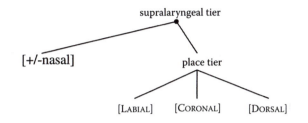

If we continue to build our structure in this way, we end up with a *feature geometry* (as introduced in Chapter 5). Since Clements's (1985) first major geometry, there have been numerous alterations and emendations, and the structure in (23) is fairly representative of recent developments. You should note that the segmental tier is now called the root tier, and we say that features in the geometry attach to the root.

(23)

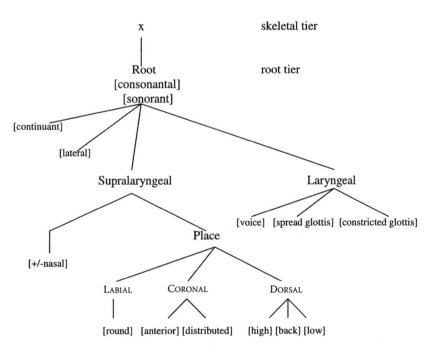

The motivation for the organization of features in the above geometric representation is purely phonological. That is, dependent features are assumed to be thus due to their participation in phonological processes/rules, not due to their anatomical location. This is to be contrasted with articulatory phonology (Browman & Goldstein, 1992; discussed in Chapter 12), where phonological organization is informed primarily by phonetic facts. That said, much of what is observed phonologically is in line with such facts.

A feature geometry like that in (23) can be used to show the feature makeup of an individual segment. Compare the representations in (24) and (25), which show the segments /ð/ and /h/, respectively. Note that the representation for /h/ has no place node whatsoever, indicating the lack of place for this sound.

(24)

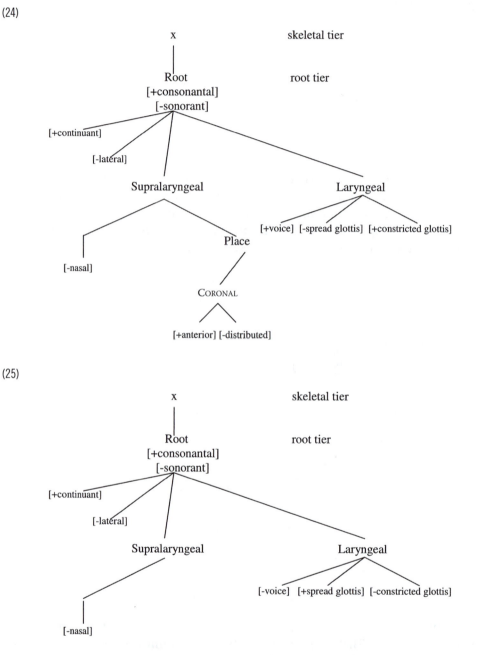

(25)

Using a feature geometry like that in (21) along with the conventions of autosegmental phonology, we can show how different classes of features behave as groups in phonological processes. We have already demonstrated in rule (17) above how the place node can spread from one segment to another, and we can also talk about laryngeal spreading, such as in cases of devoicing or cases of complete assimilation where the entire root node spreads. Importantly, when a rule targets a specific node, it affects all those features dominated by that node and no others. In cases of denasalization, only the [nasal] feature is affected, and all other features remain intact.

Bernhardt (1992a, p. 273) suggests that the progress of linguistic development in a child can be charted in terms of the ability to contrast features at stages in the geometry. She suggests that features lower down in the geometry, those dominated by the place node or laryngeal node, for example, should be mastered later in development than those higher in the geometry.* If we consider that children's early utterances are typically comprised of consonant and vowel distinctions, but little else, and that functioning voice and place contrast develop later in acquisition, this claim seems reasonable.

FEATURE GEOMETRY IN CLINICAL CASES

While autosegmental phonology maintained the use of both rules and representations in accounting for phonological processes, it seriously challenged the form and role of the representation. Rather than being a row of segments specified for distinctive features (as in SPE), representations in autosegmental phonology are made up of independently ordered tiers of features. Equally, the enriched representations were subject to constraints on their well-formedness, which could trigger processes in and of themselves (McCarthy, 1988, p. 84).

This means an account of the organization of a sound system, including a disordered sound system, is going to be quite different when viewed from this new, nonlinear perspective. In the following sections we discuss the implications for some common phonological disorders that autosegmental phonology brings about, and in turn consider their implication for the theory itself.

Cluster Coalescence

One of the most appealing accounts autosegmental phonology can offer is for the phenomenon of cluster coalescence, which sees the features of two adjacent segments attach to a single root node. The result is a single segment that has the properties of both the segments in the input of the rule, but is not identical to either one. This process is not unique to the speech of children with phonological disorders, of course, and has occurred in the history of languages to bring about sound changes, and can take place at word boundaries as a connected speech process. The words *what you*, for example, can be pronounced as /wʌt.juː/, with a consonant on either side of the syllable boundary, or as /wʌ.t͡ʃuː/,† with the affricate /t͡ʃ/ being the outcome of the coalescence. Further examples can be found in (26):

(26)

Connected speech process:	*would you*	/wʊd.juː/	→	/wʊ.d͡ʒuː/
Sound change:	*tissue*	/tɪs.juː/	→	/tɪ.ʃuː/

---

* Similar such proposals have been made regarding the acquisition of a second language (Brown & Matthews, 1997).
† We have not used the "tie-bar" elsewhere when transcribing English affricates; it is used here, however, to highlight the coalescence effect and to denote the /t͡ʃ/ as a single affricate rather than a sequence of two consonants.

Such a process is accepted in normal speech and does not cause a communicative problem; however, disordered speech can feature a great many more instances of coalescence. Dinnsen (1997) interprets data from Lorentz (1976), which involves a child aged 4;6 replacing the target consonant clusters /sp/, /sm/, and /sw/ with the singleton consonant [f], as a process of coalescence. Dinnsen argues that this process involves the place node of the second constituent of the cluster spreading to the first constituent. This is shown in (27).

(27)

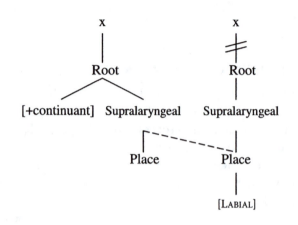

In a strictly segmental-based account, such an event is not at all easy to deal with. However, in the representation above we capture the spreading of the place node (which carries with it the labial information) to the continuant, and the decoupling of the non-continuant from the skeletal tier.

Assimilatory Errors

As with coalescence, assimilation occurs readily in normal speech. It is a common connected speech process across word boundaries, and in fast speech it will often occur word internally. In example (6) above we illustrated consonant assimilation occurring across an entire word. This is very common in the speech of children with phonological disorders, and is representative of an inability to satisfy the no-crossing constraint. The result is consonant harmony.

Assimilatory effects can also be observed between vowel and consonant segments. Dinnsen (1999) interprets data from Williams and Dinnsen (1987) using the notation of feature geometry to great effect. Consider the distribution of alveolar and velar consonants in the data in (28).

(28)

(a)	*deer*	[dɪʊ]	*dress*	[dɛ]
(b)	*cage*	[te]	*gate*	[deʔ]
(c)	*comb*	[ko]	*goat*	[goʔ]
(d)	*Tom*	[kæ]	*tooth*	[guʰ]
(e)	*pinch*	[pɪ]	*boot*	[buʔ]

You should notice that the child can properly produce the alveolar consonants /t/ and /d/, the velar consonants /k/ and /g/, and the labial consonants /p/ and /b/ (as evidenced by rows a and e). Equally, the child uses voicing appropriately at all times. However, the problem is in the use of the correct place of articulation when the target is either coronal or dorsal. Specifically, when the target consonant is either coronal or dorsal, the realization is conditioned by the place of the following vowel. The labial consonants, on the other hand, are not affected by this process.

To account for this we can adopt the unified place theory of Hume (1994) and Clements and Hume (1995). This assumes the one-mouth principle of consonant and vowel articulation, that is, that consonants and vowels should be specifiable using the same set of distinctive features. Clements (2006, p. 10) summarizes the exponents of specific distinctive features in consonants and vowels, as shown in Table 7.1.

Evidently, the data in (28) exhibit the spreading of the features [CORONAL] and [DORSAL] from the vowel's place node to the initial consonant. This is represented in (29) and (30) (modified slightly from Dinnsen, 1999).

(29)

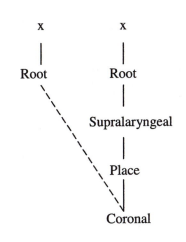

Table 7.1 Exponents of Features

Feature	Consonants	Vowels
[LABIAL]	Labials, labialized consonants	Rounded vowels
[CORONAL]	Coronals, palatalized consonants	Front and retroflex vowels
[DORSAL]	Velar and uvular consonants, velarized and emphatic consonants	Back vowels
[PHARYNGEAL]	Uvula and pharyngeal consonants, pharyngealized and emphatic consonants	Pharyngealized vowels

(30)

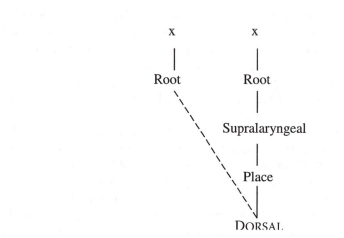

You should note that the spreading must take place below the place node to account for the fact that the process does not affect labial consonants.*

EXERCISE 7.3

Consider the following child language acquisition data and interpret it based on the unified place theory discussed in the previous section.

soup	[pup]	*short*	[wɔɹt]
sheep	[ʃip]	*keep*	[jip]
win	[jɪn]		

FURTHER READING

John Goldsmith developed autosegmental phonology in his unpublished PhD thesis (1976); however, we recommend you consult Goldsmith (1990) for a general overview of nonlinear phonology (including autosegmental phonology's theoretical counterpart, metrical phonology). McCarthy (1979) first introduced the CV tier, and Levin (1985) developed the ideas behind the skeletal tier that is used in this chapter. Goldsmith (1995) contains numerous chapters concerning the state of generative and nonlinear phonology in general, as does Goldsmith (1999).

The development of feature geometry began with Clements (1985) and Sagey (1986), and continued with McCarthy (1988) and Clements and Hume (1995). A modern feature geometry incorporating the unified place theory can be found in Roca and Johnson (1999). Clinical studies involving the use of feature geometry include Chin and Dinnsen (1991), Bernhardt and Gilbert (1992), Gierut, Cho, and Dinnsen (1993), and Heselwood (1997).

---

* This differs from Dinnsen's representations, which show the spreading of the entire place node. This would incorrectly predict that the labial consonants would also be affected by the rule.

A review of the implications for language development of nonlinear phonology in general can be found in Bernhardt (1992a), and clinical applications can be found in Bernhardt (1992b) and Dinnsen (1997).

REVIEW QUESTIONS AND STUDY TOPICS

Review Questions

1. What is nasal place assimilation and why does it support a nonlinear approach to phonological representation?
2. What is the absolute splicing hypothesis and how does it relate to autosegmental phonology?
3. What are the three possible mapping associations in autosegmental phonology?
4. What are the characteristics of a complex segment? Give an example.
5. What is the skeletal tier intended to encode?
6. Give an example of an autosegmental rule. What are its components?
7. What is the difference between a rule and a well-formedness constraint?
8. What is the unified place theory, and what does it help to account for?

Study Topics

1. Part of the motivation for autosegmental phonology was that features may apply to varying parts of a word rather than simply the segment. Draw up a list of words from English or any other language that you think demonstrate this point. Why would assigning feature values to only segment-sized units fall short of a full analysis of these words?
2. Using acquisition data from any child, consider the proposal that phonological acquisition can be regarded as a movement from high to low on the feature geometry tree. Do your data support this proposal?

8

METRICAL PHONOLOGY

INTRODUCTION

In the previous chapter we introduced the theory of autosegmental phonology. This was a progression of the ideas originally proposed in Chomsky and Halle's *Sound Pattern of English* (SPE) (1968), and introduced a multitiered approach to phonological representation. While SPE was strictly linear in its account of phonological description, autosegmental phonology was nonlinear, with multiple, parallel tiers of autosegments associated with nodes on a skeletal tier. Each node on a skeletal tier corresponds to one timing slot and is comparable to a segment. In this chapter we explore a method of establishing organization above the level of the segment, and so tackling the issue of stress assignment and rhythm.

In SPE, stress was dealt with as a distinctive feature of the segment, akin to [±nasal] or [±round]. The feature [+stress] was assigned to the vowels of stressed syllables, with [−stress] being a feature of the vowels of unstressed syllables. There were no limitations, or constraints, on how many, or indeed which, vowels could be stressed in a word. In time, this proved to be a wholly inadequate approach to accounting for the stress patterns of the world's languages, as we will demonstrate in the next section. What succeeded SPE's overly simplistic method was an approach called metrical theory, or metrical phonology (Liberman, 1975; Liberman & Prince, 1977; Goldsmith, 1990). In metrical phonology stress is regarded as hierarchical, structuring syllables into rhythmic sequences. As a result, words are represented as binary tree structures (similar to those used to model phrase structure relations in syntax) with several levels of organization. Terminal nodes are labeled as either strong or weak, denoting the stressed or unstressed syllables themselves. The well-formedness of these representations in a particular language is determined by the settings specified for a number of parameters. What arises is a theory that accounts for the attested linguistic rhythms in the world's languages.

Work in metrical phonology has focused on accounting for the stress assignment rules of individual languages, processes such as stress shift, and other phonological processes that are sensitive to stress patterns. The theory has also offered valuable insights into the prosodic development seen during the course of child language acquisition. Specifically, rhythmic structure can be shown to influence errors such as syllable or sound omissions. In this chapter we will outline the motivations for the development of a new theory of rhythm, and draw your attention to its applicability to clinical cases.

THE MOTIVATION FOR METRICAL PHONOLOGY

The approach to stress assignment in SPE was straightforward. The vowels of stressed syllables were to be specified with the feature [+stress], with the vowels of unstressed syllables given [–stress]. In this sense, stress in SPE operated no differently than features such as [±nasal]. This can be seen in (1), which is a portion of a feature matrix for the English word *melon*.

(1)

	C	V	C	V	C
[syllabic]	–	+	–	+	–
[voiced]	+	+	+	+	+
[stress]	–	+	–	–	–
[nasal]	+	–	–	–	+

etc.

We can see clearly that a vowel is stressed if it is specified as [+] in the feature column [stress]. Consonants, by definition, must be unstressed, and so they will be necessarily specified with a [–]. The constituent of the syllable is absent in SPE, and so the notion of a syllable, as opposed to simply its nucleus, being stressed is not possible.* Unfortunately, this technique fails to account for a number of important facts regarding stress assignment in languages. To explain these we need to deal with the important distinction between primary and secondary stress.

When talking about stress, we can distinguish between so-called *primary stress* and *secondary stress*. Secondary stress is a property of the syllable and, in a *stress-accent* language like English, takes the phonetic exponents of duration, intensity, and pitch.† Stressed syllables, then, are typically longer, louder, and have a pitch movement on them. Unstressed syllables are often produced with a lax manner of articulation, leading to vowel reduction. Primary stress is also assigned to the syllable, but is a property of the word. That is, there is one primary stressed syllable in each word. For this reason, you will sometimes see primary stress being referred to as *word-level* stress. In pairs of words like *caterpillar* and *permutation* you should be able to perceive the difference in the location of the primary stress. Both words are comprised of a strong-weak-strong-weak alternation of secondary stressed syllables, but in *caterpillar* the first syllable has word-level stress, whereas in *permutation* it is the penultimate syllable.

Languages vary as to where the preferential location of their primary stress falls. Hayes (1995) identifies the positions of initial (e.g., Finnish), postinitial (e.g., Dakota), antepenultimate (e.g., Macedonian), penultimate (e.g., Polish), and final (e.g., French) as possible locations. Importantly, unattested primary stress placements include the syllable that is fourth from the edge of the word, or that is in the "middle" of the word (Ewan

---

* Following the publication of SPE, the absence of a syllable-sized unit attracted much criticism. See Fudge (1969) and Anderson (1969) for immediate reaction.

† This is to be contrasted with Japanese, which is a pitch-accent language. In Japanese the main correlate of stress is pitch.

& van der Hulst, 2001, p. 217).* Equally, words only have one primary stressed syllable, never more. A theory such as SPE that only allows us to specify syllables as stressed or unstressed is falling short of a complete account of stress assignment. First, there is no possible way of making the three-way distinction between an unstressed syllable, a syllable with both primary and secondary stress, and one with purely secondary stress. Stress in SPE, as with all features, is specified in a purely binary fashion. Second, there is no inherent constraint in the theory that outlaws the assignment of [+stress] to *all* the vowels of a word. Crucially, this fails to account for the tendency of languages to avoid adjacent stressed syllables. And finally, SPE fails to explain why some stress patterns are more common than others, and indeed why some stress patterns are unattested for altogether. In light of this we need to recognize constituent structure above the level of the syllable, which in turn allows us to better understand the principles governing the alternation of stressed and unstressed syllables. In metrical phonology this is exactly the approach that is taken.

Metrical Structure

The alternation of stressed and unstressed syllables in a language such as English is observable in the words *ladder* and *assume*, where the former has the pattern strong-weak (SW) and the latter weak-strong (WS). In metrical phonology we can display this by labeling sister nodes of tree structures with strong (s) and (w) labels, as shown in (2).

(2)

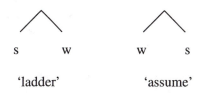

s w   w s

'ladder'   'assume'

Clearly the two words in (2) have the opposite rhythmic structure. Both words are bisyllabic, with a different syllable receiving stress in each. You should see that the weak syllable in both words is similarly reduced in its phonetic form. In British English, both weak syllables are reduced to the vowel schwa, the most lax vowel. In fact, schwa is never found in stressed syllables and is the least prominent of all English vowels.

If we are presented with a word that has four syllables and two strong syllables, we can usually detect which of these two syllables is the strongest relative to the other. This means there is a degree of discrepancy in the relative strength of the strong syllables. In order to represent this we need to establish a second level of structure that intervenes between the syllable and the word. We call this constituent the *foot*. The foot groups syllables in a binary fashion. The foot in turn has a strong-weak pattern, and offers its stress to the stronger of the two syllables inside it. In (3) we demonstrate a strong-weak foot structure and a weak-strong foot structure.

---

* Words can have primary stress on the middle syllable, but as a token of the length of the word, not because it is specified that the middle syllable be stressed.

(3)

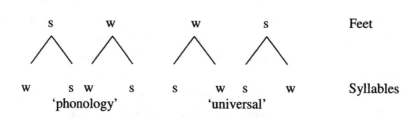

In the word *phonology* the first foot is strong and the second weak. This means the strong syllable of the first foot, *no*, receives the strength of the foot. In the word *universal* the reverse is true, where the second foot is the stronger, giving its strength to the syllable *ver*. Another way of phrasing this is to simply say that the syllable dominated by only strong nodes is the syllable with primary stress. You should note here that stress in this sense is used simply in a relative fashion. That is, to say one syllable is weaker than another is to simply make a claim relative to the span of that word.

Above the level of the foot, we can group feet into phonological words, and in turn group words into a phonological phrase. The principle, originally formulated by Nespor and Vogel (1986), is a simple one, namely, that mother nodes comprise one or more daughters in the below category, and this gives rise to the *prosodic hierarchy* (4).

(4)

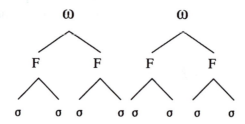

The representations used in (2), (3), and (4) are tree-like, or *arboreal*; however, we could just as well represent the distribution of both primary and secondary stressed syllables in a grid-like structure, or *metrical grid*. For comparative purposes, the grids in (5) show again the stress patterns in *phonology* and *universal*.

(5)

	.	x	.		.	.	x	.	primary stress
	.	x	.	x	x	.	x	.	secondary stress
	x	x	x	x	x	x	x	x	syllables

        'phonology'   'universal'

As we mentioned above, words only have one syllable taking primary stress. This means that in a word containing, for example, six syllables, only one syllable will take primary stress. In turn, this means two of the feet will be weak, and only the foot dominating the primary stressed syllable will be strong. The placement of this primary stress, and indeed the alternation of strong and weak feet below it, is a matter of linguistic preference. That is, languages vary in terms of their preferred rhythmic structure, and this can be shown to be governed by a set number of parameters.

EXERCISE 8.1

Construct metrical grids for the following English words. Pay particular attention to the assignment of primary and secondary stress to syllables.

merger
persuade
horizontal
investigate

PARAMETER SETTING IN METRICAL PHONOLOGY

The preference of stress alternation found in individual languages is captured in metrical phonology using a technique similar to that of the *principles and parameters theory* (Chomsky & Lasnik, 1993). A simple idea that has emerged from thinking in universal grammar (UG), the basis of the principles and parameters movement, is that languages differ according to the parameter settings of a finite number of linguistic principles. In metrical phonology, our principles relate to the potential placement of secondary and primary stress, and our parameter settings govern the tendencies found in any individual language. In turn, this relates directly to language development, in that if children learn language according to these formalisms, their behaviors during the course of acquisition can be more easily explained. We will come to this shortly, but first we need to explore the parameter settings needed to classify linguistic rhythm.

We saw in (3) above that a foot can be either left- or right-headed, yielding two different rhythmic structures. This is represented in the first metrical parameter, shown in (6), which we call here foot-headedness, and which can select either left- or right-headed feet.

(6)

    Foot-headedness: A foot is either left-headed (F:LH) or right-headed (F:RH).

The foot-headedness parameter assumes the existence of the foot types shown in (7).

(7)

This is supported by work in poetics, for example, where the LH foot is deemed a trochaic foot, or trochee, and the RH foot an iambic foot, or iamb. English and Dutch are languages that have a preference for left-headed feet, and so the parameter is set to F:LH. French, on the other hand, prefers right-headed feet.

Alert readers will have noticed that thus far we have dealt purely with words containing an even number of syllables (two, four, six, etc.), meaning a binary-based constituent structure is sufficient. However, given a word with an odd number of syllables, there will be one syllable that is not contained within a foot, or is *unfooted*. Such orphaned syllables are dominated by a *degenerate foot*, as shown in (8).

(8)

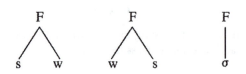

The existence of degenerate feet necessitates the next parameter: directionality. The setting of the directionality parameter, shown in (9), dictates the direction from which syllables are grouped into feet. As with the foot-headedness parameter, this also is a binary setting.

(9)

   Directionality: Erected from left to right (D:L→R) or from right to left (D:R→L).

Depending on the setting for the directionality parameter, a string of five syllables could be parsed as in (10), with a F:LH setting and a D:L→R setting, or as in (11), with a F:LH setting but a D:R→L setting.

(10)

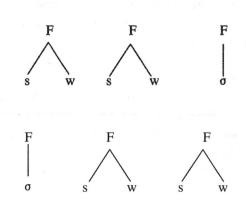

(11)

English is a language that erects feet from right to left, meaning that, combined with the foot-headedness setting, the parsing in (11) is what would be typical for an English speaker. The problem of what to do with the degenerate foot is discussed in Hayes (1995), and languages differ in this respect. English and Spanish are among those languages that permit the existence of an initial unfooted syllable. If we take the word *banana*, for example, we find it represented as in (12), with the unfooted initial syllable /bə/. Such unfooted syllables are extremely susceptible to deletion, and in the speech of young children are often omitted (yielding *nana*).

(12)

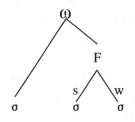

The following parameter settings involve the placement of the primary stress. Recall that primary stress is assigned to a single syllable in each word, and hence we call that syllable the head of the word. As with the foot-headedness parameter, word-headedness can either be left-headed or right-headed, as shown in (13).

(13)

> *Word-headedness*: A word is either left-headed (W:LH) or right-headed (W:RH).

According to the word-headedness parameter, then, the head of the word will be either the leftmost or rightmost secondary stressed syllable. For example, the word *phonology* is left-headed while the word *universal* is right-headed.

EXERCISE 8.2

When an adjective and a noun are regarded as an actual compound in English, the primary stress is typically heard on the first syllable of the construction. This yields a different pronunciation for *a blackbird* (the specific species) as opposed to *a black bird*, a simple description of a bird as being black. Decide whether the following examples are treated as compounds or simply as an adjective modifying a noun.

> *carrot cake*
> *apple pie*
> *snooker table*
> *an English man*
> *an Englishman*
> *a leather jacket*

The next parameter is concerned with the constituent structure of the syllable itself, something we have not dealt with explicitly in this chapter so far. However, if you refer to Chapter 2 on sonority theory, you will find an introduction to the syllable constituents of the onset, rime, nucleus, and coda. Recall that a rhyme can be either branching or not, and we state that a syllable containing a branching rhyme is a heavy syllable. Conversely, a light syllable has a nonbranching rhyme. This is represented in (14), where an x corresponds to any material in the rhyme, be it a nucleus or a coda.

(14)

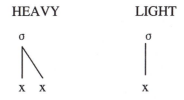

Languages differ with respect to whether heavy syllables are necessarily stressed or not. This can be expressed by the weight-sensitivity parameter, shown in (15).

(15)

Weight-sensitivity: Heavy syllables demand to be under the strong node of a foot.{yes/no}

We call languages with a {yes} setting for this parameter quantity sensitive. A quantity-sensitive language would outlaw constructions such as that in (16), where a branching rhyme is dominated by the weak node of a foot.

(16)

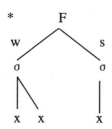

English is a quantity-sensitive language that seems to recognize a sequence of a short vowel with up to one consonant in the coda as being light, and a heavy syllable as comprising a short vowel plus two or more consonants, or a long vowel or diphthong with zero or more consonants in the coda. We can see that words ending in heavy syllables tend to have final stress (e.g., *complete*, *exist*), whereas words ending in light syllables tend to have penultimate stress (e.g. *erratic*, *exhibit*). Interestingly, we find that words ending in a short vowel plus an affricate tend to have penultimate stress (e.g., *manage*), thus proving the status of the affricate as a singleton consonant rather than a cluster (Harris, 1994, p. 40).

EXERCISE 8.3

When a suffix is added to a word, the location of primary stress can sometimes shift. Compare the two lists of suffixed words and decide whether the suffix has attracted the primary stress of the root form or not (examples from Clark & Yallop, 1990).

allowance (allow)   inhibition (inhibit)
deliverance (deliver)   dedication (dedicate)
existence (exist)   edition (edit)

CLINICAL INSIGHTS USING METRICAL PHONOLOGY

Applications of metrical phonology to phonological disorders have been fairly limited in number. This is not at all surprising, given the fact that the framework is limited to the characterization of stress patterns only, whereas theories such as autosegmental phonology deal with the more general segmental component of phonological representation. Moreover, those applications that do exist seem to limit themselves to the behavior of syllables according to the alternation of strong and weak foot nodes, with little attention given to anything above the level of the foot. That said, there have been a number of studies published looking at the occurrence of syllable omission and syllable repetition in disordered speech that are worth discussing, and we review their major findings below.

One of the first studies to consider the metrical patterns found in the speech of a childhood disordered population was Velleman and Shriberg (1999), who looked at the patterns of syllable omissions by English-speaking children with speech delay and with suspected developmental apraxia of speech. Specifically, the authors tested the hypothesis that error patterns similar to those found in the speech of younger, normally developing children would be found in the disordered children. They found that more syllable omissions were found in (1) weak as opposed to strong syllables, (2) right-headed as opposed to left-headed feet, and (3) non-word-final syllables as opposed to word final syllables.

The susceptibility of right-headed feet to errors was also found by Nickels and Howard (1999), who tested the production of bisyllabic words by aphasic patients. They found that unstressed syllables in general were more susceptible to error than stressed syllables, and that unstressed syllables in words of a weak-strong pattern were especially vulnerable. Such errors typically involved the weak syllable being omitted altogether, or replaced by a reduplicated form of the strong syllable. An example is the realization of *romance* as [momæns]. Interestingly, the authors did find that if a weak syllable was present, it was always produced with the correct stress. That is, they didn't find evidence of stress shifting. The authors interpret this as going against the suggestion by Butterworth (1992) that metrical structure is assigned to lexical items as a unique entity and that if words are retrieved without the correct metrical structure, a default metrical structure will be imposed upon them based upon the parameter settings of the language. As discussed above, English selects a left-headed foot setting, and so WS feet would surface as SW if Butterworth's hypothesis were correct. However, it is worth bearing in mind that English is also quantity sensitive, and realizing a WS pattern as an SW pattern may violate the specification that branching rhymes cannot be dominated by a weak node.

Further research into the stress patterns found in aphasic speech also pointed to the vulnerability of unstressed syllables (Patte, Safran, & Martin, 1987). Niemi, Koivuselka-Sallinen, and Hanninen (1985) found that 84% of phoneme omissions in Finnish Broca's aphasics appeared inside unstressed syllables.

FURTHER READING

The foundations of metrical phonology are to be found primarily in Liberman (1975) and Liberman and Prince (1977). Metrical phonology was developed and expanded in Prince (1980, 1983) and Hayes (1981). An attempt to combine the nonlinear models of both autosegmental phonology (Goldsmith, 1976) and metrical phonology can be found in Halle and Vergnaud (1981). Goldsmith (1990) offers a unique volume focusing on both autosegmental and metrical phonology, but maintains the separation between the two.

As mentioned in the chapter, clinical applications of formal metrical theory are rare. Rather, most studies looking at stress in disordered populations focus simply on syllable omissions and errors with regard to the alternation of strong and weak syllables. Such studies include Nickels and Howard (1999) and Velleman and Shriberg (1999).

REVIEW QUESTIONS AND STUDY TOPICS

Review Questions

1. How was stress dealt with in Chomsky and Halle's *Sound Pattern of English*?
2. What is the difference between primary and secondary stress?
3. How is foot-headedness related to the notion of stress patterns in poetics?
4. What are the different tiers of the prosodic hierarchy?

5. How can the metrical structure of English explain why the initial syllable of the word *banana* might be omitted?
6. What two main clinical phenomena can metrical phonology shed light on?
7. What does the literature on syllable errors in clinical phonology suggest regarding foot-headedness?
8. What did Butterworth (1992) propose regarding lexical retrieval and metrical structure?

Study Topics

1. Using some data from a normally developing child, look for evidence of the deletion of unfooted, initial syllables. Does this seem like a common occurrence to you?
2. There is a considerable lack of work in clinical phonology looking at the role of primary stress in disordered speech. Collect some data of your own from a client who you know is likely to omit syllables or make errors affecting syllable structure or stress placement, and analyze the status of primary stressed syllables in the data. Are primary stressed syllables less susceptible to omissions/errors, and does there seem to be a preference for left- or right-headed word stress?

9

PROSODIC ANALYSIS

INTRODUCTION

In this chapter we look at a theory of phonology that was developed primarily between the 1930s and 1960s. Referred to by its practitioners as prosodic analysis and by others as the London school, it was a movement led by John Rupert Firth and centered around the School of Oriental and African Studies (SOAS) in London. Since Firth's death in 1960, the theory has continued to develop and has been practiced recently as prosodic phonology (Waterson, 1971, 1987) and Firthian prosodic analysis (Ogden & Local, 1994), and has been used as a basis for the synthesis of natural speech (Ogden et al., 2000). In this chapter we deal predominantly with the original ideas of the London School and outline the foundations of the theory. Specifically, we will draw attention to the distinct differences between prosodic analysis and the more popular theory of the time, phonemic analysis. Indeed, prosodic analysis was very much a movement against the philosophy of phoneme theory, which Firth found to be overly transcription oriented and reliant on a complete segmentation of the speech stream (Waterson, 1987, p. 4). For Firth, more was to be gained through the analysis of whole units (*pieces* in his terminology), such as syllables, words, or word junctures. Firth also encouraged a nonmodular approach to linguistic analysis, and one should regard prosodic analysis as forming the phonological component of a much larger, integrated description of language.

Prosodic analysis is one of only a handful of the theories discussed in this book that does not fall within the general movement of generative grammar. It does not, for example, posit underlying representations, or incorporate the notion of derivation. Rather, variability in form is explained using simple alternation. There are, however, a number of Firth's ideas that seem to foreshadow more contemporary developments of generative grammar, and indeed of mainstream linguistics in general. Specifically, the tiered representations employed in autosegmental phonology (Goldsmith, 1976) have many similarities to the ideas underpinning prosodic analysis, and it has even been argued that the use of autosegments is essentially a "notational variant" of prosodic analysis (Lass, 1984, p. 269).* Outside generative linguistics, the increasingly popular clinical

---

* The relationship between prosodic analysis and autosegmental phonology is discussed in Goldsmith (1992, 1994) Ogden and Local (1994). See also Coleman (1998, p. 21).

tool of systemic functional grammar, developed by Halliday (1961), a student of Firth's, shares a great deal with prosodic analysis (see Chapter 14). Specifically, Halliday adopts the distinction between system and structure and places it at the center of his theory. Equally, the insistence by prosodic analysts on a nonsegmental view of speech can also be related to gestural phonology (Browman & Goldstein, 1992), and both theories share a common pursuit for uncovering the syntagmatic aspects of phonology.

In this chapter we provide an introduction to prosodic analysis, discussing the state of phonology at the time of its development, and highlighting the major principles of the theory. We then demonstrate some practical applications of the theory, focusing on vowel harmony, the notion of juncture, and its potential insights for the study of disordered speech.

PROSODIC ANALYSIS: HISTORICAL CONTEXT

To fully appreciate prosodic analysis as an approach to phonological description, it is necessary to understand at least something about the state of phonology in general at its time of development. In particular, the positions that Firth held in different universities, and his reaction against the general climate of linguistic theory during the early to mid 20th century, are central to understanding the motives behind the ideas he developed.

After fulfilling a series of short-term appointments in Britain and abroad,* Firth was offered the post of senior lecturer in the Department of Phonetics at University College of London (UCL) in 1928. The department was headed by Daniel Jones, the first professor of phonetics in Britain, and instrumental in the spread of the concept of the phoneme. For Jones, the phoneme was a theoretical tool that was to be used for almost entirely practical purposes. Specifically, the phoneme provided a straightforward method for the transcription of speech and for devising alphabets for languages (Jones, 1957). Robins (1957, p. 191) outlines the importance of this, pointing out that from the offset, the bond between the phoneme and transcription led to "the representation of a language in terms of its phonic material by means of discrete and consecutive letters or symbols on paper." This, as Robins alludes to, is perhaps best highlighted by the title of Kenneth Pike's book *Phonemics: A Technique for Reducing Language to Writing* (1947).

For Firth, this was deeply disconcerting. Specifically, Firth objected to the generally accepted principle that strings of phonemes mapped neatly onto sequences of phonetic events, and seemed concerned that the characteristics of the Roman alphabet were governing the formation of phonological theory (Firth, 1936, p. 73). Firth's opinion was that a great deal of phonological phenomena seemed decidedly uncharacterizable as individual, segment-sized units. Due to these frustrations, it is probably not surprising that Firth left Jones's department and moved to the School of Oriental and African Studies (SOAS) in 1938, where he was appointed as lecturer, and later as the head of the department of linguistics and phonetics (Anderson, 1985, p. 177). It was at SOAS that Firth really developed his theory of language, and 1948 saw the publication of "Sounds and Prosodies," the paper usually cited as the cornerstone of prosodic analysis. This paper, along with a series of publications by many of Firth's students and colleagues, developed the theory of prosodic analysis. Specifically, Firth introduced the idea of language comprising a "plurality of systems" (Firth, 1948, p. 137), rather than one unique inventory of

---

* Most notably in India, where Firth was involved in the development of modern Indian linguistics during this time.

sounds. In the discussion that follows we will refer to this as *polysystemicity*. Equally, the distinction between the segment-sized *phonematic units* and the long-domain features of *prosodies* was conceived. In both of these we see quite a radical reaction against the transcription-oriented practices of phoneme theory and, specifically, the idea that language can be reduced to a sequence of discrete units, with much of a phonologist's work representing a quest for the single inventory of these units.

Unfortunately, for Firth and his followers at least, mainstream phonological theory has indeed been dominated by the phoneme. However, while being practically suited for transcription purposes, the phoneme's failure to account for a vast range of phenomena observable in natural language has gradually risen to the surface over the course of the last century. This is evidenced by more recent developments in mainstream phonology, particularly nonlinear phonology, which have sought to remedy the problems associated with absolute segmentation. In other, more applied areas, such as speech-language pathology, the phoneme is often regarded as a given and is introduced in undergraduate textbooks as a matter of fact. This has had implications for the way in which articulation disorders are assessed and treated, with therapy techniques such as minimal pair treatment directly borrowing from the phonemic principle.

PROSODIC ANALYSIS: THE BASIC PRINCIPLES

The distinguishing factors of prosodic analysis are its (1) polysystemic and (2) nonsegmental nature. These serve to mark the theory as distinct from more generative and nonlinear models of phonology.

A Plurality of Systems

Polysystemicity is the notion that the most convincing analysis of language is to be gained when multiple systems of elements are established. It emerged from the work of Firth (1948) and Henderson (1949), and has been advocated more recently by Hawkins (2003), Local (2003), and Ogden (1999). Put simply, it means the analyst is encouraged to think about language not as *one* complete system of elements and structures (as being monosystemic), but as comprising *several* distinct but interacting systems (polysystemic). This concept is central to prosodic analysis and manifests itself in a number of ways.

The first broad sense in which prosodic analysis is polysystemic is evidenced by the fact that it was common for prosodic analysts to set up different systems of contrast for different places in a word or syllable. Take some language, for example, which allows syllables of the shape C_1VC_2, where one system of consonants appears at C_1 and a second at C_2. Are we better combining these two systems and positing them as one complete system of the language? Or rather, taking a polysystemic approach and positing two distinct subsystems, one that operates in the syllable onset and one in the syllable coda? For Firth and his colleagues the latter is preferable. Indeed, Henderson (1948), in her paper on Siamese, proposes an analysis just like the abstract one sketched above. In realizing that Siamese has certain properties common to the syllable beginning and some common to the syllable end, she proposes two distinct systems of contrast at the two places in structure.* This approach is quite distinct from the endeavors of phonemic

---

* Articulatory phonology can yield a similar approach, where the gestures comprising a segment at the syllable onset may be different from those gestures comprising the same segment in a syllable coda. Bybee (2001, pp. 86–88) also alludes to a polysystemic approach to the analysis of certain English consonants.

analysts, who strive to provide a single inventory of all the phonemes of a given language (Bloomfield, 1933).

As well as bringing about a markedly different approach to phonological analysis, adopting a polysystemic stance means a series of traditional conundrums associated with phonemic analysis disappear. Lass (1984, pp. 163–166) discusses the case of neutralization in particular. Neutralization occurs when a contrast between two phonemes in one word position is not exploited in another, with those two phonemes in fact functioning as allophones of the same phoneme in that position. After Trubetzkoy (1939), we say the phonemic contrast in that position has been *neutralized*. Final devoicing in German serves as a classic example. Word initially and intervocalically, German utilizes a voice contrast between the bilabial, alveolar, and velar stops. Word finally, however, only the voiceless variant surfaces. Under polysystemicity, there is nothing remarkable about this, as we would simply posit three systems of contrast (cf. Lass, 1984, p. 165); see example (1).

(1)

# _____		V _____ V		_____ #
p	b	p	b	p
t	d	t	d	t
k	g	k	g	k

By allowing for these multiple subsystems, it can be argued that the meaning, or value, of some element is dependent on what it contrasts within its own system. A commonly cited example of this is the distribution of nasal consonants (Anderson, 1985, p. 181). In English specifically, /n/, /m/, and /ŋ/ are permitted syllable finally, but only /n/ and /m/ can be found syllable initially. Because /n/ contrasts with two other nasal consonants syllable finally, but only one syllable initially, its treatment in a prosodic analysis should reflect this. In other words, part of the meaning of /n/ is not just what it is, but what it could have been, and isn't. While this claim might strike some readers as somewhat counterintuitive—that two phonetically similar segments should yield differing phonological analyses—it is important to consider the fact that the segments can be more easily reduced in connected speech if they are in contrast with fewer other segments. An example is the present progressive suffix -*ing* in English, which is regularly realized as [ɪn], as opposed to the more standard form [ɪŋ]. Importantly, this only happens to this particular morphological ending, and not when the string /ɪŋ/ forms part of the stem of the word, as in *sing* or *thing*. This can be explained simply using the principles of polysystemicity, as the realization of *sing* or *thing* with [ɪn] would bring about a different lexical item, namely, *sin* and *thin*. The nasal of the progressive suffix, however, is generally not in competition with any other segments, and is hence more easily altered.

Interestingly, Grunwell (1987) advocates a polysystemic approach similar to the one described above to the analysis of disordered speech in children. In her assessment tool *Phonological Assessment of Child Speech (PACS)*, Grunwell encourages the analysis of a client's speech not in terms of a single inventory of sounds, but rather in terms of the contrasts achievable at different places within the word and within the syllable (specifically syllable initial word initial, syllable initial within word, syllable final within word, and syllable final word final). She makes the point that regularities and patterns may well be missed by merely carrying out a traditional analysis of phoneme omissions, substitutions, and additions. Equally, simply identifying the position medial, as is traditional in speech-language pathology, is inadequate, and hence the distinction between syllable initial within word and syllable final within word. Such an approach to assessment (see Müller, Ball, & Rutter, 2006, for a recent example) seems to evolve directly from the ideas of prosodic analysis.

EXERCISE 9.1

Look at the data below from a 7;0-year-old boy with highly unintelligible speech. What are the possible realizations of the fricatives /s/ and /z/? Is there any pattern as to where they occur within the word or syllable?

biscuits	ˈbe?de?	ice cream	ˈaɪçβ̥ɹi
thirsty	ˈbɜfd̥i	glasses	ˈjahd̥ə
scissors	ˈjeɪd̥ə	sleeve	jːəi
zipper	ˈjɪ?b̥ʌ	zero	ˈjeɪβ̥ɹoʊ
ice	?ʌɪç	mouse	mæʊh
zebra	ˈjeɪwʌ̰	yes	jeç

(Data from Müller, Ball, & Rutter, 2006)

The second sense in which prosodic analysis can be said to be polysystemic is the fact that different phonological statements can be formed for different portions of the language. In this sense, variation in phonetic detail can be considered as having the potential to indicate not just lexical but also grammatical structure (Hawkins & Smith, 2001). For example, consider the distribution of the voiced dental fricative /ð/ in English. Word medially and finally, it can occur freely in content words, such as *brother, mother, bathe,* and *loathe.* In the word initial position, however, it is limited to a set of words called function words (e.g., *the, then, these, those, that*). It is evidence such as this that prosodic analysts use to justify positing different phonological statements for such systems as function versus content words and suffixes versus roots. Local (2003) suggests that the bilabial nasal [m] of *I'm* is less resistant to assimilatory effects than the [m] of lexical items such as *lime.* The cause, he suggests, could be that the [m] of *I'm* is in a grammatical system, whereas the [m] of *lime* is doing lexical work.

Clearly, there are a number of appealing aspects to the polysystemic approach. However, it is not without its theoretical drawbacks. Predominantly, the question arises as to how many systems we need to posit. If we desire a theory that allows statements of similarity to be made about systems of oppositions, we may end up breaking the language down into its most basic components. This has, however, been recognized and discussed by the theory's more contemporary practitioners (Halliday, 1967, p. 11; Ogden, 2001).

Sounds and Prosodies

In many theories of phonology we can talk about the *phonological prime,* the smallest unit of analysis. Depending on our theoretical position, we could talk about the phoneme, the distinctive feature, or the gesture. In prosodic analysis we talk about phonematic units and prosodies. In order to understand these elements, however, we must first appreciate the idea that there are two distinct aspects of phonological organization that any theory needs to account for: the *paradigmatic* and the *syntagmatic*.

Above we discussed the multiple systems of prosodic analysis and the places in structure they operate at. To be clear, a system is a set of potentially exchangeable elements. They are specific to a particular place in structure. The place in structure is usually expressed with reference to syllable shape, although we can also talk about word initial systems, word medial systems, word final systems, or even systems appearing at the word juncture. Essentially, phonematic units are the elements that are in system with each other at specific places in structure. In this respect, they are "placed." Phonematic units are hence functioning paradigmatically, as they are alternative possibilities at a particular place in the structure of a language; exchanging one unit for another brings about linguistic contrast. A prosody, on the other hand, is a feature of language that is abstracted above the level of phonematic unit due to its higher level of function—a function that serves to characterize, or synthesize, the structure of the language. In recognizing prosodies, Firth insisted that the syntagmatic, or "horizontal," aspect of phonology would be accounted for.

The higher level of function of a prosody may well be a feature, such as stress or tone, that cannot be assigned to a single place in structure. In prosodic analysis it may also be one of a great number of other features, such as nasalization or palatalization. We can call this type of prosody an *extensional prosody*. What we are calling here a prosody is similar to what we have called a *suprasegmental* elsewhere, and indeed the term *suprasegmental*, meaning "above the segment," does align with our notion of a prosody. However, as mentioned above, prosodies can be identified for a number of other reasons. If lip-rounding, for example, extends over a stretch of speech such as an onset, or entire syllable, we may want to call it a prosody of that structure. Equally, nasality has commonly been treated as a prosody by prosodic analysts (Robins, 1957).

A second type of prosody is the *demarcating prosody*. This is a feature of the data that is not extensional in scope, but which has a higher function due to being confined to a certain place in structure. It therefore serves to delimit or identify that place. These features are abstracted as prosodies of that place in structure because a native speaker may identify that place in structure by the feature. Henderson's paper on Siamese (1949, p. 30) serves as a particularly good example of the use of demarcating prosodies. She identifies the phonetic features of plosion, aspiration, voice, affrication, frication, lateralization, rhotacization, and labialization as prosodies of the beginning of a syllable, while identifying closure without plosion as a prosody of the end of a syllable. The presence of any of the syllable beginning prosodies indicates to a listener that a syllable is beginning, while closure without plosion always indicates the end of a syllable. Henderson combines the use of such demarcating prosodies with extensional prosodies of the syllable, word, and sentence.

Considering both phonematic units and prosodies together then, we have a system of analysis that recognizes oppositions along a vertical axis and along a horizontal one. This is summarized below:

Phonematic unit: Elements in system with each other at places in structure.
Prosody: Properties of the structure itself.

EXERCISE 9.2

Consider the following list of English words. Which of the following phonetic features do you think should be treated as phonematic, and which as prosodic: lip-rounding, nasalization, plosion, voice? What are the scopes of the prosodies?

home
room
lamp
sink
man

PROSODIC ANALYSIS IN PRACTICE

Vowel Harmony

One of the most commonly cited linguistic phenomena for which prosodic analysis is said to account for very succinctly is vowel harmony (Goldsmith, 1994). Vowel harmony is found in languages such as Turkish, Finnish, and Hungarian, and is a process through which the vowels in a word agree with each other in some respect. Traditional accounts of vowel harmony have recognized this as an assimilatory process, where a trigger vowel causes target vowels to assimilate, or change, according to the qualities of that trigger vowel. Turkish is a classic example of vowel harmony, and was analyzed in Waterson (1956/1970). By setting up a system of word prosodies, Waterson used the principles of prosodic analysis to cast vowel harmony in an innovative way. Using this analysis, certain properties of both the vowels and, notably, the consonants in a word are determined by which of the prosodies are realized. Importantly, Waterson uses palatographic evidence (pp. 185–186) to support her claim that both vowels and consonants are affected by such word prosodies. Specifically, she suggests that when vowels are front, surrounding consonants tend to be somewhat palatalized, whereas when vowels are back, there is a lack of such palatalization. This reflects theories of coarticulation, where delays in the alignment of gestural postures bring about periods of coarticulation. We noted in Chapter 7 on autosegmental phonology that recent versions of feature geometry have adopted the unified place theory (Hume, 1994; Clements & Hume, 1995) to account for interactions between consonant and vowel constituents.

The Vowel System of Turkish

Traditional analyses of the Turkish vowel system posit eight vowels: four front vowels and four back vowels. For each set of four there are two rounded vowels and two unrounded vowels. This system is outlined in (2), with the IPA symbol on the left and the orthographic symbol bracketed on the right.

(2)

	Front		Back	
	Unrounded	**Rounded**	**Unrounded**	**Rounded**
High	i (i)	y (ü)	ɯ (ı)	u (u)
Low	e (e)	œ (ö)	ɑ (a)	o (o)

Vowel harmony is said to cause vowels in noninitial syllables to copy the features for [front/back] and [rounded/unrounded] from the vowel in the initial syllable. Vowels in noninitial syllables are specified only for [high/low], while the vowel in the initial syllable is fully specified. In her prosodic approach, Waterson (1956/1970) deals with this by abstracting the features for [front/back] and [rounded/unrounded] as prosodies of the word. Two word prosodies are established: a y prosody and a w prosody. It is common practice in prosodic analysis for prosodies to be given full statements of phonetic exponency, detailing their phonetic realizations. Here, the y prosody corresponds to words with front vowels only, and consonants having some degree of palatalization. The w prosody corresponds to words having back vowels, with consonants having no palatalization. This yields representations like those shown in (3).

(3)

tunç	^{w}CVCC	*ast*	^{w}VCC
denk	^{y}CVCC	*üst*	^{y}VCC

A second prosodic distinction, that of o ~ o̲, is then set up to account for the rounded/ unrounded alternation, and this too is a property of the word. Specifically, an o prosody designates the presence of lip-rounding (roundness) in an entire syllable, whereas an o̲ prosody designates the absence of lip-rounding (unroundedness) in an entire syllable. Again, it should be noted that this prosody brings about lip-rounding, or its absence, in both the vowels and the consonants in its span.

The front/back distinction and the rounded/unrounded distinction are both being treated as properties of the word (i.e., they are prosodic); only the high/low distinction is specific to the vowel position itself (i.e., is phonematic). Here vowels are classified as either α (taking the exponent of lowness) or ɪ (taking the exponent of highness). Finally, Waterson (1956/1970) states that the o prosody operates with ɪ in all syllables of the word, but with α only in the first syllable of the word. That is, for low vowels, only those in the first syllable will be rounded. The o̲ prosody operates with both ɪ and α in all syllables of the word. This yields the representations such as those below.

(4)

	o----------------
	w----------------
yolumuz	CαCɪCɪC
	o-----
	y-----
önü	αCɪ
	o̲--------------
	w--------------
kalabalık	CαCαCαCɪC

The above example successfully demonstrates the use of the distinction between prosodies and phonematic units in prosodic analysis to characterize phonetic events that take place over varying domains. Specifically, we can see that only the high/low distinction is operating in a paradigmatic fashion, while the features of frontness/backness and lip-rounding are prosodic.

Juncture

Mainstream phonological theories are unanimous in their focus on the phonetic properties of individual words. This bias toward single-word production is also observable in studies of language acquisition, clinical phonology, and speech-language pathology. From this perspective, speech is often regarded as a succession of idealized productions, invariable and context insensitive. However, naturally occurring speech is noted for its continuity, with no decipherable pauses and gaps, but a continuous, running stream of physical movements. As a result, our impressions of how individual words are realized are often confounded, as sounds at the edges of words are merged with one another. Traditional phonological theories have generally avoided dealing with such phenomena, with connected speech processes often dealt with as a subbranch of phonetics. Prosodic Analysis differs in this sense, and from its inception, the theory has paid much attention to the properties of word *junctures*.

Following Sprigg's (1957) study of Burmese, prosodies can be analyzed as properties of the juncture itself, rather than explaining connected speech processes using notions of assimilation. As discussed above, prosodies are phonetic features that span more than a single sound, and can stretch across entire syllables or words. They may also be properties of a juncture piece, where they are associated with the linking of two successive units in speech. Importantly, the juncture prosodies are not properties of any particular phonematic unit, but rather properties of the coalescence of multiple phonematic units.

One particular observation that has been shown to be particularly useful for the study of disordered speech is that of the distinction between *closed* and *open* juncture (see Howard, 2004; Howard, Wells, & Local, 2008). Open juncture prosodies serve to preserve the distinction between two units and are particularly common in the clear speech used during repair (Rutter, 2008). Examples include the full release of stop consonants, the presence of glottal closure between the words, or pausing between words. Closed juncture prosodies operate in the opposite way, serving to smooth the progression from one unit to another. The so-called linking *r* of English has been analyzed as a closed juncture prosody (see Sprigg, 2005). It is important to note that positing this as a property of the juncture means the analyst is freed from having to decide whether it would be a property of the end of the first word in the juncture or the beginning of the next.

EXERCISE 9.3

The distribution of the labial-velar approximant /w/ in English is extremely interesting, especially when viewed from a prosodic analyst's perspective. Consider the presence of /w/ in the following data set and specify its distribution.

win	power	how	how and why
twin	sandwich	low	low and behold
squint	persuade		

CLINICAL INSIGHTS FROM PROSODIC ANALYSIS

In the following section we look at several aspects of prosodic analysis and consider their implications for a view of phonological disorders. One should bear in mind that applications of prosodic analysis to clinical data are not abundant; however, adopting a prosodic analyst's perspective can be seen to shed new light on many commonly observed behaviors in the speech clinic.

Polysystemicity

As discussed above, polysystemicity has already been proposed by Grunwell as a means of assessment, where the recognition of the numerous, interacting systems of a phonological system is essential. If we view language acquisition as being polysystemic, that is, that children are acquiring the many different systems of contrast in parallel rather than simply acquiring a single inventory of consonants and vowels (as proposed in most classical treatments of language acquisition), then much of what is seen in the speech clinic becomes nonremarkable. For example, Dinnsen (1999, p. 650) presents data demonstrating the "omission" of final obstruents "even though those same sounds can and do occur in other word positions." Below is a sample of the data:

(5)

target: *cup* [kʌ]	~	target: *pie* [paɪ]
target: *hide* [haɪ]	~	target: *dish* [dɪ]
target: *duck* [dʌ]	~	target: *cars* [kɔ]

Using a generative framework, Dinnsen (1999) states that one of two potential causes can be used to explain the data: (1) The child has no final obstruents in the underlying forms, and hence they don't surface phonetically, or (2) the child does have the obstruents underlyingly, but there is a deletion rule operating on the forms, which destroys the final consonant. Clearly, both the insistence on monosystemicity and the derivational nature of generative phonology are influencing the diagnosis. That is, because a supposed phoneme appears in one position, it is assumed that it should be available in all positions. Moreover, if it doesn't surface, it must be accounted for by either positing an erroneous underlying form or inventing a deletion rule. In prosodic analysis, the possibility of derivation is not an option. Rather, we can simply state that the system of contrasts for the word final position has yet to be acquired. Put differently, the child has not yet acquired the ability to close a syllable.

Similarly, Ingram (1997) constructs an identical argument regarding pairs of words like those in (6): that final consonant deletion can be due to the fact either that there are no consonants in the underlying forms of words or that the consonants are present underlyingly but are deleted by rule.

(6)

    cab [kæ:]   *cabby* [kæbi]

Here, the fact the [b] has emerged in the intervocalic position in *cabby* is treated as evidence that it is present in the underlying form of *cab* but has been deleted by some context-sensitive rule. In contrast, some children would produce forms such as [kæi] for *cabby*, and hence have no consonant underlyingly. Again, using prosodic analysis we would not be forced to account for such a disparity. Rather, the two positions in structure, C# and VCV, are given different systems of contrast, and should be expected to develop at different rates. A speech-language pathologist in this situation would be encouraged to treat the systems at the two places in structure as distinct, and undertake therapy accordingly.

Phonematic Units and Prosodies

The distinction between system and structure also seems to lend itself well to many phonological disorders. Consider, for example, consonant harmony processes, which see the consonants in a word agreeing with each other for some feature. We can view the word as being characterized by a "word prosody," which enforces certain articulatory features on those segments inside it. There are a number of advantages of this approach over standard generative accounts as well. First, by setting up a word prosody, we don't have to make the decision as to the directionality of the process, which is often based on nothing but arbitrary factors (Sprigg, 1957). Equally, if vowels and consonants alike were to be affected by the process, this would not be a problem for the theory, but a direct prediction of it. Waterson (1956/1970) showed that both the vowels and the consonants in Turkish vowel harmony are affected by the process, and the same is often true of harmony processes in children. Consider the following examples of place harmony (Ferguson et al., 1973).

(7)

| *doggie* | [gɑgɑ] | *body* | [bɑbi] |
| *raccoon* | [gækum] | | |

Using prosodic analysis, a simple phonological formula could be proposed, one assigning information regarding place of articulation to the level of the word via a prosody.

(8)

```
          ┌── x/y ──┐
          CVCV(C)        x: backness    y: labiality
```

As mentioned earlier, such prosodies of the word predict similar exponents to surface in vowels as in consonants, and hence such consonant-vowel interactions as those discussed in Williams and Dinnsen (1987) and Dinnsen (1997) are easily handled.

(9)

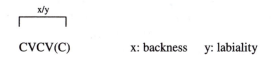

'Tom'   [kɑ]   'cage'   [te]   CV

Here, back vowels surface with back consonants, and front vowels with coronal consonants.

CONCLUSIONS

Prosodic analysis was initially developed as a reaction against the phonemic principle. While the theory never replaced the phoneme, many of Firth's original ideas have gradually found their way into more mainstream approaches to phonology. Moreover, prosodic analysis still has a healthy modern-day following, with work in speech synthesis, conversation analysis, and child language still being conducted using the basic ideas of the theory.

FURTHER READING

Firth (1936) is commonly cited as the starting point for prosodic analysis, although many of the theory's main principles were discussed in Firth (1948). Much of what we know about the theory is due to the work of Firth's colleagues, and Henderson (1949), Waterson (1956/1970), Sprigg (1957), and Carnochan (1960) can be considered as classic applications of the theory. Modern interpretations of the theory can be found in Ogden (1995) and Local (2003), and the theory has been combined with declarative phonology in Coleman (1998) and Ogden (1999). General overviews of the theory are sparse; however, readers are encouraged to consult Robins (1957), Lass (1984, pp. 163–166), and Anderson (1985, chap. 7). The theory was given a critical review from the viewpoint of generative phonology by Langendoen (1968). In an exchange of papers, Goldsmith (1992, 1994) and Ogden and Local (1994) discuss the relationship between autosegmental phonology and prosodic analysis.

Waterson (1987) is a collection of papers applying the theory to child language acquisition and speech processing, and Grunwell (1987) adopts the principle of polysystemicity in her analysis of disordered speech productions by children.

REVIEW QUESTIONS AND STUDY TOPICS

Review Questions

1. What were the original uses for the concept of the phoneme?
2. What specifically did Firth object to about the phoneme?
3. What is polysystemicity and how does it relate to linguistic structure?
4. What do the terms *system* and *structure* mean?
5. How do prosodies differ from suprasegmentals?
6. What is the difference between an extensional prosody and a demarcating prosody?
7. What are the implications for language acquisition when taking a polysystemic stance?

Study Topics

1. Gather some data from a child in the process of language acquisition. Look for evidence that segments appearing in one position in structure may not appear, or are realized differently, in other places of structure.
2. Using the same data from topic 1, look for phonetic events that seem to operate over longer domains than a single segment. For example, you may observe that lip-rounding frequently occurs over the course of a syllable onset, or nucleus. Contrast these with phonetic events that are specific to a single segment. Based on your observations, decide whether the separation of phonematic unit and prosody is justified.

10

NATURAL PHONOLOGY

INTRODUCTION

Natural phonology is another approach to linguistic sound systems that is outside the dominant generative paradigm that we have followed through Chapters 2 to 8. David Stampe was the prime mover behind this theory (see, for example, Stampe, 1969, 1979), and his work came out of the study of cross-linguistic patterns in phonology, especially in the acquisition of phonology by children. He noticed that similar patterns tended to occur irrespective of the target language. This led him to believe that certain aspects, at least, of phonology could be deemed to be natural, while others were idiosyncratic aspects of a particular language—a characteristic so far tackled only at the segmental level through markedness.* Naturalness, however, was not confined to merely occurring often, but had to have some kind of phonetic plausibility also. This approach to phonology has proved to be very popular with speech clinicians; however, as we will discuss below, it is not always clear that those who apply natural phonology to clinical data have fully understood the theory as Stampe outlined it.†

PROCESSES AND RULES

In natural phonology a distinction is made between phonological *processes* (natural) and *rules* (idiosyncratic). Stampe (1969, p. 443) defines a phonological process as follows: "A phonological process merges a potential phonological opposition into that member of the opposition which least tries the restrictions of the human speech capacity," and further (1979, p. 1): "A phonological process is a mental operation that applies in speech to substitute, for a class of sounds or sound sequences presenting a common difficulty to the speech capacity of the individual, an alternative class identical but lacking the difficult property." However, as we have noted, it was not intended that processes would be *ad hoc* devices; rather, they should be grounded in naturally occurring patterns and phonetically realistic changes. These patterns could be found through investigating

---

* Natural phonology should not be confused with natural generative phonology, a version of the generative paradigm described, for example, in Hooper (1976).
† Parts of this chapter follow closely the arguments about natural phonology put forward in Ball (2002).

phonological acquisition across languages, and by looking at systemic and structural constraints across languages. In other words, if in phonological acquisition cross-linguistically, children replace fricatives with plosives, this can be considered a natural process. Also, if adult phonologies cross-linguistically display a preference for final voiceless obstruents over voiced, that too can be considered a natural process. It is worth noting that Stampe believed that processes were not just helpful descriptive labels but linguistically innate.

However, in his description of natural phonology Stampe did not restrict himself to natural processes as descriptive devices. He also believed that you needed phonological rules that could describe language-specific (morpho)phonological changes that could not be grounded in natural, phonetic explanations. For example, Stampe notes that changes such as palatalization in fast speech in English (/t/ + /j/ → /tʃ/ in "what you ...") are a natural process, whereas /k/ → /s/ in *electric, electricity* is not natural and so must be accounted for via a rule. Generally, Stampe and adherents of natural phonology eschew the formalism of other approaches to phonology. Therefore, we do not encounter rule or process formalisms in their expositions; rather, phonological changes tend to be written out as descriptions (e.g., fricative stopping—all fricatives are realized as stops). This should not be taken to mean, however, that natural phonology operates at the level of the segment. As we noted above, Stampe sees processes as replacing the difficult property of a class of sounds with an easier property. We can only interpret this to mean some kind of phonological (or maybe phonetic) feature.

EXERCISE 10.1

Which of the following English phonological patterns would be classed as a process, and which as a rule?

   a. Plural *mouse-mice, louse-lice*
   b. Plural *cat + [s], dog + [z]*
   c. Juxtapositional assimilation: *te[n] dogs, te[m] men, te[m] boys, te[ŋ] cups, te[ŋ] kids*
   d. Vowel change: *prof[eɪ]ne–prof[æ]nity, obsc[i]ne–obsc[ɛ]nity*

DERIVATIONS

What is difficult to ascertain, however, is whether natural phonology is derivational in the sense we have explored in previous chapters. In describing phonological acquisition, natural phonologists would claim that the child has access to the full adult system, but that different sets of natural phonological processes operate at different stages to simplify this target phonology. Indeed, phonological acquisition can be seen as a procedure whereby natural processes are eliminated one by one, until the only ones left are those still operating on the adult target phonology. In this sense, then, acquisition can be thought of as derivational in that the adult phonology is realized by the child through a filtering layer of natural processes.

But what about the target system itself? We would argue that as far as natural processes are concerned (that is, the set of processes that still apply, or are supposed to apply, for that particular language, and these will differ from language to language), natural phonology is nonderivational. The processes act as constraints (see Chapter 11) on the set of phonological units available to the language (the phonological system) and on the combination of these units at the syllable or word level (the phonological structure). Only in the sense of the link between all possible units and all possible combinations can these processes be seen as derivational. On the other hand, the phonological rules (as far as these have been described) are presumably derivational, as seen in the *electric, electricity* example given earlier. Such a hybrid approach to phonology may be viewed as a drawback to a coherent theory of speech organization, although there has also always been support for polysystemic approaches to linguistics—so different theories for different aspects may be a strength (see Chapter 9).

TYPES OF PROCESSES

Processes can be broadly divided into those that effect systemic simplification (that is, simplify the set of units available to the phonology) and those that effect structural simplification (that is, simplify the possible combinations of units allowed at the syllable or word level). We can illustrate this distinction with some typical natural processes found both in language acquisition and in adult natural language phonologies.

Examples of systemic simplification can be seen in the following processes:

1. Fricative stopping. All fricatives are realized as stops, found cross-linguistically in phonological acquisition. It can also be noted that 6.6% of languages in the UPSID database (see Maddieson, 1984) lack fricatives, although this cannot be classed as fricative stopping, of course. In the acquisition data, fricatives are normally replaced by stops at the nearest place of articulation (e.g., /f/ by [p], /s/ by [t]), so that it is the fricative property that is being simplified here. In binary feature systems of the SPE type, we would need rules specifying that both [+continuant] and, where appropriate, [+strident] were changed to negative values, as well as rules to adjust for place differences (e.g., /ʃ/ to [t]). The process is much simpler, though the lack of formalism does not make explicit within the theory how the simplification works, or its phonetic motivation, or how classes of sounds may be grouped together.

2. Velar fronting. All velar consonants are realized further forward (usually as alveolars/dentals). Again, this is widely found in acquisition data. There are also many languages that do not utilize the velar place of articulation for all, or some, of their consonant types. English, for example, now lacks velar fricatives (though a velar fricative phoneme did exist in Old English). Historically, some kind of fronting of English velar fricatives does appear to have happened, in that the spelling *gh* (a sign that originally a velar fricative was present) can be realized as /f/ in some cases (*rough, cough*). However, a total deletion process also appears to have occurred; see *though, through*. It can be noted that velar to alveolar changes in SPE phonology requires changes to the four features [anterior], [coronal], [high] and [back].

3. Liquid gliding. Liquid consonants (e.g., /l/, /ɹ/) are replaced by glides (e.g., [j], [w]). The liquids (especially /ɹ/) are not among the earliest consonants acquired in normal phonological acquisition, and are often replaced by glides. Indeed, in English /ɹ/ may be realized as [w] or [ʊ] until quite late and may need therapeutic intervention.

Structural simplification can be seen in the following processes:

4. Final consonant deletion. Commonly occurring in acquisition, and there are also languages, like Italian, where no (or very few) words can end with a consonant.
5. Final devoicing. It is also common in acquisition to encounter only voiceless obstruents in word final position. This is mirrored in some Germanic (German, Dutch) and Slavonic (Russian, Polish, Czech) languages, among others, where only voiceless obstruents may occur word finally. Devoicing, indeed, does occur to some extent with final obstruents in English, but differences in the length of the preceding segment still allow us to contrast fortis and lenis sounds in this position.
6. Cluster reduction. This process covers a variety of subprocesses whereby clusters of consonants are simplified at different positions in the word. Children acquiring English will display cluster reduction in word initial position in the following two ways: /s/ plus consonant clusters will simplify by deleting the /s/ (e.g., *stop* [tɑp], *snow* [noʊ]), while consonant plus approximant clusters will usually delete the approximant (e.g., *blue* [bu], *quick* [kɪk]). At first, these two subprocesses may co-occur, but later the first may be retained while the second is discarded. In natural language, too, we may find a range of constraints on consonant clusters, in terms of both the number and type of consonants allowed. For example, Arabic only allows two consonants in word final clusters (English can have up to four), while Hawaiian has severe limitations on consonant clusters of any kind.

Processes such as these are claimed to occur cross-linguistically by natural phonology. The order in which these processes are suppressed during acquisition is also claimed to be fairly regular across languages (although the actual date in months will differ from child to child and language to language). Languages with a fairly large phonemic inventory and fairly wide range of phonotactic possibilities (such as English) will delete more processes during acquisition than languages like Hawaiian, with a low inventory and restricted range of phonotactic possibilities. More processes are listed in Exercise 10.2, and others still are described in Grunwell (1987, 1997).

EXERCISE 10.2

Which of the following processes effect systemic simplification, and which structural simplification?

    a. Weak syllable deletion, for example, *umbrella* → ['bwɛlə]
    b. Reduplication, for example, *bottle* → ['bɒbɒ]
    c. Consonant harmony, for example, *doggy* → ['gɒgi]
    d. Context-sensitive voicing, where obstruents are voiced initially and voiceless finally

Note: The [ɒ] in (b) and (c) is standard in RP, where General American would have [ɑ].

THE USE OF PROCESSES IN CLINICAL PHONOLOGY

The application of natural phonology to disordered speech has a long history (see Grunwell, 1997, for discussion). It has been seen as a relatively formalism-free (and so nonthreatening) approach to the description of disordered speech. Many of the processes used to describe disordered speech are the same as those used in language acquisition and natural language description. They are thus grounded in cross-linguistic data as well as in phonetic simplicity effects. Further, because we have a relative chronology of process deletion for certain languages, we can examine process use by children in the speech clinic and ascertain if their phonological patterns show typical or atypical order of acquisition. Indeed, many researchers have assigned age ranges to specific processes, so clinicians can calculate not only phonological delay, but also delay by a certain time period. This is clearly useful in screening clients to ascertain whether their phonology is delayed enough to warrant therapy, and in deciding which phonological errors one should tackle first. Grunwell (1997) provides a chart listing common phonological processes and the age range whereby they should be deleted in normal acquisition, based on English norms. We reproduce a version of this in Table 10.1.

Grunwell used charts such as these to assign one of three overall categories to children with phonological disorders: delayed (process suppression is behind normal rates, but following usual pattern), uneven (some later processes have been dispensed with while some earlier ones are still persisting), and deviant (patterns are in use that do not follow natural processes) (Grunwell, 1997). Grunwell notes five characteristics of disordered phonology that can be used in assigning clients to these groups. *Persisting normal processes* is the main criterion used to assign a client to the delayed group, whereas *chronological mismatch* between processes is a sign that the uneven category is required. The deviant category is used if clients demonstrate any, or any combination of, *unusual processes*, *variable use of processes* (excluding variation that shows movement toward the correct target forms), and *systematic sound preference* (for example, the child who uses palatals and palatalization wherever possible, thus producing *Christmas tree* as ['cɥɪçməç 'cɥi]).

Table 10.1 Deletion Dates for Natural Processes, Based on Data for English.

Process	2;0-2;6	2;6-3;0	3;0-3;6	3;6-4;0	4;0-4;6	4;6-5;0	5;0 →
Weak syllable deletion	███	███	███	■ ■ ■ I			
Final consonant deletion	███	███	■■ ■■ I				
Reduplication	███ ■ ■ I						
Consonant Harmony	███	███ ■ ■ I					
Cluster reduction (initial)							
obstruent + approximant	███	███ ■ ■ ■	■ ■ ■ ■ ■	■ ■ ■ ■			
/s/ + consonant	███	███	███	■ ■ ■ ■			
Stopping							
/f/	■ ■ ■ ■	■ ■ ■ ■	■ ■ I				
/v/		■ ■ ■ ■	■ ■ ■ ■ ■				
/θ/	███	███	■ ■	/θ/→ [f] ■ ■	■ ■ ■ ■	■ ■ ■ ■	■ ■ ■
/ð/				/ð/→ [d]/[v]	■ ■ ■ ■	■ ■ ■ ■	■
/s/	███ ■ ■ ■	███ ■ ■	■				
/z/	███	███	███ ■ ■				
/ʃ/	███ ■ ■ ■	■	/ʃ/→ [sʲ]	■ ■ ■ ■	■ ■		
/tʃ/, /dʒ/	███	███	■ ■ ■ ■	[ts̪ dz̪] ■ ■	■ ■ ■ ■	■	
Velar Fronting	███	███ ■ ■ ■	■ ■ ■ I				
Liquid Gliding /r/ → [w]	███	███	■ ■ ■ ■	■ ■ ■ ■	■ ■ ■ ■	■ ■ ■ ■	■ ■ ■ ■
Context sensitive voicing	███ ■ ■	■ ■ ■ ■					

Not only are natural processes used in the analysis of disordered phonology, they also inform remediation. The normal timetable of suppression of processes is used as a metric; thus, the therapist will usually start remediation with the earliest process still being used by the client, and then moving through the remaining processes in the order they would normally be suppressed. (In many manuals adopting a process account, other factors, such as the functional load of particular contrasts, would also be taken into consideration when planning therapy.)

EXERCISE 10.3

Consider the following sets of data, and decide which of the three categories (delayed, uneven, and deviant) the clients could be assigned to. For each client, list the processes being used. Note: In many items more than one process will be operating.

K (4;4)

bed	[dɛs]	jug	[dʌs]
catch	[dats]	pig	[dɪs]
dress	[dɛs]	roof	[dus]
fish	[dɪs]	glass	[das]
teeth	[dis]	vest	[dɛs]

S (4;3)

shop, top, pop, chop	[bɒp]	cot	[dɒt]
face, case	[deɪt]	slide	[daɪt]
cat, grass	[dat]	picture	['dɪdə]
brush	[dət]	dougall	['gugʊ]
pig	[gɪk]	stable	['beɪbʊ]
dress	[dɛt]	pussy	['dʊdi]

J (5;0)

clouds	[klaʊdz]	flowers	['flaʊəz]
thread	[fwɛd]	cat	[kak]
dog	[gɒg]	card	[kɑg]
donkey	['gɒŋki]	middle	['mɪgʊɫ]

(All data adapted from Grunwell, 1987; the target accent is British West Midlands.)

PROBLEMS WITH THE CLINICAL USE OF NATURAL PHONOLOGY

We have just noted that not all disordered speech is of a simple delay type: So how does Stampe's theory of natural phonology deal with unusual or idiosyncratic patterns, or patterns that do not immediately appear to have a phonetic simplification motivation? Our understanding of Stampe leads us to assume that we should call these phonological rules, but it is not easy to know from published work in natural phonology precisely how these differ from processes in their formalism or their ordering. Usually, work on natural phonology as applied to disordered speech has coined new processes as and when needed to cover whatever unusual patterns are encountered.

If processes are being used as simple shorthand devices to remind a speech-language therapist what a pattern looks like, and if all pretensions to the innateness of processes as opposed to rules are abandoned, then coining new processes as and when required presents no problems. If, however, we are attempting to use natural phonology as a theory of the structure and control of sound systems, then such an approach negates any theoretical integrity, and we cannot claim to provide any coherent insights on phonology or therapy. We will provide two illustrations of the problematic use of processes in clinical phonology.

Vowel Disorders

Disorders of vowels in child speech has been a largely neglected area, but one that has become more in focus in recent years (see, for example, Ball & Gibbon, 2002, for a collection of work on this issue). While a variety of patterns of realizations of target vowels have been described, a common thread appears to be movement toward what have been termed the corner vowels, that is, [i], [ɑ], and [u], together with monophthongization. Reynolds (1990), who undertook one of the first large-scale studies of vowel errors, proposed the following three natural processes for vowels:

1. Lowering of (mid-front) vowels to /æ/
2. Fronting (of low back vowels) to /æ/
3. Diphthong reduction (or monophthongization)

It appears that the first two of these processes fit into the general movement to the corner vowels noted above, which could be described by three processes, as follows:

1. Front vowel raising
2. Back vowel raising
3. Open vowel lowering

Indeed, we might want to argue that these three processes are manifestations of a single substitution pattern, which could be termed vowel cornering.

Clearly, the problem we are encountering here is that clinical natural phonologists have fallen into a trap of inventing a process to deal with their data without grounding this process in the way Stampe outlined. Until more work on vowel acquisition has been undertaken, we are not able to say that a vowel cornering process is as well motivated as velar fronting or final consonant deletion. Such *ad hoc* labeling may supply us with a handy descriptive label for what is going on, but it has no theoretical value and, further, cannot inform the clinician's intervention strategy.

Stridency Deletion

The anterior section of the fricative system as displayed on the IPA chart (see the appendix) is crowded compared to other manners of articulation, with fricatives listed at the bilabial, labiodental, dental, alveolar, postalveolar, and retroflex positions (not to mention the alveopalatals that are confined to the "Other Symbols" section). This reflects the fact that, for many languages, there are several anterior fricatives that have contrastive function. For example, English contrasts /f, v, θ, ð, s, z, ʃ, ʒ/, while Polish has the following front fricative phonemes, /f, v, s, z, ɕ, ʑ, ʃ, ʒ/, and Putonghua, /f, v, s, z, ʃ, ʒ, ʂ, ʐ/.

Traditionally, phoneticians have distinguished between these fricatives not only by place of articulation, but also through appeal to channel shape or percept of the frequency range of the frication. Channel shape is normally divided between slit and groove, though slit fricatives may also be described in terms of narrow or broad (see Ball & Müller, 2005, for example). The acoustic correlate of a grooved fricative channel is a higher-pitch range for the frication, and the traditional term given to this kind of fricative is *sibilant*. Nonsibilant fricatives are those with a lower top limit to the frequency of the friction component. Most of the slit fricatives are of this type, but the postalveolar fricatives, having generally a narrow slit channel, are classed with the sibilants (we may also encounter these classified as an intermediate category of *shibilant*; see Ball & Rahilly, 1999).

In modern phonology too, fricatives have been divided into two classes. Partly this derives from the use of binary feature systems in many models of theoretical phonology, as we have seen in earlier chapters. Due to the large number of fricative places of articulation, economy of description is lost if we need to posit binary features to account for place distinctions that only operate with this one manner of articulation. The way around this problem is to divide fricatives into two by the use of a type of friction feature, which in most approaches is the feature [strident] (see Chapter 3). Unfortunately, the term *sibilant* and the feature [strident] do not co-occur in their application. Taking the English fricative system as an example, the sibilant fricatives are /s, z, ʃ, ʒ/ and the nonsibilants are /f, v, θ, ð/. On the other hand, [+strident] fricatives are /f, v, s, z, ʃ, ʒ/ and [–strident] fricatives are /θ, ð/.

Clearly, these two approaches differ in their resultant analysis of anterior fricative systems, and this may impact our analysis and subsequent treatment of commonly occurring disorders to these systems that we encounter in the clinic. Among clinical phonologists who espouse a natural processes approach, some researchers claim there is a phonological process they term *stridency deletion* (see, for example, Bauman-Waengler, 2000, Creaghead, Newman, & Secord, 1989). The use of this process suggests first that the data from phonological disorders support a division of fricatives into strident and nonstrident (as opposed to sibilant and nonsibilant, as no sibilant deletion process is described), and that disordered phonological systems often display patterns peculiar to [+strident] fricatives.

The name *stridency deletion* seems to derive from work by Hodson (e.g., Hodson & Paden, 1991). However, the description of this process given by those authors is complicated by the fact that, unlike most other processes, different patterns of realizations of target strident fricatives are covered by the same label. For example, Hodson and Paden state, "Stridency deletion may be observed in a number of different forms" (1991, p. 51). They then go on to list the alternatives: total omission of the relevant segment, stopping, replacement with nonstrident continuants (they give the examples of /s/ → [h] and /s/ → [θ]), and gliding (/f/ → [w]). This description appears flawed to us in several ways. First, a general process of segment deletion (final, initial) has been reported often enough in the literature that it would appear superfluous to have a consonant deletion process as well as a strident consonant deletion process. Clearly, there may be occasions where consonant deletion processes affect only certain types of consonants, but it is generally not felt necessary to posit a whole raft of different deletion processes to deal with this, but rather to restrain the process to the class of sounds concerned.

Second, stopping of fricatives is commonly reported. However, the separation of strident fricatives from nonstrident ones in this regard is tantamount to claiming that nonstrident /θ, ð/ are pronounced correctly while strident /f, v, s, z, ʃ, ʒ/ are realized as stops. The evidence, in fact, points the other way, in that the dental fricatives may be among the last to be realized correctly. An alternative reading of this claim would be that while the strident fricatives are stopped, the nonstrident ones undergo some other process. However, stopping of dental fricatives is noted as a common pattern by Hodson and Paden (1991, p. 52), along with realization as labiodental or alveolar fricatives (a process termed fricative simplification by Grunwell, 1987, who also notes that all fricatives can undergo this simplification to the labiodental or alveolar place). It seems, therefore, unjustified to separate this aspect of stridency deletion from an overall stopping process that might affect all fricatives, affricates, and occasionally liquids as well. Hodson and Paden describe a variety of stridency deletion that applies to target affricates as deaffrication; again, it is surely more straightforward to consider it as another manifestation of stopping.

Third, we can consider the replacement of strident by nonstrident continuants. Hodson and Paden's first example of /s/ → [h] is, of course, commonly reported in the historical and dialectology literature. It is reflected in the /s/ ~ /h/ cognates between Latin and Greek (*septem* ~ ἑπτά), and in modern changes between standard Spanish and dialects such as Cuban Spanish (*dos* ~ *doh*). It is one step on a general lenition process whereby there may be an eventual complete weakening to zero. The other example, /s/ → [θ], is rare (according to Hodson & Paden, 1991) and may simply be an example of general fricative simplification patterns referred to below.

Finally, the gliding of strident fricatives can be considered. Hodson and Paden (1991) note that this is comparatively rare, and indeed, it seems more commonly found with liquids (Grunwell, 1987). Nevertheless, examples of fricative gliding may be encountered. Again, it would seem more economical and insightful to simply note that a general gliding process has been extended to fricatives for the instances that Hodson and Paden note. Indeed, there are instances reported of the voiced dental fricative being replaced by a glide (Smith, 1973), so there again seems little reason to set this aspect up as specific to strident fricatives.

This brief survey of the claimed actualizations of the stridency deletion process has demonstrated that there is little evidence to support treating the strident fricatives differently from the nonstrident ones. Indeed, we have to recall that the grouping strident itself is an artifact of a feature label emergent from a particular view of phonological theory. As we noted above, there is phonetic evidence of both an articulatory and acoustic/perceptual nature to suggest that a division into sibilant and nonsibilant fricatives is better motivated.

EXERCISE 10.4

A child of 6;0 presents with the following natural processes: velar fronting, final consonant deletion, liquid gliding of /ɹ/, and /s/ cluster reduction. Using normal acquisition as a metric, plan the order of intervention for these processes. Then, using functional load as a metric, draw up a second plan. How do the two plans differ (if they do)?

CONCLUSION

The application of processes to disordered speech proved so popular that many assessment protocols were devised to this end. Grunwell (1997) notes six of the more commonly encountered: Weiner (1979), Hodson (1980), Shriberg and Kwiatkowski (1980), Ingram (1981), Grunwell (1985), and Dean, Howell, Hill, and Waters (1990) (though some of these are hybrid assessments not restricted to process analysis). One can also note the KPPA2 (Khan & Lewis, 2002). However, because the proponents of the theory of natural phonology have not been as concerned with formalism as those in other schools, there has not been an effort to draw up a standard list of processes in natural language. This means such a list cannot be taken over into clinical phonology. That, coupled with the tendency to invent processes at will, noted earlier, results in a widely differing number of process labels used in the assessment procedures listed above. These vary from 8 (Shriberg & Kwiatkowski, 1980) to 27 in Ingram (1981).

Clearly, a process approach can be considerably simpler to use for a clinician than one of the more formalistic accounts of phonology. However, if researchers cannot agree how many processes there are, if the distinction between innate natural processes and idiosyncratic rules is ignored, and if clinical phonologists invent new process labels that do not seem grounded in naturalness, then we have to ask ourselves whether what is being used is natural phonology, or just verbal labels of patterns in the data.

FURTHER READING

The best account of natural phonology is that given by Stampe (1979), although there have been several works of interest in the area in the 1980s and 1990s. The most interesting of these, perhaps, are Donegan's (1985) investigation of vowels and the collection of papers in Hurch and Rhodes (1996). Grunwell has been the most important writer on natural phonology in clinical linguistics. Her books (1981, 1987) and chapters (1992a, 1992b, 1997) are all clear expositions of the approach. Other applications of the theory to clinical assessment were referred to in the conclusion to this chapter.

REVIEW QUESTIONS AND STUDY TOPICS

Review Questions

1. The study of what aspects of linguistics lay behind Stampe's development of natural phonology?
2. What is the difference between a *process* and *rule*?
3. Is natural phonology derivational?
4. What are the two main types of processes?
5. Which process is suppressed earliest by children learning English?
6. What are the three categories of disordered child speech according to Grunwell?
7. What are the realizations of *stridency deletion*?
8. Give one example each of an *unusual process* and *systematic sound preference*.

Study Topics and Projects

1. Using the data you collected for the study topics in Chapter 1, undertake a natural process analysis. Outline a remediation plan using the developmental metric described in this chapter.
2. Compare and critically contrast natural phonology with any other approach to phonology described in the book so far. Examine the application of the theories to both normal and disordered data, and to both assessment and remediation in the latter case.

11

OPTIMALITY THEORY

INTRODUCTION

Within the general framework of generative phonology there has been a gradual shift from the complete reliance on language-specific rules to the introduction of linguistically universal constraints. In phonology at least, these constraints, or well-formedness conditions, were first seen in autosegmental phonology (Goldsmith, 1976; see Chapter 7 of this book). Their aim was simply to limit the set of forms the theory could classify as well-formed. In optimality theory (OT) this trend reached its inevitable conclusion, with the total abandonment of rules in favor of a fully constraint-based phonology.

Arguably the first major OT publication was Prince and Smolensky (1993), and the approach has since become the dominant phonological theory of mainstream linguistics. Much of the initial appeal of OT was its potential applicability to other areas of linguistic analysis, and indeed research has been conducted in optimality theoretic syntax and semantics. Equally, OT has also been applied to, among other things, first and second language acquisition, language change, and most importantly for our purposes, speech pathology. In almost all of these areas OT has generated an extraordinary body of work, much of which can be found in the Rutgers Optimality Archive (available online at http://roa.rutgers.edu/index.php3). It should probably be considered the state of the art as far as mainstream linguistics goes, and is certainly the most contemporary theory included in this particular textbook. However, the theory is not without its doubters (see, for example, McMahon, 2000), and many of the potential problems encountered when applying OT are a result of its theoretical background; it was developed initially as a computational model for learnability. It is true that Tesar and Smolensky (2000) represent an attempted bridge between OT as a theory of formal learning and natural language acquisition; however, many of the ideas that underpin OT are still heavily computational in nature. This explains much of the vocabulary and notation associated with the theory. It has, nonetheless, been extensively applied to speech disorders and continues to influence clinical phonology.

In this chapter we look at the ideas underlying OT as a general framework, and specifically those concerned with phonology. We look at the notion of language acquisition in OT, and we then consider approaches to commonly occurring phonological errors.

First, though, in order to appreciate the aims of OT, it is essential to review the concept of universal grammar, with which OT is so closely associated.

OPTIMALITY THEORY IN UNIVERSAL GRAMMAR

Work in generative grammar (of which generative phonology is a subset) can be defined very broadly as the search for:

a. a way of describing what defines the well-formed utterances in one particular language, *and*
b. a way of describing what defines a possible natural language.

That is, generative linguists aim to describe what is possible and what is impossible in languages, and in a language itself. In considering (a) generativists typically come up with a description of an individual language, say English, which accounts for grammaticality in that one language. We call this simply a grammar, or a generative grammar. In *The Sound Pattern of English* (SPE) it takes the form of a set of rules, and an order in which they apply. But it is in considering the second endeavor, (b), that the notion of universal grammar (UG) (see Chomsky, 1981, for example) has come to the fore. UG comprises a finite set of laws, or principles, which define the degree to which individual languages can vary. At the same time, UG is said to be innate in children. That is, children are predisposed with the boundaries of UG, and the process of acquisition is one of identifying where their native language falls within these boundaries. As such, UG aims to explain the paradox of language acquisition: the fact that children master such complexities with such impoverished exposure or instruction (deemed Plato's problem by Chomsky). The question, then, is what substance do these complexities take? If the boundaries of possible languages are set, what are these boundaries made of? In syntax, we can talk of principles and parameters. A principle is a property of UG, part of a finite set, and is essentially a choice. A parameter is the selection of a specific choice by some language. The principle may be that languages are either head initial or head final, the *head directionality principle,* for example, while the parameter setting in English is that of head initial. But what of phonology? Attempts at an answer lie in the individual theories of generative grammar, and have in fact changed over the course of the 20th century.

Initial work in generative phonology (based primarily on the SPE model) characterized a phonological system as a series of rules taking the form A → B/C____D. The grammar of the language instigates the change B when an underlying form contains the string A and the location C_D. The output of the rule is said to be grammatical in that language. Languages were seen as varying simply due to the rules that they utilized and the order in which they were applied.

Work in autosegmental phonology enriched the phonological representations with which practitioners could work, making them essentially multidimensional, and also introduced the notion of well-formedness constraints. These constraints were not language specific, like rules, but were properties of the theory. They limited the set of possible output forms, those forms said to be grammatical, by doing such things as blocking rule application. You will recall from Chapter 7 the no-crossing constraint, for example. Simply put, this constraint prevented rules operating over an inappropriately large distance. In autosegmental phonology, such constraints had to be abided by; no surface form could violate them.

In 1993, Prince and Smolensky wrote a seminal paper that would again alter the direction of generative grammar. Indeed, for many, their paper, entitled "Optimality Theory: Constraint Interaction in Generative Grammar," represented the major event in mainstream linguistics of the 1990s. In OT, constraints are not peripheral or secondary to rules, but are the sole tenant of the theory. Prince and Smolensky suggested that UG "consists largely of a set of constraints on well-formedness, out of which individual grammars are constructed" (1993, p. 2). Crucially, Prince and Smolensky insisted that many constraints of UG are highly conflicting, meaning not all of them can be satisfied. This presupposes that any surface form is likely to violate at least some of the constraints of UG. Languages differ purely in how they resolve these conflicts. This is achieved through *constraint ranking*, a system by which languages select how important it is to satisfy certain constraints. Highly ranked constraints are more frequently satisfied at the expense of lower-ranked constraints. OT's response to the questions posed in (a) and (b) above, then, is expressed by the following distinction:

Universal grammar: A finite set of violable constraints.
Individual grammars: A ranking of these constraints into a hierarchy.

We note here that OT is not necessarily an approach to defining phonological representations (in the sense that autosegmental phonology or Firthian prosodic analysis is), but rather a theory of how grammars could be generated. It simply posits the mechanism by which this happens. The form of the input on which the constraints are operating is potentially variable, and often ill-defined in the OT literature. It is true that the vast majority of work in optimality theoretic phonology has assumed the basic representations proposed by Goldsmith in autosegmental phonology (along with some geometry of features); however, Gafos (1999) proposes a model where the gestures employed in articulatory phonology (Browman & Goldstein, 1992; see Chapter 12 of this book) are the representations on which the constraints of an OT grammar operate.

We can picture OT operating something like that shown in (1). GEN, short for generator, takes some underlying form, called the input, and generates a set of possible candidates for its surface form. These candidates are formed according to very basic principles of well-formedness.

(1)

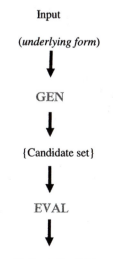

Input

(*underlying form*)

GEN

{Candidate set}

EVAL

Optimal Candidate

The candidate set is then evaluated, by EVAL, according to which constraints of the language each candidate violates. Candidates are then ranked according to *relative harmony*. That is, the more higher-ranked constraints that they violate, the least harmonic they are. The optimal candidate is hence at the top of the relative harmonic ranking, and is said to best fit the constraint ranking of the language in question. The constraint ranking can be represented as in (2) (where higher-ranked constraints appear on the left), and the results are shown in a table, similar to that shown in (3).

(2)

$$\text{CONSTRAINT}_1 > \text{CONSTRAINT}_2 > \text{CONSTRAINT}_3$$

(3)

/input/	CONSTRAINT$_1$	CONSTRAINT$_2$	CONSTRAINT$_3$
☞ Out$_1$			*
Out$_2$	*!		
Out$_3$		*!	

The members of the candidate set run down the leftmost column while the constraints run along the top row. The constraints are ordered such that the leftmost constraint is the most highly ranked. A constraint violation is shown by the symbol *, and if this violation is fatal, then the symbol *! is used. The optimal candidate is then the form considered grammatical for the language in question, and is shown by the symbol ☞. In the abstract example above, Out$_1$ is optimal as it violates the lower-ranked constraint, CONSTRAINT$_3$. Conversely, Out$_2$ would be the least optimal form, as it violates the highest ranked constraint.

CONSTRAINT-BASED PHONOLOGY

To further explore OT and its application to phonology, we will start with a simple example. Dekkers, van der Leeuw, and van de Weijer (2000) discuss the case of how loan words from Dutch are handled in Sinhalese (or Sinhala, the main language of Sri Lanka). Loan words often provide interesting evidence as to the differing constraint rankings of languages (Archangeli, 1997). When a word is borrowed from one language by another, as has been the case with many words coming from French into English, for example, its form is often altered to satisfy the constraints of the host language. For similar reasons, beginning second language learners often alter the form of words in the target language so they accord with their own first language. From an OT perspective, it is the differing constraint rankings of the languages that cause this. In the case of Dutch words being borrowed into Sinhalese, we need to consider three specific constraints, as shown in (4).

(4)

    *COMPLEXONSET : Consonant clusters are prohibited in the syllable onset.
    MAX-IO   : Segments in the input must be in the output.
    DEP-IO   : Do not insert a vowel.

    *COMPLEXONSET constrains words from having more than one consonantal segment in the onset of a syllable. MAX-IO and DEP-IO prohibit the deletion of segments from the input, and the insertion of vowels (epenthesis), respectively. These three constraints serve as examples of the two general types of constraints found in OT, shown in (5):

(5)

Output: Constraints that assess the well-formedness of the output.

Faithfulness: Constraints that maintain faithfulness to the input.

Output constraints are often referred to as *markedness constraints*, as they aim to make the output as unmarked as possible. Because they militate against markedness, output constraints usually take the form of flagging marked structures (typically with a *). Faithfulness constraints, on the other hand, are in direct opposition to this. Their aim is to simply preserve the content of the input as best as possible. Hence, faithfulness constraints typically act to prevent the insertion and deletion of material. Logically, output constraints and faithfulness are destined for conflict. If the input contains a marked structure, then output constraints will strive to remove it while faithfulness constraints will strive to preserve it. The solution thus lies in the ranking of the constraints.

Returning to the Sinhalese example, *COMPLEXONSET clearly is an example of an output constraint, while MAX-IO and DEP-IO are faithfulness constraints. Given the Dutch word /plan/ (English gloss: *plan*), there is essentially a conflict between the satisfaction of *COMPLEXONSET, which would be violated by virtue of the complex onset /pl-/, and satisfying the faithfulness constraints. As is often the case in OT, all possible candidates will violate at least one constraint, so the ranking of the constraints in the language is critical. This is one major difference between the constraints of OT and those of autosegmental phonology, as the latter must always be satisfied. What is crucial in OT is the ranking, as whichever candidate violates the lowest ranked constraint will "win out." This will then be the form that is used by the speaker. Stemberger and Bernhardt (1997, p. 216) suggest that constraint rankings of languages can hence be seen as expressions of "ease of articulation." Different speakers of different languages have different constraint rankings, and thus find different words easier to say than others. The process of learning the phonology of a second language, then, can be regarded as overcoming the tension between the ease of articulation of the first language and the difficulty of the second.

We can represent the constraint ranking in Sinhalese as in (6). This is called, in OT terms, a *strict dominance hierarchy*. It assumes that when some constraint is ranked higher than some other constraint, that dominance is absolute.

(6)

*COMPLEXONSET > MAX-IO > DEP-IO

Given the hierarchy in (6), with DEP-IO the lowest and hence the most violable, the table in (7) is generated. The form [päläna] violates only DEP-IO and is hence the form that Sinhalese speakers use for Dutch /plan/.

(7)

/plan/	*COMPLEXONSET	MAX-IO	DEP-IO
[plän]	*!		
[pan]		*!	
☞ [päläna]			*

Obviously, if the constraints were ranked differently, as they are in other languages, then the optimal candidate would have been a different word. This is the essence of OT: While the constraints are provided by UG, languages differ in how they rank them.

Constraint Interactions in English

We will now consider an example of constraint hierarchies at work in English. In the example above, *COMPLEXONSET was the highest ranked of our constraints, meaning any violation of it was automatically fatal. In English we find a quite different state of affairs. Indeed, many English words have complex onsets (*play, split*) or complex codas (*rent, tints*), or even both (*sprints*); therefore, the constraint *COMPLEXONSET and its partner *COMPLEXCODA (which can be collapsed into *COMPLEX, a constraint that forbids any complex syllable constituents) can't be as highly ranked as in Sinhalese. Instead, English has the constraints in (8), along with DEP-IO and MAX-IO, all ranked higher than *COMPLEX, giving English the constraint hierarchy in (9).

(8)

> NO-CODA: Syllables are prohibited from having codas.
>
> ONSET: All syllables must have an onset.

(9)

> DEP-IO > MAX-IO > ONSET > NO-CODA > *COMPLEX

You should note that English has a completely different strict dominance hierarchy than Sinhalese, meaning forms like [pleɪ] and [plan] are permitted. An OT table for underlying /pleɪ/ is shown in (10).

(10)

	/pleɪ/	DEP-IO	MAX-IO	ONSET	NO-CODA	*COMPLEX
☞	[pleɪ]					**
	[pe]		*!*			
	[ple]		*!			*
	[pə.leɪ]	*!				
	[pə.le]	*!	*!			

** denotes that a constraint is violated twice.

The optimal form for /pleɪ/ in English is [pleɪ]. Even though it violates *COMPLEX twice, on account of its complex onset and nucleus, this constraint is the lowest ranked of all the constraints shown here, and unlike the other members of the candidate set, it satisfies all the other constraints. The candidate [pe] violates MAX-IO twice, because two of the segments from the input have been removed, while [pə.leɪ] and [pə.le] both violate the highest ranked constraint, DEP-IO.

EXERCISE 11.1

Using the constraint hierarchy in (9), sketch an OT table similar to that shown in (10) for the word *spit*. What are the words at the top of the candidate set and why is [spIt] the optimal form?

OT AND PHONOLOGICAL ACQUISITION

Before discussing applications of OT to speech-language pathology, it is appropriate to outline some of the implications the OT framework has to bear on language development in general. Indeed, OT is a theory of UG, which in turn is an attempt to tackle the so-called logical problem of language acquisition: the claim that there is a mismatch between the linguistic data to which a child is exposed and the grammatical rules he or she manages to acquire (Chomsky, 1986). As a result, a reasonable testing ground for OT is perhaps the area of language acquisition. Moreover, there has been a great deal of work done in the area of OT and language acquisition, with much of it (see, for example, Barlow & Gierut, 1999) proving very interesting.

Because UG is theorized to be a means of reducing the potential grammars a child could consider to be correct, it stands to reason that the fewer possible grammars that could be learned makes learning the correct grammar more achievable. OT is a variety of UG that proposes that learning a language is the task of ordering the universal constraint set (deemed CON in formal models). Archangeli and Langendoen (1997, p. 15) state that CON "is posited to be part of our innate knowledge of language." This means children, at birth, are endowed with all the constraints of UG, and the act of language acquisition is simply the act of acquiring the constraint ranking that is true of the child's native language. And according to the principle *richness of the base*, this even excludes any acquisition of language-specific lexical variation.

Simply put, richness of the base (Prince & Smolensky, 1993, p. 191; Smolensky, 1996) states that it is the grammar of the language (i.e., the constraint rankings) that is solely responsible for enforcing the well-formedness of the output, not the input (the underlying forms contained in the lexicon). This predicts that if a language does not allow surface forms with coda constituents, the lexicon can still contain forms with a coda, but that the grammar must flag these forms as illegal (by having a high ranking for the constraint NO-CODA) and generate forms without codas. Equally, apparent variation in the phoneme inventories of languages is not due to a restricted set of phonemes appearing in lexical forms, but to the ranking of constraints. Smolenksy (1996, p. 4) gives the example of whether or not languages permit output forms to surface with voiced obstruents. This, he claims, is determined by the ranking of two constraints: (1) an output constraint, permitting the co-occurrence of the distinctive features [voice] and [sonorant], and (2) a general faithfulness constraint, requiring features in the input to be in the output (which we referred to earlier as MAX-IO). All languages have voiced obstruents in input forms, but regarding permissible output forms, the relative ranking of these two constraints gives rise to the following language types:

MAX-IO > ([voice] + [sonorant]) = languages that permit both voiceless and voiced obstruents

([voice] + [sonorant]) > MAX-IO = languages that only permit voiceless obstruents

You should note that no language can be generated where only voiced obstruents are permitted. This is due to the markedness component of OT. Voiceless obstruents are unmarked segments, and hence no output constraint militates against their inclusion in the output form. This is generalized to all segment types, and hence the set of input forms in OT is universal, with all variation in the surface forms being accounted for by the differing constraint rankings of languages. As a result of this *universal theory of input*, acquisition in the OT framework is not the business of acquiring the correct input forms, or even of acquiring the phonemes of a language, but of ordering the universal constraint set correctly.

Such a view of language acquisition gives rise to two questions: (1) What is the initial state of the constraint set at birth? (2) By which process do the constraints come to be ordered correctly? Because constraints are ordered in a language-specific way (indeed this is the very premise of the theory of OT), the answer to the second question is one of learnability. We deal with this as a process of acquisition. First, however, we must consider the ordering of the constraint set in its *initial state*.

Constraint Ranking at Birth

Unsurprisingly, early thoughts regarding the initial ordering of constraints centered around the notion that they simply had no ranking at all (Tesar & Smolensky, 1993). However, research supporting this hypothesis was predominantly supported by experiments using the acquisition of artificial language by machines. More recently, empirical data (see, for example, Levelt, 1995) have been used to suggest that in the early stages of acquisition, the set of output constraints generally outrank the set of faithfulness constraints (Smolensky, 1996). Recall from the section above that output constraints assess the well-formedness of surface forms, keeping them as unmarked as possible, while faithfulness constraints strive to eliminate disparity between the input and the output.

Under the view that the child is born with a universal set of constraints, with output constraints ranked above faithfulness constraints as default, language acquisition can be regarded as the gradual development from unmarked, unfaithful forms to more marked, but faithful forms. This in turn predicts that language-specific effects should not be observable in the early stages of language production. Equally, as acquisition progresses, the marked structures of the adult language start to appear in the child's utterances (Smolensky, 1996). In the example we gave above of voiced obstruents, we would expect these segments to appear later in the acquisition process than their voiceless counterparts. This certainly seems to be supported in the literature on the order of phoneme acquisition, in which marked constructs are almost always reported to appear relatively late. The question remains, however, as to how the rankings are reordered, and what information the child uses in order to go about this reordering.

Acquisition as Constraint Reranking

If output constraints outrank faithfulness constraints in the earliest stages of language acquisition, infants are faced with the task of reordering the constraint set. It has been suggested that they do this via a process of *constraint demotion* (Tesar & Smolensky, 1998). Constraint demotion is an error-driven hypothesis, positing that infants are sensitive to the similarities and differences between their own production of a word and those of the adults around them. If there is a lack of correspondence between their own form and that of an adult, the infant has the potential to use this negative evidence. One approach may be to demote the constraints that are satisfied by the infant's own production, in turn promoting (indirectly) those constraints that are satisfied by the adult form. This approach has been proposed as a learning mechanism, or algorithm, in the OT literature.

Dinnsen (2002) demonstrates how this might work in practice. He cites the case of a child who at the age of 4;2 correctly produced the voiceless dental fricative /θ/, but replaced it for all other fricatives, yielding productions like [θoʊ] for *sew*. The situation three months later, however, at age 4;5, was quite different. The alveolar fricative /s/ had been introduced into the inventory at this point, but was now being produced in place of /θ/. Consider the data in (11):

(11)

Age 4;2

soup	[θup]	*mouse*	[maʊθ]
thumb	[θʌm]	*bath*	[bæθ]

Age 4;5

soup	[sup]	*mouse*	[maʊs]
thumb	[sʌm]	*bath*	[bæs]

At 4;2 [θ] is used initially and finally for targets /s/ and /θ/, whereas at 4;5 [s] is used initially and finally for target /s/ and /θ/. To account for this progression we need to consider the constraints in (12):

(12)

*s	: Avoid coronal fricatives.
*θ	: Avoid dental fricatives.
*f	: Avoid labiodental fricatives.
IDENT[cont]	: Preserve the feature continuant.
FAITH	: Preserve all features.

The first three constraints are output constraints, which together outlaw fricatives in general. The final two constraints are both faithfulness constraints. The first is a specific requirement that the feature [continuant] be maintained in the output, while the second is an umbrella constraint, requiring faithfulness across the board. In the OT literature, FAITH is often used in this way to represent the general class of faithfulness constraints. Above, we referred to it as MAX-IO. When needed, specific faithfulness constraints will be specified, as with DEP-IO in the example earlier in the chapter, and IDENT[cont] here. In this example, IDENT[cont] is specified because it is ranked higher than FAITH. That is, the feature [continuant] is always maintained in the output, meaning stops are realized as stops and fricatives as fricatives. This can be seen in the constraint ranking (13) that is posited for the child at 4;2 (the sign = denotes an equivalence in rank).

(13)

Constraint ranking at 4;2:

IDENT[cont] = *f = *s > *θ > FAITH

The constraints IDENT[cont], *f, and *s are all equally ranked above *θ, which is in turn above FAITH. Essentially, the child is operating such that the feature [continuant] will have the same value in the output as in the input, and the fricatives /s/ and /f/ are more severely erroneous than is /θ/. The general constraint FAITH is ranked such that other than the feature [continuant], it is more important to avoid fricatives than to remain faithful to the input. In simple terms, then, the child will generate output forms that will avoid the fricatives /f/ and /s/ more than /θ/. For the underlying form *soup*, this would generate the table in (14) (the constraint IDENT[cont] has been excluded for the sake of simplicity, but suffice it to say that this constraint would be violated by any candidates that altered /s/ to [–continuant]).

(14)

/sup/	*f	*s	*T	FAITH
[fup]	*!			*
☞ [θup]			*	*
[sup]		*!		

The table in (14) brings about an incorrect production of the underlying form *soup*; however, the table in (15) shows how the correct production for underlying *bath* would be generated.

(15)

/ bæθ/	*f	*s	*T	FAITH
[bæf]	*!			*
☞ [bæθ]			*	
[bæs]		*!		

Because *θ is ranked below both *f and *s, the candidate [θup] is the winning form. This is the pronunciation the child uses. According to the principles of constraint demotion, however, the child will be motivated to demote the constraint *s, because she will hear adult productions of the word using this fricative. The demotion will bring about a new constraint ranking, (16), which now sees *s ranked below *θ in the equivalent position to FAITH.

(16)

Constraint ranking at 4;5:

IDENT[cont] = *f > *θ > FAITH = *s

With *s now placed at the bottom of these constraint rankings, the child will produce the fricative /s/ rather than violate the more highly ranked constraints of *f and *θ. This means a correct production for *soup*, seen in (17).

(17)

/sup/	*f	*θ	FAITH	*s
[fup]	*!		*	
[θup]		*!	*	
☞ [sup]				*

However, constraint demotion involves the constraint for which the child received evidence of violation, in this case *s being demoted lower than *θ, and now the form *bath* that was previously produced correctly is incorrect (18).

(18)

/ bæθ/	*f	*θ	FAITH	*s
[bæf]	*!		*	
[bæθ]		*!		
☞ [bæs]			*	*

EXERCISE 11.2

What constraint ranking would be required to generate the correct forms of both /bæθ/ and /sup/?

OT AND PHONOLOGICAL DISORDERS

Just as OT has become the dominant theory of mainstream linguistics, so too has the literature concerning clinical phonology become inundated with applications of OT to clinical data. This is to be welcomed if only because clinical phonology should explore current developments in descriptive linguistic theory, and outcomes of such work can be positive for both clinicians and linguists (Ball, 2003). However, there is a danger when applying linguistic theories to clinical data of modifying the principles of the theory in order to account for disordered speeech. There seems to have been a tendency in clinical phonology to adopt the terminology, notational devices, and schemata of phonological theories but adjust the way they work in order to accommodate disordered speech patterns. This is particularly apparent in clinical OT. Strictly speaking, for an OT grammar to be "in error," there can only be one thing wrong; the constraints must be incorrectly ranked. Regarding child language, it is usually claimed that errors are caused by output constraints being ranked inappropriately highly over faithfulness constraints, causing simplified (unmarked) utterances that deviate from the target form (Dinnsen, 2001, p. 15). In the following section we will consider the plausibility of constraint ordering being responsible for the kinds of phonological impairments that are found in the speech clinic.

Consonant Harmony

Consonant harmony involves the sharing of a distinctive feature by two consonants in a word for whom that distinctive feature should be different. The feature can be [place], [voice], [nasal], or [continuant], and in the most extreme cases of consonant harmony, the harmonizing can be absolute. Examples of each are given in (19).

(19)

[place] harmony:	*bat*	→	[dæt], [bæp]
[voice] harmony:	*bat*	→	[pæt], [bæd]
[nasal] harmony:	*mat*	→	[mæn]
[continuant] harmony:	*sap*	→	[sæf]
complete harmony:	*sap*	→	[sæs]

In accounting for harmony processes such as those above, OT practitioners have been faced with a simple problem. Why does harmony occur in the speech of children but not adults? Several approaches to this problem have been formulated. In the first, a child's specific output constraint is posited, which demands agreement in, for example, place of articulation between consonants in a word. Pater (1997) calls this REPEAT while Pater and Werle (2000) call it AGREE. In the grammar of a child who harmonizes consonants, this constraint is highly positioned, outranking faithfulness constraints that would demand input-output correspondence.

In the second, Stemberger and Bernhardt (1997, 1999) use a constraint called SINGLYLINKED, which "prevents an element from being produced for an extended period of time" (1997, p. 220) or, in other words, makes it illegal "to prolong a gesture" (1999, p. 13). Consonant harmony is explained via a low ranking of this constraint, allowing for its violation.

Finally, a constraint is used that aligns a particular feature with the edge of some domain. Dinnsen (2001) posits ALIGN, which aligns a manner feature with the left edge of a prosodic domain, while Goad (1997) suggests ALIGN(DORSAL/LABIAL/CORONAL), which aligns the place of articulation of a consonant with the left edge of a foot.

Such "invention" of constraints is problematic for a number of reasons. The GEN of OT has access to a supposedly universal constraint set, which should permit no language- or child-specific constraints. To sanction the invention of constraints to handle specific phenomena is to seriously reduce the strength of the theory. Proposals have been put forward, however, to account for such a nonrestrictive OT model of language acquisition. Pater (1997) has suggested that constraints may be able to come and go, so to speak, and that this is likely during the acquisition of language, and while the lexicon is expanding.

Final Consonant Deletion

Unlike consonant harmony, consonant deletion is relatively simple to account for in the OT framework. Such an account rests upon the relative markedness of the coda constituent, and the subsequent output constraint NO-CODA that serves to outlaw the existence of a coda in surface forms. The table in (20) demonstrates how a child's production of *cat* may surface as [kæ].

(20)

/kæt/	NO-CODA	DEP-IO	MAX-IO
[kæt]	*!		
☞ [kæ]			*
[kæti]		*!	

In (20) the output constraint NO-CODA outranks the faithfulness constraints DEP-IO and MAX-IO (as is predicted in the early stages of acquisition), yielding the failure to realize the final consonant. A process of constraint demotion would bring about the constraint ranking in (21), which would in turn generate the correct form [kæt].

(21)

N̶o̶-C̶o̶d̶a̶ > DEP-IO > MAX-IO > NO-CODA

EXERCISE 11.3

In some children final consonant deletion is not found, but the form [kæti] will often be preferred to [kæt] (this can continue with words like *cat* and *dog* for some time). What ranking of the following constraints would bring about a preference for the forms like [kæti]?

No-Coda
Max-IO
Dep-IO

FURTHER READING

Optimality theory was introduced in Prince and Smolensky (1993) and developed in McCarthy and Prince (1993). Approachable textbooks on the theory include Archangeli and Langendoen (1997), Kager (1999), and McCarthy (2002), while a critical review of it can be found in McMahon (2000).

The richness of the base and universality of the input are discussed in Smolensky (1996), and the theory was given a full application to language acquisition in Tesar and Smolensky (1998, 2000). Further studies on acquisition can be found in Pater (1997), Boersma (2000), and Dinnsen (2001). More clinically orientated approaches include Stemberger and Bernhardt (1997) and Bernhardt and Stemberger (1998, chap. 4).

REVIEW QUESTIONS AND STUDY TOPICS

Review Questions

1. What is universal grammar, and how might it explain how children acquire language?
2. According to optimality theory, on what basis do individual languages vary?
3. Why can loan words be important in discovering the constraint rankings of different languages?
4. Explain the difference between faithfulness constraints and output constraints.
5. What are the implications of the richness of the base and the universality of the input for language acquisition?
6. What is the relative ranking of output and faithfulness constraints at birth, and how does this impact the child's speech?
7. What is constraint demotion and what is it supposed to account for?
8. The relatively high ranking of which constraint is responsible for the process of final consonant deletion in children?

Study Topics

1. Gather some data from a child who is in the early stages of language acquisition. Try to find evidence for the ranking of output constraints above faithfulness constraints.

12

ARTICULATORY PHONOLOGY

INTRODUCTION

Articulatory phonology is considerably different from many of the other theories discussed in this book, as it is so heavily grounded in the physical act of articulation. The theory's architects, Browman and Goldstein (1986), insist that phonological description should be organized around articulatory activity, and hence bring phonetics and phonology closer together. Browman and Goldstein insisted on a very phonetic model of phonology, and so assumed gesture to be their phonological prime, that is, their smallest unit of phonological description (for this reason, the theory is sometimes referred to as gestural phonology). Crucially, the gesture is considered to be an actual articulatory event, with inherent duration. This is quite unlike the abstract, atemporal units of more traditional, feature-based accounts of phonology. Using this approach, Browman and Goldstein were able to offer a very rich, albeit powerful, theory of how speech is organized. This has significant implications for the way in which lexical contrasts, phonological processes, and natural classes can be expressed and understood. Indeed, much of the appeal of articulatory phonology is a direct result of its phonetic grounding. Furthermore, while theories such as autosegmental phonology (Goldsmith, 1976) have tended to analyze such phenomena as harmony and morphophonological alternations, articulatory phonology has been readily applied to the less mainstream, and arguably more challenging, areas of connected speech processes (Browman & Goldstein, 1990) and speech errors (Browman & Goldstein, 1992). Such applications undoubtedly serve to ease the transition of the theory's principles to the field of speech-language pathology.

This chapter outlines the background to the theory of articulatory phonology and considers some of the arguments for assuming that phonology is organized around concrete phonetic events. We will also draw your attention to the key differences between the gesture and its alternative, the feature, and consider the implications for assuming one over the other. Applications of a gestural account to speech disorders are then considered, and you may well find that the theory of articulatory phonology is among the more appealing approaches to phonology discussed in this book.

THE GESTURE AS PHONOLOGICAL PRIME

Phonology is distinct from phonetics in that it is the study of how individual languages combine a finite set of primes in order to form the lexical items of the language. This set of primes are those units that, when alternated, can bring about *lexical* change, not simply acoustic change. Models of phonology differ in what they assume to be the prime. Traditionally, the segment or phoneme has been the unit of analysis. Phonologists sought to define the set of contrastive phonemes in a language, claiming their combinatory nature allowed for the formation of each and every word of the language. Like the splitting of the atom, however, the internal structure of the segment became of interest, and the notion of the distinctive feature emerged (Jakobson, Fant, & Halle, 1952; Jakobson & Halle, 1956; Chomsky & Halle, 1968). More recently, phonologists working with nonlinear representations have argued for an internal structure of these subsegmental features, as in the movement of feature geometry (Clements, 1985; Sagey, 1986).

Articulatory phonology addresses the problem of phonological organization from a phonetic perspective, and proposes the notion that "phonology is a set of relations among physically real events" (Browman & Goldstein, 1992, p. 156). These real events are called gestures in articulatory phonology, and constitute the prime of the theory. They are neither feature nor segment, but represent "the formation and release of constrictions in the vocal tract" (p. 156). The gesture is distinct from the feature in a number of ways, and yields quite a different approach to phonological analysis. In the sections that follow we consider the fundamental properties of the gesture.

The Articulatory Nature of Gestures

Broadly speaking, a gesture is the formation of some degree of constriction at some place in the vocal tract. In this sense, the gesture is substantiated through articulatory activity. Distinctive features, on the other hand, are properties of a segment that are responsible for phonological contrast. They are atemporal and are defined in a present or absent manner. The gesture is defined using *task dynamics* (Saltzman & Kelso, 1987; Saltzman & Munhall, 1989). Task dynamics is an approach to describing goal-oriented systems. Specifically, in humans, such goal-oriented behavior is observable in the skilled, coordinated movements used in such acts as reaching and, crucially, speaking. Articulatory phonology uses the principles of task dynamics to define gestures according to a series of *tract variables*. A tract variable defines one element of the formation of a constriction in the vocal tract. The tract variables (lip protrusion, lip aperture, etc.) and the articulators that are involved in conducting them (upper and lower lips, jaw, tongue tip, etc.) are shown in Table 12.1.

Gestures in articulatory phonology are defined according to their effect on a set of the tract variables in Table 12.1. Related tract variables begin with the same letters, yielding five *tract variable sets*: lips, tongue tip (TT), tongue body (TB), velum (VEL), and glottis (GLO). For each tract variable set, a series of parameter values is set. For example, if a gesture involves the tongue tip (TT), we need to specify both the location of the constriction (CL) and the degree of the constriction (CD). Alternatively, if a gesture involves nasality, we need only specify the degree of constriction for the velum, as the place of constriction is self-evident.

Despite the introduction of such terms as *tract variable* and *gesture*, nothing particularly remarkable has so far emerged about articulatory phonology. Rather, it seems speech is being defined according to the movement of a series of articulators—explicitly,

Table 12.1 Tract Variables and Articulators

	Tract Variables	Articulators
LP	Lip protrusion	Upper and lower lips, jaw
LA	Lip aperture	Upper and lower lips, jaw
TTCL	Tongue tip constrict location	Tongue tip, tongue body and jaw
TTCD	Tongue tip constrict degree	Tongue tip, tongue body and jaw
TBCL	Tongue body constrict location	Tongue body, jaw
TBCD	Tongue body constrict degree	Tongue body, jaw
VEL	Constriction degree	Velum
GLO	Constriction degree	Glottis

Source: Adapted from Browman & Goldstein (1992, p. 157).

the specification of degrees of constriction being formed at the lips, tongue tip, tongue body, velum, and glottis, with the location of this constriction being given for the tongue tip and tongue body. It is worth noting, though, that gestures are consistently defined using articulatory information. Features, on the other hand, often make use of acoustic information. The feature [±strident], for example, specifies the presence or absence of stridency in a sound, a purely acoustic property. For speech-language pathologists, the gestural approach seems advantageous, as articulatory disorders are consistently defined according to abnormalities in the act of articulation, not in the acoustic properties. However, Clements (1992, p. 183) does question the significance of this difference, concluding that it is nonessential in nature. In support of this, the articulatory correlates of such features as [strident] are made explicit in the distinctive feature literature (e.g., Halle & Clements, 1983).

The Parameter Settings of Gestures

As you'll recall from Chapter 4, the features of *The Sound Pattern of English* (SPE) are binary in nature.* For example, the feature [±nasal] indicates either the presence or absence of nasality in a segment. As a result, oral consonants such as /p, d/ are specified as being [−nasal], while nasal consonants such as /n, m/ are specified as being [+nasal]. Rules can subsequently alter the feature for a segment to account for surface forms, as in the nasalization of vowels in English. In articulatory phonology, we find a quite different state of affairs. Gestures are defined not just by the presence of some tract variable, but are specified for how the gesture is achieved. That is, constriction degree, constriction location, damping, and stiffness are all specifiable along a continuum.

Browman and Goldstein (1992, p. 159) use the term *parameter* to refer to the differences in the way gestures can be articulated. For example, consider constriction degree (CD). It is not sufficient to state that there exists a degree of constriction at some place in the mouth. Rather, we need to specify how much constriction is present. The accepted parameter distinctions are fivefold: CD: clo(sed), CD: crit(ical), CD: mid, CD: narr(ow), and CD: wide. This particular parameter allows us to express differences between stops, for example, which have complete closure, and fricatives, which have a critical constriction degree that is close enough to create turbulence. The values mid, narrow, and wide are used for the differentiation of approximants, close vowels, and open vowels. Such an

---

* Recall, though, that Ladefoged (1971) did subsequently develop a system of distinctive features that used both binary and multivalued features.

approach leads us to analyze the difference between the English words *tad* and *sad* as being simply a difference in the parameter value for the first TT gesture (closed in *tad* and critical in *sad*). In contrast, the difference between the words *tap* and *gap* involves the same constriction degree but uses different tract variables (TT and TB). This, you should note, is a much richer approach to accounting for lexical contrasts than merely positing a change in segment (lexical contrasts in articulatory phonology are discussed further below).

If a difference in constriction degree is parameterized at the phonological level, it follows that other gestures should select a particular parameter setting. Constriction location (CL) selects from the following parameter values: CL: lab(ial), CL: dent(al), CL: alv(eolar), CL: palatal, CL: velar, CL; uvula, and CL: phar(yngeal). Equally, stiffness can be used to contrast vowels from glides, while damping can contrast flaps from stops (Browman & Goldstein, 1992, p. 159).

A gesture, then, if present in the articulation of a word, needs to be specified for certain articulatory parameters. We can schematize this as in (1), where the makeup of a complete closure at the alveolar ridge is shown (as in the onset to the English word *tip*).

(1)

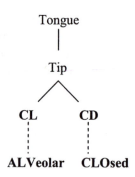

You should notice that the representation in (1) is not dissimilar to the sort of feature geometries we introduced in Chapters 5 and 7. In feature geometric terms it specifies the place and manner of the articulation of an individual segment. If (1) were to be associated with a particular slot on the skeletal tier, then it would be no different than describing a segmental unit occupying a single timing slot. However, in articulatory phonology representations are not formed using timing slots, as gestures vary in their individual duration. This property of the theory is crucial to understanding its potential for accounting for graded phonological variation.

The Internal Duration of Gestures

A crucial difference between articulatory phonology and feature-based systems is the fact that gestures have internal duration. This allows gestures to vary in how they co-occur. Crucially, it means gestures can overlap not at all, partly, or completely, and are perhaps the element of articulatory phonology that is responsible for the incredible richness (or rather, power, in generative terms) of the theory. Such richness has been regarded as advantageous in nature, but also as being the Achilles' heel of the theory (see, for example, Steriade, 1990).

Recall from Chapter 7 the description of association lines in autosegmental phonology. They serve to indicate that two autosegments on two separate tiers of the autosegmental graph are articulated simultaneously. Moreover, they allow multiple autosegments on one tier to be mapped onto a single segment on another, as in, for example, the case of a single vowel being associated with two tonal segments (2).

(2)

In articulatory phonology we talk about the *phase relations* of different gestures, and the way they occur in time. Remember that a gesture is an actual event, and so it stands to reason that some gestures may take longer to reach a completion point than others. Equally, gestures will not always completely align with each other, and may well overlap. Take, for example, the representation in (3), which shows the gestures (along with their parameter values) for the tongue body and tongue tip tract variable sets in the production of the English word *add*. The tongue body gesture is the vocalic production, with a pharyngeal constriction location and a wide constriction degree. The consonantal gesture involves a closed constriction degree and a location of alveolar.

(3)

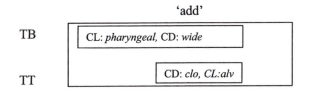

What is important to note in (3) is that the gesture for the tongue tip is only half the duration of the gesture for the tongue body. This is how representations are formed in articulatory phonology, and (3) is a portion of a complete *gestural constellation* (defined and discussed in the next section). Specifically, gestures are coordinated with each other at three possible points: the onset of movement toward the target, the achievement of the target, and the beginning of the movement away from the target (we will refer to these from now on as the *onset, achievement,* and *offset,* respectively). In (3) the achievement of the TB gesture coincides with the onset of movement toward the TT gesture. Consequently, these two gestures are in a state of *partial overlap.* Browman and Goldstein (1992) have suggested that gestures can overlap minimally (i.e., not at all), partially (as in (3) above), or completely (in cases when the onset of movement toward the target of two distinct gestures coincides). What is sometimes unclear in the articulatory phonology literature, however, is the degree to which *partial overlap* can vary. The representation in (3) exhibits partial overlap commencing at the halfway point of the vocalic gesture. If we are to permit partial overlap to begin at any stage in a gesture, then the number of phonological contrasts being predicted due to overlap is simply immense. Specifically, it is in stark contrast to the more constrained approach taken in nonlinear phonologies.

Traditionally, mainstream phonology has been heavily concerned with the segmentation of the speech stream. A recent incarnation of generative phonology, the autosegmental model, did move away from this somewhat, but still posited sequences of segments at the root, with only the composite features of segments having the potential to spread across several phonemes. And even with this freedom of association, it was not possible for features to overlap with each other only partially. For example, consider the case of prenasalized stops we discussed in Chapter 7, where an autosegmental representation would be similar to that shown in (4), and a possible gestural account is shown in (5).

(4)

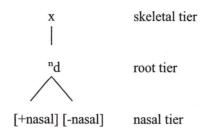

(5)

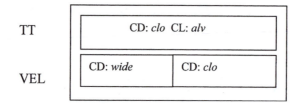

In autosegmental phonology, autosegments could be either co-registered or not. We can call this a purely *categorical* approach to representation. In articulatory phonology, gestures can vary according to the degree to which they overlap, offering a *gradient* approach. In doing so, articulatory phonology aims to capture the *syntagmatic* aspect of speech.[*] That is, the phonetic properties that span a word or utterance. The inventory of gestures serves the purpose of capturing the *paradigmatic* aspect of speech, the interchangeability of its subparts. In this respect, the aims that underpin articulatory phonology can be directly related to those of the theory of prosodic analysis (discussed in Chapter 9), where capturing the syntagmatic and paradigmatic aspects of speech were of equal importance (Robins, 1957, p. 191).

While the advantages of positing gestural overlap are abundant, it has been a property of the theory that has drawn some criticism. In a comparison of the gesture and the feature, Clements (1992, p. 185) questioned the need for such potential richness of representation. He argued that the "system predicts the existence of many more types of lexical contrasts than are actually attested." It is debatable, however, whether Clements' point is well grounded. He claims that the three potential linking points of

---

[*] The distinctive between syntagmatic and paradigmatic properties of language was made by, among others, Ferdinand de Saussure (Anderson, 1985, p. 186) and adopted by the likes of Firth (1937). You may encounter the terms *structure* and *system* used interchangeably for paradigmatic and syntagmatic (Clark & Yallop, 1990, p. 386).

gestures—the onset, achievement, and offset—yield nine different ways in which two gestures can be combined, not three, as Browman and Goldstein claimed. However, if the onset of one gesture coincides with the onset of another, that is the same scenario as if the offset of two gestures coincides, that is, complete overlap. Moreover, Browman and Goldstein make explicit the point that articulatory phonology is intended to be able to explain both the categorical (lexical contrasts, for example) and the gradient properties of speech (language change, or connected speech processes, for example). If the latter is to be successful, then the overlapping of gestures is an essential property of the theory. This is especially true in the treatment of language acquisition and clinical cases, as the next section moves on to explore.

REPRESENTATIONS IN GESTURAL PHONOLOGY

It is by using a *constellation* or *score* that the gestures of articulatory phonology are represented. A bare constellation is shown in (6), with only an abstract gesture filled in. Running vertically down the left are the five tract variables: velum (VEL), tongue body (TB), tongue tip (TT), lips, and glottis (GLO).

(6)

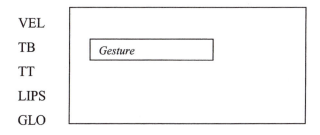

For any given word, a constellation will be formulated with the specific gestures appearing inside the box next to the appropriate tract variable. For example, if a closing of the lips takes place (as in a labial consonant), a gesture will appear on the LIPS column. In the articulatory phonology literature it is common for a box to be used. Enclosed in this box will be the parameter values for this gesture. The lip-rounding found in the segment /b/, then, would be represented as shown in (7).

(7)

Categorical Contrasts in Articulatory Phonology

Using such representations, lexical contrasts can be expressed easily. Specifically, Browman and Goldstein state that words can be contrastive due to (1) the presence or absence of a gesture, (2) differences in parameter settings of two identical gestures (e.g., constriction degree of a tongue tip movement toward the alveolar ridge), (3) differences in how the same set of gestures may be organized, and (4) differences in the duration of gestures. We will exemplify each with a commonly occurring lexical contrast from English.

The presence or absence of a gesture is a simple contrast. An example is the distinction between *bad* and *pad*, which sees the addition of a glottal gesture to *pad* to achieve the effect of aspiration (shaded in (8)).

(8)

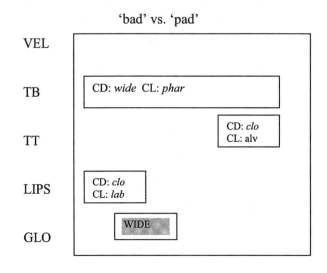

'bad' vs. 'pad'

EXERCISE 12.1

Draw a gestural score to show the Hindi word [bˢukʰ] *hunger*. The [u] vowel is represented by CL: velar; CO: nar.

The second potential contrast comes about when a parameter setting is altered. As discussed above, this allows for the distinction between such words as *tad* and *sad*, whereby *tad* selects a constriction degree value of *closed* and *sad* selects one of *critical*. Other than this, the two words are identical in terms of number and duration of gestures, as shown in (9).

(9)

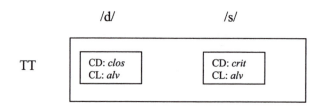

Distinction 3 involves differing organizations of the same gestures. A simple example is the pair of words *bid* and *dib*. Here the two consonantal gestures will be in the opposite positions in either word. You should note that this distinction does not apply to all words that would be traditionally dealt with as consisting of the same segments, but in differing orders. For example, *mad* and *damn* comprise the same phonemes, but in the latter word there would be an additional distinction in that the gesture causing nasality on the velum column would be longer than in the former. This contrast then encompasses both distinctions 3 and 4. A contrast that utilizes distinction 4 alone is exemplified by the difference between long and short vowels.

Adopting the gestural framework could have implications for the way phonological therapy is carried out. Traditionally such therapy has focused on the phoneme, and attempted to remedy any phonemes that are erroneous or absent in a system (van Riper, 1978). Using the system described above, speech is composed not of segments, but movements, and what we have traditionally thought of as minimal pairs may vary to the extent in which they themselves vary. Furthermore, the same segment in initial position may not have the identical articulatory characteristics as in final or medial position, due to the overlapping of gestures. This also has implications for therapy techniques.*

Gradient Contrasts in Articulatory Phonology

Perhaps most salient about work in articulatory phonology is a clear move away from a strictly segmental view of speech, and it is the potential for the overlapping of gestures that makes the gestural score so adequate for this endeavor. To explore this potential, let us consider the nasalization of vowels in English. It is well known that vowels preceding a nasal consonant become at least partially nasalized themselves. A classical SPE style account of this phenomenon needs to specify the change of the vowel's feature [–nasal] to [+nasal] when it is preceded by a nasal consonant. This, of course, fails to make explicit the fact that it is the same property of the consonant that is present in the vowel (the lowering of the velum in articulatory terms). A modern featural account remedies this somewhat and will typically indicate the spreading of the feature [+nasal] from consonant to vowel, as shown in (10).

(10)

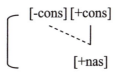

In articulatory phonology the spreading of nasality can be expressed effectively and succinctly by exploiting the potential for gestures to overlap. In the score in (11) a representation for the word *in* is shown. The gesture for the opening of the velum begins slightly before that for the movement of the tongue tip, thus indicating the nasalization of the vowel.

---

* Note that Grumwell (1986) endorses an approach to phonological intervention that emphasizes the importance of treating sounds by position rather than as individual units. Equally, the theory of prosodic analysis demands that sounds from different parts of a word should be analyzed as belonging to different systems. We call this notion polysystemicity.

(11)

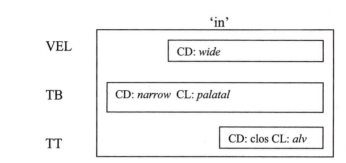

'in'

VEL	CD: *wide*
TB	CD: *narrow* CL: *palatal*
TT	CD: clos CL: *alv*

EXERCISE 12.2

What would a gestural score for the English word *man* look like? Pay particular attention to the gesture corresponding to nasality.

A second example of graded phonological variation due to gestural overlap was cited by Browman and Goldstein (1990) and involved the notion of a gesture being *hidden*. Analysis of two contextually different productions of the phrase *perfect memory* was carried out, one where the phrase was placed in a word list and the other where the list was spoken during fluent, connected speech. Perceptually, it seemed the [t] of *perfect* was deleted when the phrase was spoken in fluent speech, but was intact when the phrase was spoken in a word list (when in a word list, the two words *perfect* and *memory* would be divided by an intonational boundary). This is a commonly reported occurrence in the literature concerning the phonetics of connected speech (Clark & Yallop, 1990, p. 90; Ball & Müller, 2005, p. 259), usually being referred to as consonant elision. Interestingly, it is typically claimed that such elision occurs at the boundary between a word final consonant cluster and a word initial consonant cluster. However, Browman and Goldstein found (using x-ray evidence) that the stop closure for [t] was present but nonaudible on account of it being fully overlapped, or hidden, by other gestures, specifically, the offset of [k] and the onset of [m]. This is schematized in (12).

(12)

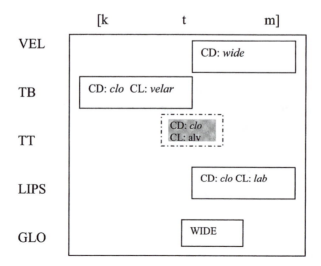

[k   t   m]

VEL	CD: *wide*
TB	CD: *clo* CL: *velar*
TT	CD: *clo* CL: alv
LIPS	CD: *clo* CL: *lab*
GLO	WIDE

As (12) shows, the gestural score has many gestural configurations at the word boundary. The result is that the gesture for the alveolar closure (filled grey in the representation) is acoustically and perceptually hidden.

CLINICAL APPLICATIONS OF ARTICULATORY PHONOLOGY

Somewhat unfortunately, there is a distinct lack of work looking at clinical data from an articulatory phonology perspective. Kent (1997) partially attributed this gap to the then newness of the theory; however, even today work in clinical phonology has been dominated by the more mainstream optimality theory (see Prince & Smolensky, 1993; Bernhardt & Stemberger, 1998), which seems to have superseded articulatory phonology. This is regrettable, as the ability of articulatory phonology to provide concise accounts of graded phonological variation has been shown to be useful in clinical cases from child language development (Studdert-Kennedy & Goddell, 1995) to motor speech disorders (Weismer, Tjaden, & Kent, 1995; Kent, 1997) through to progressive speech degeneration (Ball et al., 2004). In this section we summarize the progress that has been made in each of these areas of work.

Language Acquisition

Browman and Goldstein themselves highlight the applicability of articulatory phonology to language development (1992, p. 176), and the theory's superiority over strictly segmental approaches to language acquisition has been argued in Studdert-Kennedy and Goddell (1995). Under this view language development is regarded as the differentiation and coordination of a set of basic gestures that emerge during the babbling stage of a child's life. Language acquisition is then a continuum of mastering these articulatory gestures. This accounts for the gradient development of language and the variability in production during the early stages of childhood. As gross gestures are still undifferentiated by the child, productions are less accurate with a reduction in the fine-grained contrastivity of the adult system. The ability to produce segment-sized units comes later in acquisition, as the mastery of gestures is completed.*

Hewlett and Waters (2004) have questioned the validity of this account, however, suggesting that the solely *articulatory* nature of articulatory phonology is problematic. They cite findings where the progression toward the production of the labiodental fricative /f/ passes through a stage where the child produces /s/. Hewlett and Waters insist that the child must be attempting to replicate the high-frequency turbulence associated with /f/ by producing the similarly turbulent /s/. Implicit in this approach is a perceptual component of language development, which articulatory phonology is seemingly lacking. Regardless, it seems the approach put forward in articulatory phonology is still more intuitive than a simple mastering of an inventory of phonemes, or distinctive features, or constraint ordering.

---

* This is in line with the view held by Bybee (2001) and other cognitive linguists, who regard segments as emergent properties. See Ball (2001) and Chapter 14 of this book for a discussion of cognitive phonology and clinical linguistics.

Motor Speech Disorders

Motor speech disorders are rarely dealt with using phonological theory, as the symptoms of such conditions as Parkinson's disease and Wilson's disease do not lend themselves well to the categorical, lexicon-centric approach favored by most phonological theories. Motor speech disorders typically present with graded effects to speech, rather than the complete loss or misuse of a particular segment, for example. Articulatory phonology, however, offers great potential for the characterization of such symptoms through the use of abnormal gestural phrasing relations. Weismer et al. (1995) consider the ability of articulatory phonology in handling such symptoms, and conclude that the theory can offer much. Articulatory slowness, for example, is quite easily handled by articulatory phonology via a process of lengthening the duration of gestural components. Equally, the process of segmentalization, where segments in words appear isolated, devoid of coarticulatory and assimilatory processes, is handled well via the reduction in the amount of gestural overlap. For example, a segmentalized production of the sequence in (12) is represented in (13).

(13)

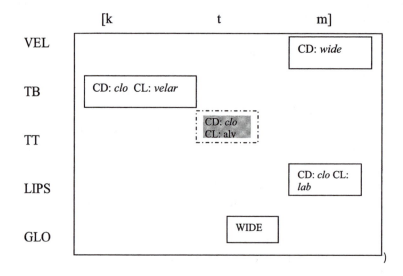

Progressive Speech Degeneration

It is fairly uncontroversial to say that a large proportion of the work in clinical phonology deals predominantly with developmental phonological/articulation disorders in children. For that reason, cases of phonological disorders occurring later in life provide interesting potential for theoretical exploration. Building on work in Ball (2003), Ball et al. (2004) provide a gestural account of the progressive degeneration (of unknown etiology) of the speech of a 63-year-old male. One of the markers of the degeneration was an inability to distinguish voiced and voiceless plosives, resulting in insignificant differences between the voice onset time (VOT) of either voiced or voiceless plosives. Specifically, the client averaged a VOT of 21 msec for the voiceless tokens and 18 for the voiced. In contrast, the authors report averages of 59.6 and 18.5 msec for the SLP. This is accounted for by positing a loss in the ability to control the duration of the glottal gesture creating voicing. Specifically, the client significantly reduces the duration of this gesture, such that the crucial contrast between voicing and voicelessnss is lost. This is represented in (14), where the arrow indicates the abnormally short duration of the glottal gesture. In articulatory phonology terms, we can call this gestural *sliding*.

(14)

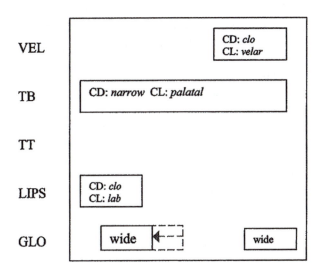

Because degeneration of speech is often progressive in nature, the gradient nature of articulatory phonology is well suited to account for such change. A featural account could simply represent the loss of a feature (in this case the change from + to − [voice]) without recognizing that this change would be gradual and would not necessarily be an all-or-nothing phenomenon.

EXERCISE 12.3

Gestural phonology can also be applied to child speech disorders. Draw constellations showing the difference between target *booth* (/buθ/) and typical disordered child speech [bup]. How does the gestural score explain the changes here?

FURTHER READING

Articulatory phonology was introduced in Browman and Goldstein (1986) and developed further in Browman and Goldstein (1989, 1990) and Kingston and Cohen (1992). A complete overview of the theory can be found in Browman and Goldstein (1992). Gafos (1999) used the representations of articulatory phonology as the input for an optimality theoretic grammar. Task dynamics for the purposes of speech is discussed in Saltzman (1986). The theory has been compared to generative phonology in Clements (1992) and Steriade (1990).

Articulatory phonology has been applied to a large range of phenomena, including connected speech processes (Browman & Goldstein, 1990, 1992, pp. 171–176) child language development (Studdert-Kennedy & Goddell, 1995), motor speech disorders (Weismer et al., 1995; Kent, 1997), and progressive speech degeneration (Ball et al., 2004).

REVIEW QUESTIONS AND STUDY TOPICS

Review Questions

1. According to articulatory phonology, what do the terms *gesture*, *tract variable*, *parameter*, and *gestural constellation* mean?
2. What is the difference between the syntagmatic and paradigmatic aspects of speech?
3. What are the three possible ways in which gestures can overlap?
4. What did Browman and Goldstein mean when they said they wanted to account for gradient as well as categorical change? What is an example of each?
5. What is gestural *hiding* and how is it related to the notion of connected speech processes?
6. How is language development regarded in articulatory phonology?
7. What is segmentalization and how might a gestural approach account for it?
8. What is gestural sliding and what can it be used to account for?

Study Topics

1. Carefully compare the chapters in this book on autosegmental phonology and articulatory phonology. Draw up a list of similarities and differences between the two. How much do you agree with Kent (1997, p. 248) when he says that articulatory phonology "embraces certain principles of autosegmental phonology"?
2. Use the list of phrases provided below and embed them first as part of a word list, and then in a series of sentences. Record a few of your friends saying the word list and then some other friends saying the sentences. Listen to the recordings and see if you can find evidence for gestural hiding occurring at the end of the first word.

passed by	finished work	cold night
next week	soft cushion	raised them
last night	East Texas	refused them
finished work	found them	old car

13

GOVERNMENT PHONOLOGY

INTRODUCTION

In previous chapters, where we have examined the development of generative models of phonology (Chapters 3–8), we have seen that the basic prime of phonological structure has been the distinctive feature (mostly binary equipollent features)—this feature only being phonetically interpretable in combination with other features (and only at a stage during derivation when underspecified features have been filled in). Relations between features were expressed via feature geometry trees, but not between the individual features within the feature matrix for a particular segment. However, alternative models of phonology, within the overall generative school, were developed from the 1980s onward. An early such approach, called *dependency phonology* (Anderson & Durand, 1986, 1987; Anderson & Ewen, 1987), allowed a range of dependency relations to hold between the primes of phonological description. This wide range proved to be too powerful, as it allowed too many combinations of primes. *Government phonology* (Kaye, Lowenstamm, & Vergnaud, 1985, 1990; Harris, 1990, 1994; Harris & Lindsey, 1995) can be seen to some extent as a development of dependency phonology, with the aim of constraining the generative power of this latter approach.

Government phonology (GovP) is seen by its supporters to be within the generative tradition (and thus part of universal grammar), and it shares with other approaches the insights and developments of feature geometry (Chapter 5), autosegmental phonology (Chapter 7), and metrical phonology (Chapter 8). In particular, we should note that the theory distinguishes a skeletal tier that contains the terminal nodes of syllabic constituents (termed constituency) from a segmental one (termed melody), and that the equivalent of features (elements) are thought to operate on a set of tiers as well. However, despite these similarities, there are major differences—in particular, as the name suggests, the idea of governing and licensing relations between units.

In this chapter we will look at the two main areas of the theory, *constituency* and *melody*, and then turn to the application of the theory to the description of disordered speech (for a fuller sketch of the theory, see Ball, 2008). The version of GovP presented here is the one developed in the mid-1990s; more recently researchers have developed varieties of the approach using fewer elements, but we feel the fuller version, described below, is more useful in clinical terms.

CONSTITUENCY

In GovP, constituency is the level that deals with units of analysis larger than the segment, for example, onset-rime pairs, feet, and the phonological word. Unlike many other approaches, GovP does not formally recognize a syllable constituent as an organizing unit (although it does as a licensing relation; we return to licensing later). Rather than the familiar onset-rime, with rime consisting of nucleus-coda, syllable structure, GovP normally shows segments in pairs of onset-nucleus (although the rime unit is present and does need to be shown in some combinations that we describe below). The concept of the phonological word is used and consists of feet, which in turn consist of the units O (onset), N (nucleus), and rime (all of which may potentially be binary branching, depending on the language concerned). These sequences are located on the tier P^0, which dominates the timing tier (or skeleton) traditionally represented by timing slots x-x-x, which dominate the consonant and vowel segments. Kula (2002) notes that the skeleton links segmental information to the constituency level, and "the government and licensing relations that hold between them" (p. 23).

Although we see that GovP does retain the traditional terms onset, rime, and nucleus, the traditional unit of the coda is not present (at least not in terms of a unit similar in status to the nucleus that is potentially always present). Singleton consonants at the end of a syllable (in traditional parlance) are always deemed to be onsets, with an empty following nucleus (see Harris, 1994, for arguments in favor of this viewpoint; theory-independent, empirical reasons for considering final Cs to be onsets are found in Harris and Gussmann, 2002). We can show this in the following GovP syllable diagrams in (1); in the first consonant final example we show the empty nucleus, in the second we omit it, as is often done to save space; also in these examples, we show the rime unit, even though that is often omitted if no branching of the rime occurs. The words are *low, let,* and *less*.

(1)

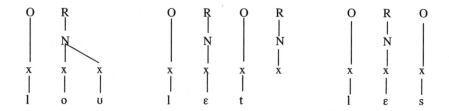

We noted in Chapter 2 that we can have binary branching of the onset, rime, and nucleus. Branching onsets account for initial consonant clusters. However, /s/ initial clusters are dealt with differently (this applies to both two- and three-consonant /s/ initial clusters). Harris (1994) and, in terms of clinical data, Gierut (1999) have argued that /s/ initial clusters are different from, for example, stop + approximant clusters. These /s/ initial clusters break the sonority sequencing principle (see Chapter 2) and behave differently from stop + approximant clusters in acquisition, disorder, and cross-linguistically. Therefore, in GovP the /s/ in these clusters is deemed to be an onset with an empty nucleus (a similar solution is proposed for /s/ final clusters, as in plurals in English). The nucleus branches to show long vowels and diphthongs (as in the first example in (1) above).

GovP also allows branching rimes. These are utilized to show consonant clusters word medially and finally. The restrictions here are somewhat complex; the right-hand branch of the rime may contain a consonant, subject to certain restrictions in the case of heavy nuclei (long vowels or diphthongs): Consonants can only be fricatives or sonorants, sonorants agree with the place of the following consonant, and the favored such place is coronal (see Harris, 1994, p. 77). These restrictions do not hold on light nuclei. We can illustrate the various possible branching units in the following examples in (2), using the words *creep, now, kept,* and *stand.*

(2)

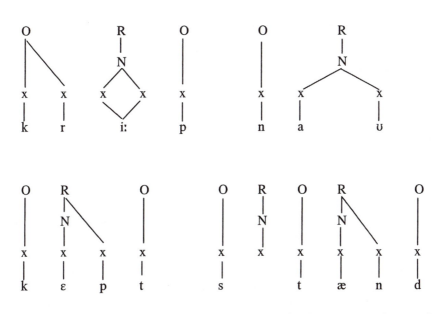

Clearly, English, for example, allows more complex final consonant clusters than the ones shown in (2), and final two-consonant clusters that do not meet the conditions on branching rimes noted above. In these cases, empty nuclei are posited between the consonants. In the example in (3) we have removed the rime unit from the diagram, as a branching rime plays no part in the word *reaped.*

(3)

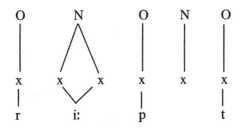

Final three- and four-consonant clusters are accounted for by combinations of branching rimes and empty nuclei dependent on which consonants are involved, as in *ponds.* (In the diagram in (4) we show the empty nucleus after /d/ but not after /z/, as is traditional. This is just a space-saving device.)

(4)

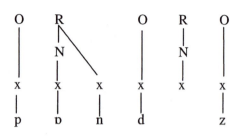

EXERCISE 13.1

Draw GovP diagrams to show the constituency of the following English words:

go, got, goat

still, steal, stops

pelt, peeled, pest, pets

texts, sculpts, prompts

This approach to phonology is termed government phonology because its units enter into governing and licensing relations with each other. *Licensing* encompasses the constraints in any one language on the combinatorial possibilities of elements. *Government* is the term used to describe the asymmetric relations between units. While this is perhaps most obvious on the melodic tier (see below), there are also relations between the various units we have been considering at the constituency level. We can look at some of the more important of these here. For example, the onset, rime, and nucleus constituents are subject to the following general principles in (5) and (6):

(5)

Every nucleus can and must license a preceding onset.

(6)

Every onset must be licensed by a following nucleus.

These two principles show that the nucleus is the head (or governor) in the combination onset + nucleus. Furthermore, as shown in (7), it is required that:

(7)

Every constituent licenser must dominate a skeletal point.

Given the above, we can derive the principle shown in (8):

(8)

Every nucleus must dominate a skeletal point.

This means that a nucleus must be linked to an *x* on the timing tier.

Related to these principles is the principle shown in (9) concerning codas, discussed above:

(9)

    Coda-licensing principle: Postnuclear rime positions must be licensed by a following onset.

These principles are concerned with the three main units of constituent structure (onset, rime, and nucleus). We may also consider principles concerned with location and direction of government between them. Kula (2002, p. 25) notes that government is subject to the conditions in (10):

(10)

    Conditions on government:

    a. Strict locality: Only adjacent positions can constitute a government relation.

    b. Strict directionality: Constituent government goes from left to right, and

        interconstituent government goes from right to left.*

The conditions in (10) constrain government relations at the constituency tier. So, for example, within a constituent, government is left-headed (so the first element of an onset cluster is the head of the relation), whereas between constituents, government is right-headed (so a nucleus governs its preceding onset).

Finally, all governing relations are subject to the projection principle, shown in (11).

(11)

    Projection principle (Kaye, 1990, p. 321): Governing relations are defined at the level of lexical representation and remain constant throughout derivation.

The projection principle implies that "constituent categories may not be altered during the course of derivation; onsets remain onsets, nuclei remain nuclei and the licensing relation between nuclei and onsets remains stable" (Kula, 2002, p. 26).

We do not have the space to examine in detail structures such as the phonological word, and foot, or analyses of prosodic features such as tone. Readers should consult Harris (1994) and Kula (2002) for more information on these areas.

EXERCISE 13.2

For the onset-rime constituents, list the governing constituent units in the words in example (2) above (there may be more than one per word).

    List the governing segment in the branching onsets and branching rimes in example (2) above.

MELODY

Melody is the term GovP uses for the segmental level of phonological description. In traditional generative phonology, the equivalent level uses the binary equipollent distinctive feature as the minimal unit of description (or *prime*). GovP, on the other hand, uses

---

* The use of the terms right and left is purely conventional, derived from Latinate left-to-right orthography. So, if dealing with Arabic, we don't find strict directionality reversed!

the unary, privative prime (see Chapter 3 for a discussion of these terms, but recall that *unary* means the prime is either present or absent, and *privative* implies the element has just one possible value, whereas *equipollent* means the feature has two values where one is not just the absence of the other). The main advantage of unary elements is that their use constrains the phonology. Binary features allow a large number of segment classes to be established (those sharing the plus value, and those sharing the minus value of a feature); unary elements only allow a class of segments that have that element, not one that does not have it. Harris (1994) also sees unary accounts as a means of reducing the range of phonological processes available to the theory to those that are observed in natural language, thus avoiding the need for theoretical add-ons such as markedness conventions.

The other main difference with the primes of GovP compared to those of traditional generative approaches to phonology is that GovP elements are phonetically interpretable; this is, the element itself has phonetic content that is pronounceable even if the element is not in a set of other elements. On the other hand, distinctive features are not by themselves phonetically interpretable (i.e., you cannot say [high]); they are only pronounceable when all the features required for a segment are together and fully specified in a feature matrix. At that point, the segment is pronounceable, but the individual features are not phonetically interpretable by themselves. (Remember, the stress laid by many researchers on underspecification means that even feature matrices are not interpretable until the final steps in a derivation.)

The advantages claimed for phonetic interpretability of elements include no longer needing to map noninterpretable distinctive features onto phonetic features late in a derivation, and the fact that we do not need underspecification (or to decide between different models of underspecification). Using phonetically interpretable elements results in all levels of derivation containing segments that are also phonetically interpretable. Harris (1994) claims that this approach is arguably more psycholinguistically plausible than traditional ones, and:

> since phonological representation uniformly adheres to the principle of full phonetic interpretability, there is no motivation for recognizing an autonomous level of systematic phonetic representation. Any phonological representation at any level of derivation can be directly submitted to articulatory or perceptual interpretation. Derivation is thus not an operation by means of which abstract phonological objects are transformed into increasingly concrete physical objects. Rather it is a strictly generative function which defines the grammaticality of phonological strings. (p. 96)

The appeal to psycholinguistically plausible models of phonology has echoes in recent work within what may be broadly termed cognitive models of linguistics (see Chapter 14). From the point of view of clinical phonology, it might well be more insightful to posit phonetically interpretable phonological elements, rather than uninterpretable binary distinctive features.

Researchers in GovP have proposed lists of elements for vowels and consonants. Whereas most within the field agree on the vowel elements, there have been disagreements about the number of consonant elements needed. Early versions of the theory had around 10 consonant elements, but more recent work has attempted to show how this can be reduced to 7, 5, or even 2 (see Ball, 2008, for more on this). We are taking a less speculative route, maintaining eight consonant elements. While this may result in a less constrained model of the phonology, we feel it is more useful for the description of disordered speech, and results in greater transparency of description. (For example, it has been proposed that the nasal element can be replaced by a combination of vocal fold and stop elements. We feel that the spread of nasality, for example, in disordered speech is more clearly shown through an element dedicated to the coupling of the nasal resonator into the speech mechanism, rather than through a more opaque combination of other elements.) We list and illustrate the elements for vowels and consonants in the following subsections.

Vowel Elements

In GovP three elements are proposed for vowels. These, with their pronunciations, are as shown in (12):

(12)

A	[a]
I	[i]
U	[u]

A fourth symbol (@, the neutral vowel) is also used, but represents a default tongue position, or the carrier signal on which the modulations represented by elements are superimposed (Harris & Lindsey, 2000; Harris, 2005). We noted earlier that, as its name suggests, GovP uses governing relations between its units of description, and this is no less true of the melodic tier than of the constituency one. The combination of elements is regulated by the concept of licensing constraints. These constraints provide restrictions on the combinations of elements, so that it is possible to derive the set of phonological representations that capture all and only those sound segments relevant to a particular language (Kula, 2002, p. 27).

So, combinations of elements provide a wider vowel set, and in combinations one element is normally considered to be the head (or governor), and others are usually dependent on the head. In GovP formalism, the head element is shown underlined; where no element is underlined then the elements are in a nongoverning relationship. English lax vowels illustrate these possibilities in (13):

(13)

[**I**, @]	/ɪ/
[A, **I**, @]	/ɛ/
[**I**, A]	/æ/
[**U**, A]	/ɒ/
[U, @]	/ʊ/
[@]	/ʌ/
[A, @]	[ɐ]

These combinations illustrate the use of the neutral element [@] as governor of vowels we traditionally term lax. Long vowels, like diphthongs, are deemed to occupy two skeletal slots (as described earlier). Typical examples from English are seen in (14).

(14)

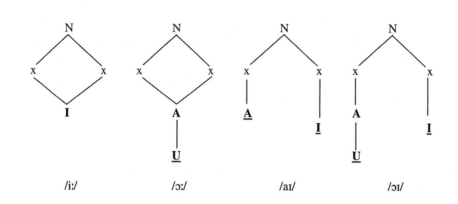

/iː/   /ɔː/   /aɪ/   /ɔɪ/

The layering of the elements in these diagrams reflects the contention that these elements (and the consonant elements of the following subsection) can be thought of as operating on separate tiers.

EXERCISE 13.3

We have not given the element combinations for all possible vowels in the text. See if you can work out the element combinations and governing relation for this lax vowel: [ʏ].
   Now do the same for this long vowel: [ø].
   And finally for these diphthongs: [aʊ], [eɪ].
   If you are unfamiliar with any of the vowels, consult the IPA chart (see appendix).

Consonant Elements

Shown in (15) are the elements most often used to characterize consonants, together with their phonetic exponence and description in more traditional phonological terms. It can be noted that the different exponences of A, I, and U result from their no longer being dominated by a nucleus node in word structure (i.e., they link to consonants rather than to vowels).

(15)

?	[ʔ]	Stop or edge
h	[h]	Noise or aperiodic energy on release
R	[ɾ]	Coronality
I	[j]	Palatality
U	[w]	Labiality
@	[ɰ]	Neutral
A	[ʁ]	Present in uvulars and pharyngeals
N	[ŋ]	Nasality

There are also two further, laryngeal node elements used mainly to distinguish voiced from voiceless consonants: **[H]** stiff vocal folds, aspiration, voicelessness, and **[L]** slack vocal folds, voicing. In the following examples we include only voiced sonorants and voiceless obstruents, and thus have no need of these last two elements.

Illustrations of both place and manner distinctions in consonants can be seen in (16):

(16)

[h, U, ?]	[p]
[h, R, ?]	[t]
[h, @, ?]	[k]
[h, U]	[f]
[h, R]	[s]
[h, R]	[θ]
[h, R, I]	[ʃ]
[h, @]	[x]
[h, A]	[χ]
[h, A]	[ħ]
[N, R, ?]	[n]
[R, ?]	[l]
[R, @]	[ɹ]

EXERCISE 13.4

We have not given the element combinations for all possible consonants. See if you can work out the element combinations and governing relation for these plosives: [c], [q].

Now do the same for these fricatives: [ç], [ɸ].

And finally for these approximants: [ʎ], [ɥ].

If you are unfamiliar with any of the consonants, consult the IPA chart.

Element Geography

We described feature geometry in Chapter 5; those working with GovP have proposed element geometries for similar reasons. As Kula (2002) notes,

> Feature geometries have ... been proposed in order to not only classify natural classes, but also to exclude unnatural ones.... The GP view that elements are directly linked to the skeleton implies that they are individually accessible to phonological processing. True as this is, it has also been observed that particular phonological processes do indeed access more than one element at the same time and thus make it necessary for us to perceive of some geometric organisation of elements. (p. 30)

In other words, element geometries allow us to constrain the possible combinations of elements that can be accessed in phonological processes, in a way complementary to how licensing constraints restrict the possible combination of elements within the description of a single segment, both being language specific. While various possible element geometries have been proposed in the literature, in (17) we illustrate the concept with an element tree combined from proposals in Harris (1994) and Harris and Lindsey (1995).

(17)

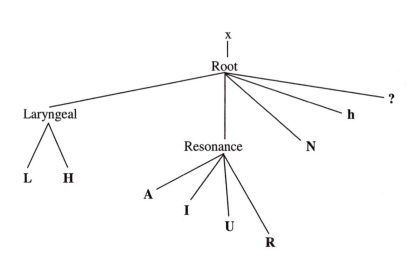

SONORITY IN GOVP

In Chapter 2 we discussed the notion of sonority and how the sonority sequencing principle (SSP) predicted the optimal shape of syllables, and the optimal combinations of consonants in clusters. Harris (1994) points out that melodic complexity could be used as a metric in GovP to account for the SSP. We can illustrate this by considering onset consonant clusters in English (this discussion closely follows that of Harris, 1994, p. 170, who uses [R] for English /ɹ/). If we consider the following four possible onset consonant clusters, we find that there is a similarity in the element complexity of the first and second segments: /dɹ-/, /tw-/, /pl-/, /fɹ-/. Look at the melody diagrams for these four in (18), and count the elements in the first consonant, and then those in the second.

(18)

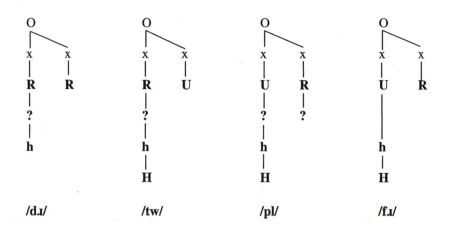

For onsets to be well formed, then, the number of elements in the second consonant must be less than the number in the first. (Harris notes that two-element /l/ is subject to historical change in some languages, possibly because two-element consonants are less optimal than one-element ones in this cluster position.) When we look at onset clusters that do not follow the SSP, we note that they breach this element complexity constraint. Let us look, for example, at */rd-/ and */lt-/ in (19).

(19)

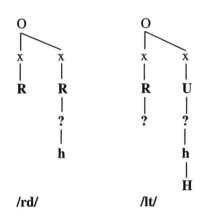

/rd/   /lt/

These two clusters have more elements in the second consonant than the first, and so do not meet the GovP requirements for the SSP in onset clusters. What happens when we look at /s/ initial clusters? In (20) are the diagrams for /st-/, /sk-/, and /sm-/.

(20)

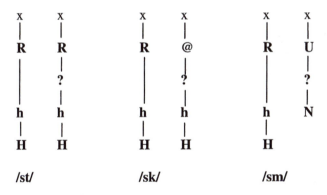

/st/   /sk/   /sm/

Instead of the second consonant having fewer elements than the first, these examples show that they have more or the same number. This metric, then, is GovP's way of showing that these sequences break the SSP, and is one of the reasons behind the adoption, noted earlier, of /s/ + empty nucleus as a description of these combinations.

EXERCISE 13.5

GovP has also worked out optimal vowel combinations (i.e., diphthongs) using a similar element counting metric.

If the diphthongs [aɪ, aʊ, iə, eɪ] are favored and [ae, io, uo] are disfavored, what generalities can you find in terms of element counting for the two parts of the diphthong?

GOVP AND DERIVATION

The less abstract approach of GovP, in terms of both the phonetically interpretable elements and the absence of underspecification, results in a phonology that is more concerned with representation (or description) of the phonology of a language, than with derivation (describing changes). In traditional generative approaches, derivations may work with abstract underlying forms that are not actually equivalent to any spoken forms. But as we noted above in (11), the projection principle limits the amount of change that can occur in derivations. Nevertheless, derivations are found in GovP. For example, we may compare careful and fast speech pronunciations of particular sound combinations, we may compare standard and regional varieties (both of which may be used by specific speakers), or we may use the theory to chart sound changes across time (where again, at least some speakers will have access to both the older and newer variants). We do not have the space to explore many such derivations here, but we will examine one change at the constituency level due to fast speech, and one common change at the melodic level that falls into the dialect/change over time categories.

First, we can consider vowel syncope (or elision). In fast, casual speech, unstressed vowels in certain words are subject to deletion. Examples include *separate* (adjective) (/ˈsɛpəɹət/ vs. /ˈsɛpɹət/), *camera* (/ˈkæməɹə/ vs. /ˈkæmɹə/), *opener* (/ˈoʊpənə/ vs. /ˈoʊpnə/), and *definite* (/ˈdɛfɪnət/ vs. /ˈdɛfnət/). The removal of the unstressed vowel might be thought to result in a resyllabification process. Considering *definite*, we could propose that in the reduced form, the /f/ could be treated as postnuclear in a branching rime. However, when we examine the example of *opener*, this solution is not open to us, as /p/ belongs to the class of stops that are not permitted in this position after a heavy nucleus. The solution best fitting the constituent structure constraints of GovP for *separate* would be to treat *pr* as a complex onset to the second syllable, as shown in (21).

(21)

```
O   N   O   N   O   N   O   N   →
|   |   |   |   |   |   |   |
x   x   x   x   x   x   x   x
|   |   |   |   |   |   |   |
s   ɛ   p   ə   ɹ   ə   t


O   N   O       N   O   N
|   |    \      |   |   |
x   x   x   x   x   x   x
|   |   |       |   |
s   ɛ   p   ɹ   ə   t
```

However, in some instances such a strategy will produce onset clusters that are not otherwise found in the language (e.g., /pn/ in /ˈoʊpnə/, /mɹ/ in /ˈkæmɹə/, and /fn/ in /ˈdɛfnət/), or even ones that break the sonority sequencing principle (e.g., /nt/ in /ˈmɒntɹɪŋ/ *mon'toring*). Harris (1994), therefore, argues that a better motivated solution is to assume that the N slot for the deleted vowel remains in structure at the skeletal tier, but is phonetically empty; that is, there is no resyllabification, just the phonetic interpretation or noninterpretation of stable syllabic positions. This would give us, for the example *separate*, the following in (22).

(22)

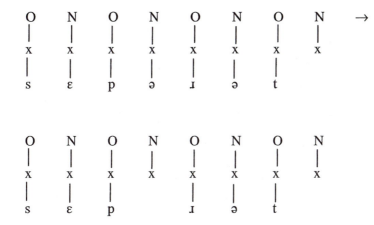

At the melodic level we can consider a commonly occurring example of lenition (or articulatory weakening). In many instances historically original /s/ in a language has weakened to [h] or even been deleted. This is a current change in certain Latin American varieties of Spanish. We also know of many instances of /h/ deletion: in modern English dialects, in fast speech in English with /h/ initial function words, and in several Romance languages historically. Lenition of /t/ has also been commonly reported, and although this is more often seen as a change to [θ] (as in Welsh aspirate mutation), a change to [ts] or [s] may also be found (as in Merseyside English and the German sound shift producing [ts] from earlier [t]). If we put all these lenitions together, we see that GovP provides in its combinations of elements an explanation of these changes through a gradual elimination of melodic material until an empty slot is obtained, as shown in (23).

(23)

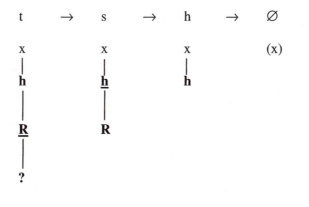

EXERCISE 13.6

In many varieties of English, the dental fricatives are replaced by either labiodental fricatives or alveolar stops. Show how GovP would describe both sets of changes (using the voiceless segments only for ease of explanation). Which change, according to GovP, is simpler? Does this answer agree with your experience of dialect differences, normal and disordered acquisition?

GOVP AND DISORDERED SPEECH

This model has not been applied often to disordered speech, but note the work of Harris, Watson, and Bates (1999), Ball (2002), and Pan and Roussel (2008), and in normal phonological acquisition the work of Ball (1996) and Harrison (1996). We will examine here some of the more commonly reported phonological patterns in disordered speech and see how GovP accounts for them.

We can start by considering some common patterns in disordered speech at the constituency level. Difficulties with onset clusters are commonly reported in the clinical literature (e.g., Bauman-Waengler, 2003), and indeed simplifications of these clusters are found in normal phonological development as well. As we have noted earlier, GovP deals with onset clusters in English in two ways: non-/s/-initial clusters are accounted for through binary branching of the onset; /s/ initial clusters, on the other hand, have the /s/ as the onset to an empty nucleus. This distinction does reflect differences in the ways English initial clusters behave in both normal and disordered phonological development (see Gierut, 1999, for evidence of this). Harris (1994) points out that GovP adopts a principles and parameters approach to grammar and so, for the cluster simplification we have been looking at, a change in parameter setting to disallow branching onsets (as is found in many languages, such as Chinese) will account for loss of non-/s/-initial clusters. As the leftmost item in the cluster is the head, this also accounts for the usual pattern in cluster simplification of this type: the retention of the leftmost item and loss of the rightmost one.

To account for simplification in /s/ initial clusters, we have to look beyond the onset to P[0] or even the skeletal tier. We need a ban on onsets with empty nuclei to account for these clusters, but all other things being equal, this ban must work only with initial instances. The operation of such a prohibition, then, would remove the /s/ onset and its empty nucleus, leaving (in this case) the rightmost consonant of the (superficial) /s/ initial cluster, as is indeed found in most cases in disordered speech. In normally developing /s/ clusters, and in delayed phonology, an epenthetic vowel may be encountered between the /s/ and the following consonant (e.g., *stop* being realized as [sə'tɒp]). GovP supplies an elegant account of these forms, whereby we assume the constraint at initial position is not on onsets *and* their following empty nuclei, but just on empty nuclei following initial onsets; the empty nuclei must be phonetically realized: in this case through the addition of the default [@] element.

Another commonly occurring simplification in both developmental and disordered phonology is the deletion of final consonants, whereby *cat* is realized as [kæ] and *dog* as [dɒ]. These, too, can be accounted for by a constraint on onsets and empty nuclei: this time in final position. If final consonant clusters are involved (and if all consonants are deleted), then the parameter setting allowing branching rimes will also need to be turned off. The label "final consonant deletion" may, however, be overused, as at least on some occasions, final consonants may be replaced by glottal stops. (It is probable that lack of training in detailed phonetic transcription may have led to this overuse in that transcribers may think that the consonant has been deleted simply because they cannot hear the glottal stop.) Final glottal replacement involves an interaction between constituency (as this realization is restricted to final position) and melody (in that these consonant slots have had all element material stripped from them except [ʔ]).

Turning now to disordered patterns at the melodic level, we will examine first the commonly reported pattern of velar fronting (we ignore for the purposes of this discussion the debate as to whether this pattern is mainly phonological or articulatory in origin). In traditional binary feature descriptions, a change from target /k, g, ŋ/ to [t, d, n] involves changing the values of the four features [high, back, anterior, coronal]. In GovP we can show that a much simpler account is available where the element [@] is substituted for [R], as shown in (24).

(24)

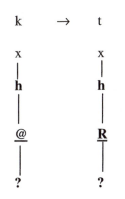

Typical lisp patterns involve the realization of target /s/ and /z/ as dental fricatives or alveolar lateral fricatives. Both of these patterns can be accounted for through simple changes at the melodic level: For the dental fricative a simple change in head is all that is required, while for the lateral fricative the simple addition of the [?] element is all that is needed. If the lisp involves realization of /s/ as the postalveolar [ʃ], then this is shown in (25) by the simple addition of the palatal element [I].

(25)

s	→	θ	→	ɬ	→	ʃ
x		x		x		x
h		h		h		h
R		R		R		R
				?		I

Whereas these lisping patterns (arguably a motoric rather than a phonological disruption) are relatively straightforward to account for in GovP, more obviously phonological patterns such as fricative simplification are not so easy to deal with. Fricative simplification is a pattern whereby (in English) target dentals are realized as labiodentals, and target postalveolars as alveolars (e.g., /θ, ð/ as [f, v], and /ʃ, ʒ/ as [s, z]). These two patterns can be seen in GovP formalism as follows in (26).

(26)

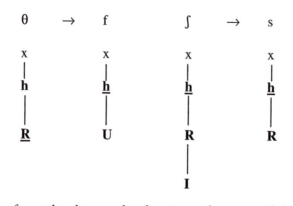

The realization of postalveolars as alveolars is neatly captured through the deletion of the [I] element, but the dental to labiodental change requires a switch of elements and a change of head pattern. The latter aims to reflect the change from a nonstrident to a strident fricative (but as argued in Ball and Howard, 2004, and Chapter 10, the classification of labiodentals as strident is not well motivated phonetically or developmentally, and so a simpler change would have resulted if dentals and labiodentals were both classed as nonsibilant fricatives).

EXERCISE 13.7

Consonant fortition (e.g., the realization of fricatives as stops) is commonly reported in normal and disordered acquisition. How does GovP show the following fortitions: /l/ to [d], /dʒ/ to [d], /z/ to [d], and /ð/ to [d]? Do you find the GovP approach explicitly shows the connection between these four different examples of fortition?

Finally, we will consider vowel disorders (see Ball, 2002, for a fuller account). While a wide range of disordered vowel patterns have been reported, we will restrict our consideration to a type commonly reported: simplification of the vowel system to the "corner" vowels (i.e., /i, ɑ, u/). (An alternative pattern, whereby vowels move from the periphery of the vowel area toward the center, has been reported in the speech of prelingually deaf speakers as well as in some hearing children.) The vowel errors show patterns of mid-vowel raising to close positions with both front and back vowels, and for lower mid-vowels there is a process of vowel lowering to an open position, again affecting front and back vowels. In a GovP account of such processes, we see a simplification of the segmental description, with vowels becoming progressively more like [I], [U], or [A], as in (27) (see Harris et al., 1999, for a detailed GovP account of a variety of disordered vowel systems).

(27)

[A, I, @]	→	[I, @]	→	[I]
/ɛ/	→	/ɪ/	→	/i/
[A, U]	→	[A, U]	→	[A]
/ɔ/	→	/ɒ/	→	/ɑ/

The converse pattern of vowel centering noted earlier is shown in (28), where we see the gradual increase in the governing power of [@].

(28)

[I]	→	[I, @]	→	[@]
/i/	→	/ɪ/	→	/ə/
[A]	→	[A, @]	→	[@]
/ɑ/	→	/ɐ/	→	/ə/

EXERCISE 13.8

The realization of /ɹ/ as [w] is commonly reported in disordered speech. Show how GovP would account for this change in terms of changes to elements and governing relations between elements. Do you find this account more insightful than that of a traditional generative rule, or less?

GOVP AND THERAPY

The clinical studies referred to above do not discuss what light GovP might shed on the treatment of phonological disorders. The theory does suggest that certain sounds are more basic than others; with vowels these would be [i, ɑ, u]. Research in normal development of vowel systems, and in vowel disorders tends to support this notion. However, the position is more complex when we look at consonants. The basic consonants (as represented by single GovP elements) include [ʔ, h, ɾ, ŋ]. We would not normally consider these to be early consonants in acquisition, or as common substitutions in disordered speech; element complexity with consonants, therefore, would not seem to be a useful clinical metric or guide to planning remediation. We await further studies using this approach to phonology to see whether the insights gained into the nature of the disorder using GovP can be translated into remediation tools.

FURTHER READING

The main textbook that we have based this account of government phonology on is Harris (1994). The emphasis of this book is on the phonology of English, and a thorough reading of it will provide more details of the approach than we were able to give here. References to later versions of GovP and its derivatives are found in the chapter. Other references within these sources to earlier versions of the theory may also be useful.

Clinical studies that have used GovP have been referred to in the chapter.

REVIEW QUESTIONS AND STUDY TOPICS

Review Questions

1. What are the two levels of description used in GovP called?
2. How are coda consonants dealt with in single-syllable words in GovP?

3. How are non-word-final coda consonants dealt with in multisyllabic words in GovP?
4. What are the directions of government constituent internally, and between constituents?
5. How do elements differ from distinctive features?
6. What are the possible governing relations between elements?
7. Consonant weakening (or lenition) is commonly encountered in language; how does GovP provide an economic description of this process?
8. How can GovP be used to describe common patterns of vowel simplification in disordered speech?

Study Topics and Projects

1. Read the chapter on floating sounds in Harris (1994), and write a paper on how this notion might be applied to clinical data.
2. Using your own clinical date, analyze where GovP provides an insightful analysis and where it does not.

14

COGNITIVE, SYSTEMIC, AND GROUNDED PHONOLOGIES

INTRODUCTION

The field of phonology has been particularly fertile over the last few decades, with new developments in theory and application regularly emerging. In this book we do not have the space to explore all of these, and some of them appear to be more clinically relevant than others. In this chapter we will explore three different approaches to phonological theory that do seem to have clinical applicability. The first of these takes a broadly cognitive approach to phonological storage and usage and, as such, would seem to be especially interesting to clinicians looking for a psycholinguistic description of phonology, rather than a theoretically simple description. The systemic aspects of phonology explored here derive from the work of systemic functional linguists and represent, to some extent, an extension of Firthian prosodic phonology, introduced in Chapter 9. Finally, the work of Archangeli and Pulleyblank (1994) on grounding phonological theory in phonetics is described. This is clearly important for clinicians, since the use of abstract feature representations, for example, may be difficult to apply to phonetically atypical disordered speech.

A COGNITIVE VIEW OF PHONOLOGY[*]

Joan Bybee (2001) has recently outlined a model of what we will call *cognitive phonology*.[†] As the name suggests, this approach is explicitly designed to model phonology as a cognitive activity, and so demonstrates a psycholinguistic approach to phonological theory. It is also a radical departure from most of the previous approaches that we have covered in this book.

Hypotheses of Cognitive Phonology

One of the most important hypotheses of cognitive phonology, as described in Bybee (2001), concerns frequency of use. Bybee notes that experience affects representation, in

---

[*] This section is closely based on Ball (2003).
[†] Note that Bybee does not actually call her approach *cognitive phonology*, preferring to avoid specifying her account too strictly, but uses the expression *usage-based phonology*.

that high-frequency forms and phrases have stronger representations in memory, and so are resistant to changes through analogy. Low-frequency forms are more difficult to access, and so may be subject to change or loss. Patterns (or *schemas*, which will be described below) that apply to more items are also stronger and more productive.

Bybee's (2001) usage-based model also claims that mental representations of linguistic objects have the same properties as mental representations of other objects. Resulting from this claim is the further claim that mental representations of linguistic objects do *not* have predictable properties abstracted away, but are based on categorization of actual tokens. It is clear that such a claim is completely opposite to the accepted wisdom of generative models (as we have discussed in previous chapters), where predictable properties of units are abstracted away through the process of derivation. As we noted in Chapter 5, underspecification approaches are claimed to have psycholinguistic validity through the minimization of storage space: This cognitive approach to phonology opposes this view. Derivation and underspecification are viewed simply as attempts to achieve descriptive elegance. The cognitive phonology described by Bybee does not object to redundant storage; indeed, it claims that this is in fact what happens. Generalizations over forms are not separate from the stored representations of forms, according to the cognitive approach, but emerge directly from them. Such generalizations are expressed as relations among forms based on both phonetic and semantic similarities. Therefore, multimorphemic words are stored *whole* in the lexicon (that is, nonderivationally).

Bybee (2001) also states that categorization is based on identity or similarity. Further, categorization organizes the storage of phonological percepts, as we will show below. The theory does not specify any particular phonological units (e.g., features, elements, etc.), but Bybee (2001) finds merit in the gestural (or articulatory) approach of Browman and Goldstein (1986, 1992), as exemplified for clinical data by Kent (1997), and described in Chapter 12 of this book. It is worth noting that the originators of gestural phonology, Browman and Goldstein, in their 1995 paper, actually link their approach to phonology to a collection of work on language and cognition. In this work they tie gestural phonology into a dynamical approach to cognition, according to which cognitive processes are the behavior of nonlinear dynamical systems, and can best be studied using dynamical modeling and dynamical systems theory.

Other linguistic units, such as morpheme, syllable, and phoneme/segment, are not basic units of Bybee's theory, but are emergent: That is, they arise from the relations of identity and similarity that organize stored units. In other words, as links between similar items in storage become stronger (due to multiple examples and frequency of access to items), these items—which may be phoneme sized, morpheme sized, word sized, and so on—become stronger, and emerge as units of storage. Storage in cognitive phonology is highly redundant (as opposed to the attempts at descriptive elegance of other approaches), so *schemas* (see below) may describe the same pattern at different degrees of generality.

Finally, among the basic hypotheses of this approach, we can note that Bybee's theory claims that grammatical knowledge is procedural knowledge. Phonology becomes a part of the procedure for producing and decoding constructions, rather than a purely abstract, psychological system. This is a model, therefore, that is not about providing descriptive economy, but psycholinguistic plausibility.

Organized Storage

Generative models of the type we examined in the early chapters of this book claim that material appearing in rules cannot appear in the lexicon and vice versa; this axiom underlies the whole principle of derivation. Although Bybee's (2001) model of usage-based phonology does not have formal rules in the way that generative models do, her model explicitly rejects any division between the type of information that appears in lexical storage and that which can appear in schemas (see below). Indeed, the claim is that predictable features do appear in schemas (patterns, rather than rules), and also in the lexicon. This means that words and phrases can be stored whole, yet still participate in the schemas that link similar forms. The reason for this is because storage is not linear but spatially networked (see Figures 14.1 to 14.3).

Schemas are nonprocess statements (i.e., not transformational rules) about stored items, and can be thought of as generalizations about linguistic units that emerge from the activity of categorizing linguistic items for storage by speakers. Figures 14.1 to 14.3 give examples of schemas linking phonological and morphological forms in the lexicon through networks. The strength of these networks is an important factor and derives partly from frequency of use. As we noted above, units such as phonemes and morphemes emerge from these schemas. The strength of connections also depends upon the degree of similarity, and this point is explored more fully in Bybee (1985).

Bybee (2001) describes four characteristics of schemas. First, schemas are patterns of organization in the lexicon, and so have no independent existence apart from the lexical units from which they emerge (and so are unlike the rules and processes of other approaches). Second, schemas can be more or less productive, dependent upon the

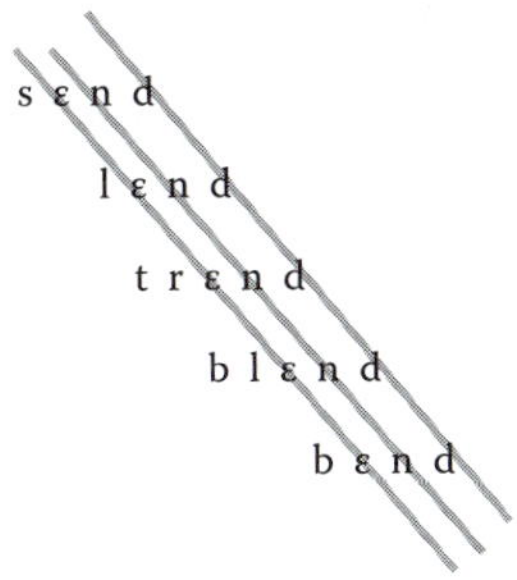

Figure 14.1 Schema for [$__ɛnd $].

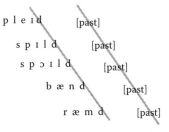

Figure 14.2 Schema for [[VERB] d]Past Tense.

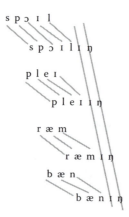

Figure 14.3 Schema for [[VERB] ɪŋ]Present Progressive.

number of items linked to the schema (for example, the English *-th* suffix of *warmth*, *length*, and *width* is much less productive than the *-ation* suffix of *formation* and *derivation*). Third, the phonological shape of the prototype exemplar of a particular class affects the members of that schema, although, finally, schemas can be gradient categories, with individual types closer or farther from the best exemplars. Indeed, the notion of prototypes can be used to account for phonetic variation between phonologically identical forms. The form *man*, for example, can be realized with assimilation affecting the final nasal, yielding a bilabial nasal in phrases such as *man bought* or a velar nasal in *man got*. The SPE approach to this was to posit a single underlying form, often chosen, it seems, arbitrarily, and then derive surface forms via rule. Bybee, alternatively, would state that the most commonly occurring form is the prototype of a set, with the other forms being peripheral members. This allows for change over time, as the prototypical member can change with experience (in, for example, language acquisition, or when a sound change occurs), and hence the typical realization of the word will change with it.

We can illustrate the notion of schemas using some of Bybee's (2001) examples. Three generalizations (among many others) emerge out of linguistic storage in English:

1. [ɛ̃nd] is a possible syllable rhyme: [$____ɛ̃nd $]. (This is diagrammed in Figure 14.1.)
2. [[VERB] d] means past tense: [[VERB] d]Past Tense. (This is diagrammed in Figure 14.2.)
3. [[VERB] ɪŋ] means present progressive: [[VERB] ɪŋ]Present Progressive. (This is diagrammed in Figure 14.3.)

Therefore, where generative models have derivational rules, cognitive phonology has schemas formed by links between forms in the lexicon. This form of cognitive phonology is, therefore, very flat in terms of derivation, but it is multidimensional in terms of networks of associations, as virtually all realizations are stored lexically. This differs, then, from most other approaches to phonological description, where the rule or process is an important device to link different levels of abstraction or description. Nevertheless, cognitive phonology, as described by Bybee (2001), does recognize some phonological processes. Two main types of processes are recognized: fast speech processes and historical change.

Fast speech processes are deemed to be lenitions (weakenings) accounted for by reduction and retiming of articulatory gestures as described in gestural models of phonology.

Examples of such processes include intervocalic flapping of /t/, and the reduction of complex word final consonant clusters.

Historical changes come about through the mechanisms of lenition and analogy. An example of historical change through lenition is the change from [s] to [h] word finally in certain South American varieties of Spanish. Analogic change can be exemplified by spelling pronunciations (such as the pronunciation of /h/ at the beginning of *herb* in British English) or the regularization of past tenses in forms such as *wept - weeped*, and *spelt - spelled*. The effect of analogy can be blocked by high-frequency use; on the other hand, high-frequency use encourages lenition.

EXERCISE 14.1

Draw some network diagrams for:

    a. Phonological characteristics of *blaze, blues, blames, bleeds*
    b. Morphophonological characteristics of *unrelated, unrequited, unrelented*

Application of Cognitive Phonology to Disordered Speech

So far, no major studies have applied Bybee's (2001) model to disordered speech. Ball (2003) and Sosa and Bybee (2008) have both speculated as to what insights this approach to phonological description might have in the clinical arena, however.

If we were to apply cognitive phonology to disordered speech, what implications would this have for assessment, diagnosis, and intervention? Looking at these three areas we can discuss three broad themes: descriptive, explanatory, and remediation planning.

Descriptive   Recall that the theory claims that units such as phonemes and syllables are emergent, and processes are either lenition or analogy. If this is so, then we would need to describe the disordered data differently in a cognitive phonology approach than we would using other popular clinical assessment types, such as natural phonology (see Chapter 10). In fact, we would need to describe data in terms of weak or nonexistent lexical networks first, assuming that this weakness has led to specific problems with segments or other units. When patterns of lenition are observed (such as in dysarthric speech), the formalisms of gestural phonology can be employed in descriptions of the clinical data. However, some child phonological disorders (and patterns of normal phonological development) appear to be better described in terms of fortitions (such as fricative stopping). These, of course, can also be accounted for through the same gestural formalisms. Bybee's model does allow for different processes in child phonological development and, presumably, by extension in child phonological disorders.

Explanatory   Assuming there is inadequate lexical storage, which has led to networks that are not strongly enough established and linked, units (phonemes/morphemes, etc.) will not emerge. Therefore, we can assume that problems arise if insufficient items are stored correctly in the lexicon, or if the categorization that creates connections does not occur. For example, an interpretation of what happens in specific language impairment (SLI) (that prevents the development of morphology) within Bybee's (1985) model of morphology is that morphologically complex words are not categorized to form the associations required. Of course, it would be difficult to know whether lexical storage is faulty because there simply are not enough items stored to create the proper networks and allow units to emerge, or because some or many items are incorrectly stored, thus disrupting expected networks.

The patterns of substitutions and deletions we see in disordered speech in children also need to be explained. As just noted, Bybee's approach to phonology lays stress on lenition as the main (or only) process of synchronic change. However, we have already commented that some disordered speech does not show lenition, but rather fortition. This can be accounted for within Bybee's account by appealing to analogy: Unestablished networks (unestablished due to insufficient or inaccurate storage) are replaced by those that do exist. The existing networks may have come about due to correct storage of a dominant pattern (e.g., when stops are realized instead of fricatives because the stop network is stronger) or incorrect storage (e.g., when sounds from outside the target system are used, as in [ɬ] for English /s/). What caused that incorrect storage is, of course, a further step back in the diagnosis process. Bybee (2001) discusses possible causes of sound changes, noting that a plausible explanation of changes that affect low-frequency forms first (such as front-rounded vowels in earlier forms of English) could well be the result of incorrect perception of the form during acquisition. As these forms are rarely heard, there are few examples for the child to correct the misperception. The other main source of sound change is rearrangement of articulatory gestures (usually lenition). This affects high-frequency forms most, as there is the greatest benefit to the user to simplify forms that are used most often. In disordered speech, therefore, we may see incorrect storage due to perceptual breakdown (although this has been a controversial area in the literature) or articulatory difficulty (or a combination of the two).

From the clinical point of view, fortitions may represent to a child acquiring speech an easier articulatory path than the target. For example, producing a [t] instead of an [s] requires considerably less articulatory precision, as no groove of a particular shape needs to be created, simply the pressing of the tongue tip against the alveolar ridge. In such a case, the weaker articulation is more difficult than the stronger one, so a fortition is more expected than a lenition.

Planning Remediation   In Bybee's account of cognitive phonology (2001), frequency of use is much more important than notions of contrast. Therefore, in remediation, minimal pair drills, the staple of many other approaches to remediation that do stress contrast, would not, it is assumed, be deemed of major importance. More important would be using sets of words that would reinforce networks and allow specific units to emerge. To some extent, this is similar to work on maximal pairs, where it may well be that the practice with widely different consonants is the most important aspect, rather than the contrast between the words (see Gierut, 1989, 1990; Barlow & Gierut, 2002).

Conclusion   Bybee's (2001) usage-based phonology is a refreshingly different approach to the psycholinguistic organization of speech. Many of its insights seem valuable, and some of these insights appear applicable to phonological acquisition and disorders in a direct way. Clearly, research comparing intervention techniques based on cognitive phonology and those based on traditional approaches, with large numbers of clients, is needed to test these ideas.

SYSTEMIC PHONOLOGY

In Chapter 9, we discussed prosodic analysis as proposed by J. R. Firth, and further developed in studies mainly originating from the School of Oriental and African Studies in London. As outlined in Chapter 9, Firth's aim was to provide an alternative and complementary theory to the dominant approaches to phonology. These centered around the paradigmatic relationships between contrastive segments, or phonemes, and the contrastive inventories of languages. A phoneme-focus requires the segmentation of the speech stream into discrete units. These units are then classified according to characteristics by which they contrast with each other. The result of this process of segmentation and classification is the description of the phoneme inventory of either a given language or, in the clinical context, a speaker with a phonological delay or disorder. Prosodic analysis, on the other hand, aims to accord the same prominence to the so-called syntagmatic characteristics of the speech stream, which cannot be accounted for by purely focusing on discrete segments and their paradigmatic relationships.

Systemic phonology is an approach to phonology that continues in the tradition of prosodic analysis and incorporates the central principles of systemic linguistics.* Tench (1992a, p. 8) summarizes the key characteristics of prosodic analysis as follows (emphasis in original):

> Prosodic Analysis is a *non-universalist* approach to the description of the phonology of a language that highlights the *syntagmatic* as well as the *paradigmatic* dimensions of the phonic material, in terms of *structures* and *systems* and is prepared to recognize *different systems* appropriate to different components of the language and to reflect *grammatical* categories wherever necessary, in such a way as to conform as fully, appropriately and elegantly as possible to a *general linguistic theory*.

The foundations provided by prosodic analysis are extended by the integration of principles from systemic linguistic theory, chiefly developed by M. A. K. Halliday and colleagues (see, e.g., Halliday, 1961; Halliday & Matthiessen, 2004). Systemic linguistic theory, most frequently referred to as systemic functional linguistics (SFL) or systemic functional grammar by proponents following in the Hallidayan tradition, has become increasingly popular among clinical linguists in the past several decades. Armstrong (2005) provides a useful overview of recent applications of SFL to the description and analysis of disordered language. Halliday (2005, p. 134) briefly summarizes some of the characteristics that make SFL relevant to clinical contexts:

> [It] presents language as a semogenic (meaning-making) resource, one governed by tendencies not rules, and whose categories (as is typical of semiotic systems) are "fuzzy" rather than determinate. It is formulated in terms of strengths, rather than of deficits or constraints: what the speaker can do (and what the language "can do").

Two major notions of systemic linguistics that feature in systemic phonology are the concept of hierarchy, and the development of system networks. Hierarchy refers to the notion of constituency, which Halliday and Matthiessen (2004, p. 5) define as "a form of order … whereby larger units are made up out of smaller ones…. We refer to such a hierarchy of units, related by constituency, as a **rank scale**, and to each step in the hierarchy

---

* Our summary of systemic phonology here draws mainly on Tench (1992b), and in particular Tench (1992a).

as one rank" (see also Tench, 1992a, pp. 8–9, and Halliday, 1961, p. 248). Halliday (1961) proposes the following phonological units, or ranks, for English: tone group, foot, syllable, and phoneme. Halliday and Matthiessen (2004, pp. 5, 14) draw attention to the circumstance that while it is possible to identify their number and location, none of these units have clearly identifiable boundaries, unambiguous points in time where one ends and the next one begins (see also Halliday's comment on fuzzy categories, quoted above). Every language has a rank scale of phonological constituents; however, the organization of the rank scale is language specific. Ranks in the phonological rank scale are the domains of prosodies (already introduced in Chapter 9), that is, characteristics of the speech stream that extend over more than one segment.*

System and structure are key concepts in systemic linguistics. Structure refers to regularities of sequencing or co-occurrence, in other words, the syntagmatic patterns or possibilities in a given language. System, on the other hand, consists in "what could go instead of what" (Halliday & Matthiessen, 2004, p. 22), that is, the paradigmatic patterns of language. A system is therefore a set of alternatives available at any given point in structure. Systemic linguistic theory views texts as the product of continuous selection in a network of systems (a system network); system networks are used to map the choices open to speakers at any given point in the production of spoken or written language. In the description of lexico-grammatical system networks, choices are conceptualized as choices in meaning making: "A language is a resource for making meaning, and meaning resides in the systemic patterns of choice" (Halliday & Matthiessen, 2004, p. 23). As Tench (1992a, p. 10) points out, at the level of phonology, the available choices are "not so much about meaning as about the actual nature of a given language." While it is possible to analyze choices in intonation in terms of meaning, "most phonological choices are not meaningful, they simply reflect the form the language takes at the level of spoken physical substance" (ibid.).

The tone system of British English, as described in Halliday (1967; see also Halliday & Matthiessen, 2004) and summarized in Tench (1992a), can serve as an illustration of how a system network is used to visualize the possibilities at a given point in structure, namely, the tone group. The internal structure of the tone group consists of an obligatory tonic segment, which may be preceded by a pretonic segment. Tonic and pretonic segments consist of at least one complete foot each. The tonic segment contains the tonic foot, which is the first foot within the tonic segment. The system network in Figure 14.4 is to be interpreted as follows.

The curly bracket at the left shows that more than one choice is to be made simultaneously. In this case, the options are that a tone group may or may not have a pretonic segment, and the choice of tone in the tonic segment, between a simple tone and a compound tone. Halliday (1967) describes the British English tone system as consisting of five simple and two compound tones (see also Halliday & Matthiessen, 2004, pp. 141–142). The five simple tones are (using Halliday's 1967 terminology) (1) fall, (2) high-rise, (3) low-rise, (4) fall-rise, and (5) rise-fall. The two compound tones are expressed as sequences of 1 and 3, and 5 and 3 (typically symbolized as 13 and 53, to be read as "one-three" and "five-three," respectively). Thus, there are five options in the simple tone system and two in the complex tone system. Within the simple tone system, tones

---

* Tench (1992a, p. 10) acknowledges that prosodies can also extend over less easily delimited stretches of speech, for example, more than one sound segment, but part of a syllable. However, prosodies that extend over only a part of a given unit are handled by system networks.

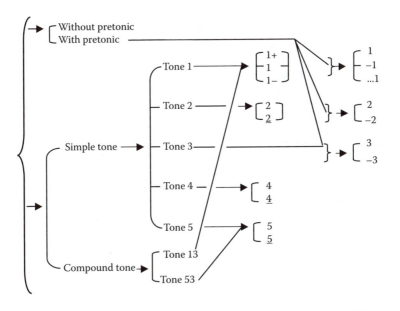

Figure 14.4 System network: Tonal system for British English. (Adapted from Tench, 1992a, p. 13)

1, 2, 4, and 5 have secondary tone distinctions (described in detail in Tench, 1992a), indicated by the three-term system at the end of the arrow to the right of tone 1, and the two-term systems to the right of tone 2, tone 4, and tone 5, respectively. The secondary tone distinctions of tones 1 and 5 are also available to tones 13 and 53, respectively; this is indicated by the lines joining up the system of tone 13 with that of tone 1, and the system of tone 53 with that of tone 5. The pretonic system also has variations that enter into the overall tone configuration. Tones 1, 2, and 3 each co-occur with a system of variations in the pretonic that depends on the selection of "with pretonic" and tone 1, tone 2, and tone 3, respectively. This is indicated in the system network by the use of right-facing curly brackets.

Graphic system networks have the advantage of permitting the visualization of the possibilities available in a fashion that is very economical of space (and words). On the other hand, it has to be admitted that reading a system network takes some practice.

Clinical Applications of Systemic Phonology

We can illustrate several of the notions introduced in this section in a clinical context by considering data first reported in Ball, Lowry, and McInnis (2006); see also Müller, Ball, and Rutter (2008). They describe a male client, age 9;8, who presented with unusual patterns of realization for target English /ɹ/. His patterns varied depending on speech style, but we will consider here his realizations when reading a word list. We give in (1) the word list and the client's pronunciations (target accent East Texas; rhotic). Note that while our analysis does examine the systems available to the client in their own right, it also utilizes the perspective of target realizations, two steps in analysis that are sometimes separated from each other (see, e.g., Grunwell, 1985).

(1)

red	[ɰːɛd]	journal	[ˈdʒɑnəl]
row	[ɰːoʊ]	word	[wɝdˠ]

rain	[ɰːeɪn]	eyebrow	[ˈaɪbˤɹaʊ]
right	[ɰːaɪt']	children	[ˈtʃɪldˤɹən]
root	[ɰːut']	january	[ˈdʒænjuɛwi]
ground	[gəˈɹaʊnd]	bark	[bɑk']
breath	[bəɹɛθ]	mirror	[ˈmɪβə]
green	[gɰːin]	water	[ˈwɑtʰə]
orange	[ˈaβɪndʒ]	your	[jɔ˞]
read	[ɰːid]	year	[jɪ˞]
robin	[ˈɰːabɪn]	labor	[leɪbˠə̞ɫ]
rat	[ɰːæt']	car	[kɑ˞]
rib	[ɰːɪb]	core	[kɔə]
ring	[ɰːɪŋk]	pure	[pjʊə]
turtle	[tɝʔtl̩]	poor	[pɔˤ]
therapy	[ˈθɛʋəpi]	are	[ɑ]
shirt	[ʃˠɝt'ˠ]	doctor	[ˈdˠɑktə]
operation	[apəˈβeɪʃn̩]	hair	[hɛə]
disorder	[dɪˈsˠɔ̞dˠə̞]	torn	[tɔn]
parent	[ˈpˠɛəɰ̞ənt']	father	[ˈfɑðə]
information	[ɪnfɔˈmeɪʃən]	mister	[ˈmɪstˠə̞]

Note: [ɰ] represents a mostly frictionless voiced velar approximant.

A systemic approach to the analysis of the varying nature of these realizations first requires the different places in word structure to be examined separately. Here we divide into syllable initial word initial, syllable initial within word, syllable final within word, and syllable final word final (and for each case, where relevant, we distinguish singletons from clusters). Figure 14.5 summarizes the system of /ɹ/ realization in the client's speech at these different places in word structure (except for syllable final word final singletons and clusters). As with the system network for tone (shown in Figure 14.4), arrows lead on to further choices, whereas straight lines denote a final node.

The use of velarization described in these networks (and shown in the transcriptions) indicates a velar prosody and can be seen spreading over neighboring vowels (marked with the tongue root retraction diacritic; see also Chapter 9).

EXERCISE 14.2

Draw systems networks for target /ɹ/ realization for this client for syllable final word final singletons, and syllable final word final clusters.

As we noted above, systemic functional linguistics has become an increasingly popular analytical and descriptive framework for clinical linguists in the recent past. Clinical phonology, in contrast, in terms of practical applications such as assessments, or approaches to intervention, remains dominated by strictly segment- or phoneme-based frameworks. The widespread insistence on an alphabetic principle, that is, the transcription of the speech stream into discrete units (sound segments), which in turn are comparatively easily quantifiable in terms of target realizations, has no doubt contributed to

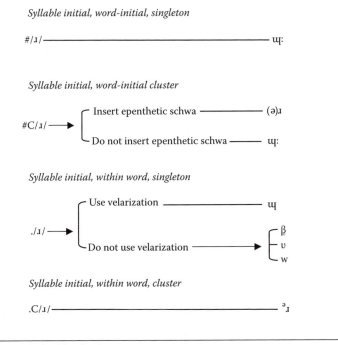

Figure 14.5 System networks for /ɹ/ realization.

this preference. However, the notion of polysystemicity (see, e.g., Grunwell, 1985; also Chapter 9 in this volume) and the analysis of speech output in its own right in terms of a resource for meaning creation, focusing on contrastivity within multiple systems, can be useful tools in the understanding of disordered speech. Likewise, the concept of prosodies (e.g., the velar prosody noted above) lends itself to the analysis of aspects of disordered speech that are difficult to handle, and may therefore be overlooked in strictly segment-based approaches.

GROUNDED PHONOLOGY

Grounded phonology was expounded by Archangeli and Pulleyblank (1994), and its application to clinical data is described in Bernhardt and Stoel-Gammon (1997). This approach to phonological analysis is firmly within the overall generative tradition, in that it is derivational, rule based, and adopts the nonlinear stance of autosegmental phonology.[*] The three main areas of concern for the authors are features and feature specifications (termed combinatorial specifications), the interface of phonetics and phonology (grounding conditions), and phonological rules (parametric rules). We shall examine each of these areas in turn.

Archangeli and Pulleyblank (1994) view a linguistic model of language as modular, with the phonology module as mediator between phonetics on the one hand and the morphology and syntax on the other. Further, they view phonology as consisting of the submodules already noted. Combinatorial specification is concerned with phonological representation. The basic units to be considered are features, the values of the features,

---

[*] The authors do show in their concluding section how their insights could be applied to a constraint-based optimality approach, which of course is nonderivational.

and the possible combinations of features. (We have seen debates on these issues already, in terms of what features to use, whether features are binary or unary, and feature hierarchies derived from feature geometry.) Another main concern of this submodule is what we have termed underspecification elsewhere, that is, whether feature values are specified, redundant, or default, and if default, whether this is a universal characteristic or a language-specific one.

Archangeli and Pulleyblank use the term *F-elements* to refer to the basic units of combinatorial specification. By this they cover the features themselves (e.g., [continuant]), the values of the feature (e.g., [+continuant] and [−continuant]*), and class nodes such as place, laryngeal, and so forth. How an F-element is realized will depend on its association with a timing slot and thereby with other features. Also, as noted above, this component contains a theory of underspecification, as only unpredictable F-elements are present in underlying representation. The authors have developed a theory of underspecification that is sensitive both to universal markedness characteristics (as discussed in Chapters 3 and 5) and to the phonological patterns of individual languages. This results in features that are unspecified in many languages having to be specified in some. For example, in many languages obstruents are by default [−voice], and no voiced obstruents are found. In languages like English, where voiced obstruents are found, voiced obstruents need to be specified for voice. Bernhardt and Stoel-Gammon (1997) point out that the ability to include language-specific underspecification can be extended to the idiosyncratic phonological patterns often encountered in disordered child speech.

Feature combinations are part of this submodule, too. Features can only be realized if they are in combination with other features (unlike in government phonology, for example); thus, feature combinations, also termed the paths between features, are also basic units of the theory. As Bernhardt and Stoel-Gammon (1997) note, features may combine simultaneously (in that they are linked to the same timing slot), as in the case of [LABIAL] and [−continuant] linked to /p/. They may also occur over more than one timing slot in cases of feature spread (e.g., [+nasal] spreading from nasal consonants to neighboring vowels). Floating segments as proposed in autosegmental and metrical models of phonology are also recognized, and these features are only realized if needed by particular words or combinations of words. Not all combinations of features are possible within the theory, and it is this area that is the concern of the submodule on grounding conditions.

This part of the authors' approach is clearly important to them in that they named the theory grounded phonology. The notion is to constrain the combinatorial possibilities of features through restrictions that are grounded in phonetics rather than *ad hoc* adjustments. Archangeli and Pulleyblank (1994, p. 177) describe two grounding conditions:

I. Path conditions invoked by languages must be phonetically conditioned.
II. The stronger the phonetic motivation for a path condition Φ,
    a. the greater the likelihood of invoking Φ,
    b. the greater the likelihood of assigning a wide scope to Φ within a grammar, and vice versa.

The first condition deals with ruling out combinations that are phonetically impossible, so, for example, the feature [+voice] cannot combine with [−voice] as the vocal folds cannot be both vibrating and not vibrating at the same time. The second condition

---

* However, the authors are neutral as to whether binary or nonbinary features are to be preferred.

deals with relative phonetic likelihood in the combination of features. Thus, we find that cross-linguistically [+voice] is much more likely to combine with [+sonorant] than with [–sonorant] for both aerodynamic and perceptual reasons. Being able to access both articulatory and acoustic reasons allows easy extension of this submodule to the consideration of disordered data. So, for example, Bernhardt and Stoel-Gammon (1997, pp. 171–172) discuss the case of the feature [nasal] in disordered speech. If a client with velopharyngeal inadequacy of some type cannot produce [+nasal] sounds (using instead [–nasal] or a combination of [+nasal] and [–nasal]), then the surface realizations of the sounds do not match the target. If the client is aware of the correct pronunciation, we might assume that he or she has the correct form stored underlyingly. So if the velopharyngeal problem is corrected, we would expect the speaker to produce the target [–nasal] forms relatively easily. However, if the speaker has reorganized his or her phonology, he or she may still overproduce [+nasal] even after corrective surgery. In this case, we see the client has replaced the phonetically grounded condition that [–nasal] is the default (except for nasal consonants) with the condition that [+nasal] is the default (or some combination of [+nasal] and [–nasal]). Bernhardt and Stoel-Gammon (1997) point to the fact that cognitive and processing factors can also play a part in grounding conditions when the theory is extended to clinical data, thus accounting for disorders that do not appear to have an articulatory or acoustic motivation.

The final submodule of grounded phonology concerns phonological rule parameters. Archangeli and Pulleyblank (1994) describe four parameters that apply to phonological rules: function, type, direction, and iteration. Rule function prescribes that insertion and deletion are the only rule types allowed, and the type of material that can be inserted or deleted is described in the second parameter: type. Type has two values: path or F-element. In other words, we can insert or delete paths between F-elements (e.g., what has been termed delinking in other models) or the F-elements themselves. The directionality of a rule (left to right, or right to left) accounts for various patterns found in phonology, such as different types of assimilation (both normal, as in the vowel harmony examples discussed in Archangeli & Pulleyblank, 1994, and disordered, as discussed in Bernhardt & Stoel-Gammon, 1997). The final parameter of iteration concerns whether a spreading rule of the types we've mentioned affects multiple or single targets. In disordered speech we can consider, for example, place assimilations, where a velar may cause a preceding alveolar to change, but only within one syllable (*tintack* ['tɪnkæk]), as opposed to where the change spreads across all syllables (['kɪŋkæk]).

The need to express the context for rule operation has been recognized in most phonological approaches. In grounded phonology both the *argument* and the *target* are covered (the argument being the F-element and the target being the location where it is anchored). These two entities are considered in terms of both content and structure. Structure refers to the presence versus absence of paths linking F-elements; if a path is present, the F-element and anchor are *linked*, and if no path is present, they are *free*.

Finally, we can consider rule formalism. Unlike the rules of traditional generative phonology, a chart-like formalism has been adopted (looking somewhat similar to the table of optimality theory; see Chapter 11). We can illustrate this with the sample chart produced by Archangeli and Pulleyblank (1974, p. 297), shown in (2).

(2)

Argument:	(Some F-element)	Default	Nondefault
Parameters	Function	INSERT	DELETE
	Type	PATH	F-ELEMENT
	Direction	LEFT TO RIGHT	RIGHT TO LEFT
	Iteration	ITERATIVE	NONITERATIVE
Structure requirements	A-structure	NONE	FREE
	T-structure	FREE	NONE
Other requirements	A-condition	(Grounded conditions/context)	
	T-condition	(Grounded conditions/context)	

An example of the use of this formalism is given by the authors (shown in (3)) when describing the rule of leftward spreading of the advanced tongue root feature in Maasai (Archangeli & Pulleyblank, 1994, p. 309):

(3)

Argument:	+ATR	Default	Nondefault
Parameters	Function	INSERT	
	Type	PATH	
	Direction		RIGHT TO LEFT
	Iteration	ITERATIVE	
Structure requirements	A-structure	NONE	
	T-structure	FREE	
Other requirements	A-condition		
	T-condition	ATR/LO	

The rule states that [+ATR] spreads leftward, but the T-condition restricts this as low vowels block the leftward spread of ATR.

EXERCISE 14.3

Maasai also has a rule of rightward spread of the advanced tongue root feature. This is not blocked by low vowels or, in fact, by any other vowels. It is iterative and has the same structure requirements as (3). Draw up a rule formalism chart to express Maasai rightward [+ATR] spread.

Application of Grounded Phonology to Disordered Speech

Bernhardt and Stoel-Gammon (1997) describe the application of grounded phonology to a case of phonological disorder. They take a particular case of a 4;6-year-old boy with highly unintelligible speech, and analyze the speech data via a phonological process approach (see Chapter 10) and a developmental inventory approach, and compare the intervention goals these two approaches suggest. The authors find that while these two approaches overlap to some extent in their identification of intervention targets, the inventory analyses failed to identify patterns in the data that the process analysis was able to do. Bernhardt and Stoel-Gammon then undertake a combinatorial specification analysis on the disordered speech data. They identify the several steps needed to draw up the combinatorial specification from the disordered data, bearing in mind that the child's defaults may on occasion be different from those of the target language. They then compare the goals suggested by their grounded phonology analysis to those from their previous analyses, and conclude that the grounded phonology approach led to a different and more precise account. They conclude that this approach was useful because, although the child's productions were variable, "this variability was shown to arise primarily from feature combination constraints and redundancies for laryngeal features" (Bernhardt & Stoel-Gammon, 1997, p. 204).

In this account, no rules were drawn up. We can, however, consider the use of rule formats proposed by Archangeli and Pulleyblank (1994) for grounded phonology, to describe disordered speech. We illustrate this in (4) with a rule describing velar assimilation, as in the case of *tintack*, referred to above. In this case the assimilation is restricted to the second syllable.

(4)

Argument:	DORSAL	Default	Nondefault
Parameters	Function	INSERT	
	Type	PATH	
	Direction		RIGHT TO LEFT
	Iteration		NONITERATIVE
Structure	A-structure	NONE	
requirements	T-structure	FREE	
Other requirements	A-condition		
	T-condition	CORONAL	

CONCLUSION

In this chapter we have looked at three approaches to phonology that have some relevance for the analysis of disordered speech, yet are not dominant in the clinical phonology arena. All three have as part of their foci attempts to move phonology to a less abstract approach, through psycholinguistic realism, phonetic grounding, or functional concerns. Particularly in the case of what we have here termed cognitive phonology, we expect that this may well be a model that will prove useful to clinical phonologists in the future.

FURTHER READING

For cognitive phonology (phonology in use), Bybee's (2001) text is eminently readable; you may also wish to consult her earlier work on morphology: Bybee (1985). Two briefer introductions to the theory can be found in Ball (2003) and Sosa and Bybee (2008). Other phonologists have also used the term *cognitive phonology*: See Lakoff (1993) and Wheeler and Touretzky (1993). For systemic phonology, you may wish to consult the collections of papers in Tench (1992b), which include both explanatory articles and worked examples of the approach with data from a variety of languages. Müller, Ball, and Rutter (2008) describe more fully the client with the /ɹ/ problem described above, including data from two other speech styles. Grounded phonology is described in Archangeli and Pulleyblank (1994). This is a dense book, and the brief description of the theory in Bernhardt and Stoel-Gammon (1997) may be easier as an introduction. The latter also contains more details on the application of the theory to clinical data than we were able to include in this chapter.

REVIEW QUESTIONS AND STUDY TOPICS

Review Questions

1. What is Bybee's approach to the debate on the size of units in linguistic storage?
2. What are schemas in Bybee's phonology?
3. What are the three aspects of clinical phonology that Bybee's approach can shed light on?
4. What are two major notions of systemic linguistics that feature in systemic phonology?
5. What are the proposed phonological ranks for English?
6. What is a system network?
7. What are the three main submodules of grounded phonology?
8. What is included under the term *F-element*?

Study Topics and Projects

1. Read the original sources on either Bybee's phonology in use or grounded phonology, then provide a detailed account of theory and suggestions of how the theory may throw light on various patterns of disordered speech and their remediation.
2. Read David Young's (1992) chapter in Tench (1992b), and then draw and describe the system network for initial consonant clusters for a client who deletes /s/ before /p, t, k/, but not before other consonants; realizes /ɹ/ as [w]; and deletes /j/ after labials and alveolars, but not after velars.

15

CLINICAL PHONOLOGY

INTRODUCTION

Having spent 14 chapters investigating theoretical phonology and its application to disordered speech, we can, in this final chapter, consider just how much of what is traditionally called phonological disorder is actually phonological. Much of what has been termed phonological errors only appears to be phonological because of three shortcomings in the analysis of disordered speech:

1. The traditional division of errors into additions, deletions, and (important here) substitutions (phonological) and distortions (phonetic). So, for example, the realization of target English /ɹ/ as [w] is termed a substitution (because /w/ exists as a sound of English), whereas an alternative realization as [ʋ] is termed a distortion because [ʋ] does not exist in English. It is more than likely that these two productions are both the result of motor difficulties with the target /ɹ/—so neither is a phonological error in terms of the linguist's use of *phonology* (an abstract level of representation).

2. The classification of errors in terms of their surface effect rather than in terms of the underlying cause of the error. So, if /k/ and /t/ are both realized by what sounds like [t], then we can argue that this is a phonological error (a phonemic merger). However, if as described in Gibbon (1990, 1999) it turns out that in many instances clients use a different (but incorrect) tongue gesture for target /k/ as opposed to target /t/, then we have a motor problem that happens to have a phonological effect.

3. The binary division into phonetic and phonological errors. We have argued elsewhere (see, for example, Ball & Müller, 2009) that adult neurological disorders would support a classification of errors into phonological (e.g., paraphasias), phonetic planning (e.g., apraxia of speech), and articulatory (e.g., dysarthria).

Dodd (1995) and Bradford and Dodd (1996) have also questioned whether child speech disorders are not ultimately motor based. They concluded that two of their four groups of subjects did display motor deficits in undertaking various motor tasks, but that two did not (and are thus described as having phonological disorders). However, we should note that the tasks undertaken by the subjects were mostly nonlinguistic and nonnaturalistic. Also, the authors used a binary distinction between an abstract phonological level and a motor level (where we have argued for a three-way division). Further, the analysis was mostly in terms of the effect rather than the cause of the error.

More recently, Gibbon (2007) has argued, from the evidence of her own and others' work, that the reliance on phonological explanations for much disordered speech needs to be challenged. She notes, "Data from instrumental studies revealing phenomena such as covert contrasts and undifferentiated gestures cast some doubt on these conclusions, suggesting that subtle phonetic difficulties could underlie many of the surface patterns that we hear in the speech of children with phonological disorders" (Gibbon, 2007, p. 254).

We expand on these points in this chapter and discuss which approaches to phonology that we have described in this book might be most useful for describing disordered data and accounting for the underlying causes of errors.

THE NATURE OF PHONOLOGICAL THEORIES

In this, our final chapter, we will draw together many of the themes that have run through the individual chapters, and give our view on the current state of clinical phonology. To begin with, we must address more fully a topic raised in Chapter 1: the nature of phonological theories. One approach to the description of linguistic data aims to be elegant and parsimonious. In this, it would follow the tradition of all scientific descriptions: Of any two approaches that account for the data, we prefer the one that is most economical. In many of the chapters of this book, we have seen how researchers have continually been refining models of phonology with this in mind: It makes for a more economical account of phonology to posit various levels of organization as developed in autosegmental and metrical phonology; it makes for a more economical description to organize features in a geometrical hierarchy; it may well be more economical to use unary rather than binary features; it may well be more economical to use constraints rather than derivations; and so on.

However, it is possible to argue for another goal for linguistic descriptions. This goal would be a model of how speakers actually communicate, or at least how they use the particular area of language under consideration (i.e., for us, phonology) to communicate. We will term this approach a psycholinguistic one. (We use psycholinguistic rather than, for example, neurolinguistic, because we are not concerned here with precise descriptions of which neurons in which part of the brain fire in which sequences during phonological organization or implementation, but rather in producing models of the various procedures speakers may go through in storing, retrieving, and implementing phonology.) Several of the theoretical approaches we have considered in this book have overtly claimed such a psycholinguistic motivation: for example, natural phonology, gestural phonology, cognitive phonology. Many of the accounts of phonology that broadly fall within the heading of generative phonology (for example, those outlined in Chapters 3–8 and 11) usually have not claimed to have more than theoretical validity. Confusingly, however, researchers within this tradition often write as if the theory did have psycholinguistic explanatory power. For example, one of the arguments in favor of underspecification (see Chapter 5) is that an underspecified feature matrix requires less storage space in the brain. Partly this blurring of the distinction between linguistic and psycholinguistic approaches stems from the use of the term *universal grammar* in generative linguists and theories developed from this school (e.g., Chomsky, 1975). So, Archangeli (1997) writing on optimality theory (OT) states, "Linguists use the term **universal grammar** to refer to the innate language knowledge humans have" (p. 2); and later, "Optimality Theory proposes that Universal Grammar contains a set of violable constraints" (p. 11). McCarthy (2002, p. 10) addresses this distinction in discussing the Eval component of OT:

> How can Eval sort an infinite set of candidates in finite time …? The error lies in asking how long Eval takes to execute. It is entirely appropriate to ask whether Eval … is well defined, captures linguistically significant generalizations, and so on. But questions about execution time or other aspects of (neural) computation are properly part of the performance model PM and must be addressed as such.

Linked to this dichotomy between theoretical linguistic and psycholinguistic approaches to the description of phonology (and other areas of linguistics) is an uncertainty over what exactly phonology is. Is it, as traditional linguistics would have claimed, a level of linguistic description that deals with the linguistic use of speech (i.e., the organization of the phonetic data obtained from the study of a language into the patterns of use that that language requires, and by extension, the study of universal aspects of such sound patterning)? Or is it, as cognitive approaches to language claim, the sound organization level within the brain? The traditional labels for childhood speech errors within speech-language pathology of *deletion*, *substitution*, and *distortion* suggest the former approach, as the errors are being classified according to whether they affect the phonetic or the phonemic (i.e., phonological) levels of description. However, accounts of acquired neurogenic disorders may well seek to situate the source of the disorder in psycholinguistic terms. For example, some types of aphasia may be said to affect the phonological component, whereas dysarthria might be claimed to affect the articulatory phonetic component. We look in more detail at this problem of what *phonology* actually stands for in the next section, when we will also consider the importance of standpoint when assigning error types to clinical data.

EXERCISE 15.1

Assign the following speech errors to the categories of *substitution* or *distortion*.

Target	Realization
soap	[ɬoʊp]
goat	[doʊt]
loop	[ɬup] ([ɬ] is a dark-l)
shoe	[çu]
key	[ti]
me	[mʷi]

DISTINGUISHING PHONETIC AND PHONOLOGICAL DISORDERS IN CLINICAL DATA

We touched on this problem in Ball and Müller (2005) and expand on that discussion here.*

Differences Between Clinical and Descriptive Linguists

We have to bear in mind that the approach of clinical linguists to their data often differs from that of descriptive linguists. Whereas descriptive linguists need to inform readers about the sound system of a particular language, clinical linguists may be primarily interested in providing a principled comparison between what a client produces and the target he or she was aiming at. In other words, they are explicitly comparing and contrasting the client's speech with the target system. For example, if the client uses the wrong variant of a contrastive speech unit (e.g., an unaspirated instead of aspirated fortis plosive), this is deemed to be a phonetic error. On the other hand, if he or she uses a different contrastive unit than the expected one (e.g., an alveolar instead of a velar lenis plosive), this is deemed to be a phonological error. In this way, clinical linguists are subtly altering the meaning of the terms *phonetic* and *phonological* as compared to their use by descriptive linguists.

Clinical linguists may also adopt the psycholinguistic use of *phonetics* and *phonology* as used by researchers in models of speech production and perception. As noted earlier, this is commonly done when describing acquired neurological disorders, as the analyst may be more interested in the source of the disorder (in terms of linguistic organization) rather than the effect it has on the speech itself. In cases such as these the terms are not being used with a contrastive function, but rather with a diagnostic one.

There are, therefore, potential problems with the use of these two terms in describing disordered speech; in particular that the terms are used in different ways by different researchers. Potentially further problems exist if a binary division is insufficient to account for the data in one or both of these approaches. Some of the previous literature that has explored these issues is referred to in Ball and Müller (2002).

In the following sections we delineate the main problems that have emerged in the use of the terms *phonetics* and *phonology* in clinical linguistics before going on to suggest solutions.

THREE PROBLEMS WITH THE PHONETICS-PHONOLOGY DIVISION

Problem 1

The descriptive linguistic approach is normally adopted in describing child speech disorders of various types. Traditionally, the phonetics-phonology distinction is manifested through error types labeled "distortions" (phonetic) and "substitutions" (phonological).† The basic notion appears to be that errors involving phonemic switches are labeled as substitutions, while those involving subphonemic switches are deemed to be distortions. However, as has been pointed out before (e.g., Grunwell, 1985), not all speech error data seem to fit this binary division. What do we do if the client uses a sound from outside the target system altogether (e.g., [ç] for /s/)? Is this a phonetic distortion because the client

---

* This section draws mainly from Ball and Müller (2002).
† The error types deletion and addition are not relevant for the current discussion, but would be considered phonological errors.

has not used another contrastive unit of his or her system, or a phonological error, as he or she has gone completely outside his or her phonological system and so can hardly be using an allophonic variant?

The normal decision in articulation tests is to claim that such instances are distortions. However, if we say it's a phonetic distortion, then what we are saying is that /s/ → [ç] is less of an error than /s/ → [ʃ], which in terms of articulation seems nonsense: [s] has the tongue tip/blade at alveolar ridge, [ʃ] has the tongue blade at palatal/alveolar area, while [ç] has the tongue front at hard palate. Of course, /s/ → [ʃ] causes a loss of contrast in the client's phonology while /s/ → [ç] does not, so in phonological terms it would seem justified to claim the former is more disruptive to the client's attempts to be understood. But what if we have /s/ → [ç] and /ʃ/ → [ç]? Here we also have a loss of contrast, and the use of a sound from outside the target system. Are these changes simultaneously distortions and substitutions? If not, how can we classify them?

So, with Problem 1 we need to address these questions:

1. Is a binary phonetic (distortion) and phonological (substitution) classification sufficient to deal with errors?
2. If it is not, what should we use instead?

Problem 2

Turning to acquired neurological disorders, we see a range of different speech error patterns. For example, certain types of aphasia may cause paraphasias, where sounds may be substituted, exchanged, or added. If we then try to assign these sorts of errors to an organizational level within the speech production process, it might appear they are best characterized as being situated at a level where the contrastive units of the phonology are put together.

In apraxia of speech, on the other hand, we have errors that seem to be connected with subsystems of phonetic implementation. An example of this is reported in Code and Ball (1982, 1988), where the subject was unable to implement the voicing subsystem when producing obstruents (though this was no problem with sonorants); nevertheless, she was able to use appropriate differences in segment quantity. Errors in apraxia of speech are inconsistent, which would suggest they are at a level of planning motor activity, rather than either an incorrect choice of phonological unit or an impairment at the neuromuscular level.

In dysarthria, however, we do have errors deriving from an impairment of the speech motor mechanisms. These errors are consistent, suggesting, therefore, that the level of interest here is the implementation of motor commands at the neuromuscular level of organization.

The questions we need to ask for Problem 2 are:

3. How does a binary phonetics/phonology distinction work when classifying neurogenic speech disorders?
4. What might we put in its place?

Problem 3

Any description of disordered speech has to take account of the fact that there may well be a difference between what we hear and what the speaker intends. By this we mean that the perceived effect of disordered speech may suggest one sort of classification, whereas the underlying cause of the error may suggest another. We can illustrate this point with examples from two different disorders: one that appears at first sight to be a classic case of child phonological delay, and another that appears to be an example of phonetic errors derived from a physical impairment (cleft palate).

In the first example we analyze a child as producing the phonological process termed velar fronting, and transcribe target /k/ as [t], /g/ as [d], and /ŋ/ as [n]. We assume that this is a phonological disorder, because the substitutions result in a threefold loss of contrast between alveolars and velars. However, electropalatography (EPG; see Hardcastle & Gibbon, 1997) may show that this is not the case, as in cases like this the speaker often has a different tongue palate contact pattern for target alveolars and target velars, so has clearly not merged these two target sounds. However, the release stage of the target velars results in them sounding like alveolars because the contact at the back of the tongue is released slightly before that at the alveolar region.

In our second example, we can imagine a child who presents with the classic characteristics of cleft palate speech: hypernasality, inability to produce plosives or fricatives, heavy use of glottal stops, and so on. The tendency would be to classify the errors as mainly phonetic, deriving from the physical impairments, and to assume the target system is intact.

However, then we learn that the cleft was repaired some time ago. The errors that we hear are learned behavior; that is, phonetic characteristics that were an automatic result of the cleft palate became phonologized and are now the normal way of speaking for this client.

These two cases show that what appears to be a phonological problem to the perceiver may be a motor (phonetic) problem for the producer, and what may appear to the perceiver to be phonetic disturbances may in fact be phonological behavior for the producer.

The questions we need to address for Problem 3 are:

5. Does a binary distinction between phonetics and phonology account for the perspective of producer versus perceiver?
6. If not, how can we deal with this?

SOME POSSIBLE ANSWERS

In this section we suggest ways to address the problems outlined above and, further, how we might attempt to unify these solutions so that we might have consistent usage of the terms *phonetics* and *phonology* as applied to a whole range of disordered speech. In doing this we will adopt a problem-solving approach, showing how it is necessary to apply a step-by-step metric along the lines of a flow diagram. We will first address each individual problem, and then demonstrate how the answers to these can be brought together.

Answer 1

This problem revolved around the need to discriminate between phonemic and subphonemic (i.e., allophonic) errors on the one hand, but also, on the other hand, around whether the realization of the target sound was within or outside the target phonology (defined broadly to mean both the phonemic units and their allophonic realizations). This implies that a two-way distinction is insufficient: We need to note both whether contrastivity is lost and whether the speaker goes beyond the target phonology. We suggest that a hierarchy of decision making is needed here. The first decision needed is whether the speaker for any particular error is using a sound from within or outside the target system. The second is whether the realization results in a loss of contrastivity or not.

For example, if the target contrast /s/ - /ʃ/ is realized as [s] - [s], then we see that the speaker has stayed within the target system but has lost contrastivity; if the same contrast is realized as [s] - [sʷ], we again see that the subject has stayed within the target system but this time contrastivity has been retained (even though the phonetic difference is slight). On the other hand, if target /s/ - /ʃ/ is realized as [ç] - [ç], then the subject has gone outside the target system and lost contrastivity, but if the realization is [s] - [ç], then there is use of a sound outside the target system but contrastivity is retained.

We clearly need a new classification, and we have suggested the following:

1. Internal allophonic: Target /t/ realized as dental in all positions [t̪].
2. Internal phonemic: Target /t/ realized as [d].
3. External phonetic: Target /z/ realized as [ʐ].
4. External phonological: Target /v/ and /ð/ realized as [β].

Clearly, for all these categories, but especially the external phonetic, we may need a further classification that accounts for the closeness versus remoteness from the target. For example, we need to distinguish between a General American target /t/ that is realized as a slit-t ([θ̠]; see Pandeli, Eska, Ball, & Rahilly, 1997, for an explanation of this transcription), a variant found in some Hiberno-English varieties and phonetically quite close to the target, and a realization of [ɬ], clearly considerably less like the target. Attempts to achieve this through distinctive feature counting may often be unhelpful (see Harris & Cottam, 1985), and the binary distinctive feature seems not best suited to the analysis of disordered speech (see Ball, 1996, 1997, 2002). Traditional articulatory labels may well work best to achieve any required subcategorization of closeness to target.

Answer 2

Research into models of speech production and their connection to acquired communicative impairments has long suggested the need to move beyond a binary approach (see Code & Ball, 1982, for an early such account). As suggested above, it became clear that phonological paraphasias, apraxia of speech, and dysarthric symptoms were mostly affecting separate levels of organization. More recently, Kent (1996) has demonstrated that we need to be aware of the interactions between different levels when considering these different types of impairments; nevertheless, it seems clear that a three-component model is justified. Such a model would contain a phonological organization module, a phonetic planning module (termed cognitive phonetics by Tatham, 1984), and an articulation module.

Paraphasia type errors would implicate the phonological module as the primary site of the disorder, apraxia errors would be mainly at the phonetic planning level, while dysarthric errors would be situated at the articulatory level.

Answer 3

As the examples above demonstrated, we clearly need to discriminate between the source of the error and the effect of the error whenever possible. In other words, we need to decide whether what we are labeling is the effect the error has on the listener in terms of loss or otherwise of contrastivity, or the site of origin of the error in terms of the modules of speech organization. Of course, making this distinction is not always easy. It is relatively straightforward to provide a description of the effect speech errors have on the listener; after all, this is what most impressionistic transcription of speech does. However, an impressionistic transcription will not always disambiguate

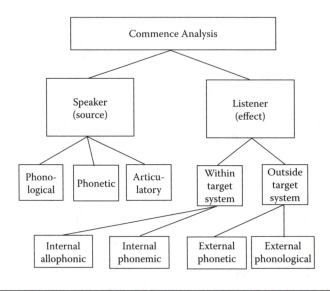

Figure 15.1 Unified method of speech error analysis.

between differing articulatory gestures that result in identical or very similar percepts. Nevertheless, the great advances that we have seen in instrumental speech assessment (see Ball & Code, 1997) mean that it is increasingly possible to couple impressionistic transcription with instrumental analysis that potentially can throw light on any differences between source and effect.

Unifying the Approaches

Clearly we wish to avoid a situation where, instead of having a binary division between phonetic and phonological error types, we have three unrelated sets of terms. It is, however, relatively straightforward to unify the suggestions made in the previous subsections, provided we retain the idea of a step-by-step analysis in the form of a flow diagram. We suggest that these steps should be as follows (as illustrated in Figure 15.1): First, we need to establish the viewpoint we are taking in the error description (the speaker or the listener). While we would encourage both approaches where possible, each will follow separate paths of description. If we follow the source of the error, then we have to identify the level of organization that has been affected (phonological, phonetic planning, or articulatory). If we follow the effect of the error, then we need to establish which descriptive category we need (internal allophonic, internal phonemic, external phonetic, or external phonological).

Such an approach provides a principled way of disambiguating the terminology applied to disordered speech, and situates any reader of a case description clearly in direct relation to the clinician's descriptive process. In order to see how such an approach translates into terminology, we can repeat some of the examples from above:*

/t/ to [d]: Phonology component source with internal phonemic effect.
/t/ to [t̪]: Phonology component source with internal allophonic effect.
/ʃ/ to [ç]: Phonology component source with external phonetic effect.

---

* Naturally, any client may exhibit several of these categories of error; further, we would of course require more than a single instance of a particular realization before saying that a speaker demonstrated this error type.

/s/ and /ʃ/ to [ç]: Phonology component source with external phonological effect.*

Target alveolars realized as velars: Phonetic component source with internal phonemic effect.

Phonologized cleft palate speech: Phonology component source with external phonetic effect.

Aphasic paraphasias: Phonology component source with internal phonemic effect.

Apraxia of speech: Phonetic component source with internal phonemic effect.

Dysarthria: Articulation component source with external phonetic effect.†

EXERCISE 15.2

Using the data in the previous exercise, analyze the speech errors in terms of *internal allophonic*, *internal phonemic*, *external phonetic*, and *external phonological*.

DESIDERATA FOR A CLINICAL PHONOLOGY

Naturally, as Grunwell (1987) points out, clinical phonological analysis requires first the input of reliable and detailed phonetic information. Whatever approach is taken to the analysis of the disordered data, none will be successful if the phonetic data are inaccurate and misleading. Assuming that we have good input data, what do we want a clinical phonological analysis to provide us with? Among the important features must be:

a. an ability to group together errors in a way that shows their commonality;
b. a means of providing an explanation of the error;
c. a metric that allows us to measure different errors in terms of severity, or deviation from a norm (such as a developmental norm); and
d. guidance in planning therapeutic intervention.

Clearly an analysis that lists errors phoneme by phoneme is going to be less insightful than one that utilizes some device to group together all those errors that are phonologically similar. So, a traditional phoneme approach that tells us a client realizes /p/ as [b], /t/ as [d], and /k/ as [g] is less useful than one that states all target voiceless plosives are voiced (whether this is expressed as a rule, a constraint, a prosody, or an articulatory score). Similarly, if we know that certain vowels in a client's speech are nasalized, we learn why such a thing might have happened if our analysis shows that it is only those vowels before a deleted target syllable final nasal consonant that undergo this process. Such explanatory power is provided by many of the theories we have examined in this book, for example, the derivational processes of generative phonological accounts, as well as gestural phonology, government phonology, and others.

The provision of severity metrics in clinical phonology has not always been simple. As we have pointed out in earlier chapters, traditional phoneme analyses (such as deletion,

---

* It is assumed for the sake of illustration that these first four examples have their origin in the component of phonological organization, rather than in phonetic planning or articulation, i.e., that they derive from phonological delay or disorder.

† It is assumed for the sake of illustration that these last two examples are restricted to the effects listed. Clearly, both apraxia of speech and dysarthria may have other effects.

substitution, and distortion) have not been very successful in this regard, as the categories used are too broad, and there is no way to explicitly show that, for example, the substitution of [t] for target /s/ in child speech is much more usual than the converse. Attempts at counting distinctive feature errors proved no more successful, but developments in underspecification and feature geometry did add to the ability to distinguish between more and less commonly occurring bundles of features. These developments have had less of an impact on clinical phonology, however, than on theoretical phonology. Natural phonology, as used with clinical data, has provided such a metric: in terms of the delayed use of natural processes or the use of deviant processes, and indeed the overall mix of processes used by a client. The functional load of a sound or group of sounds is also an important consideration in terms of assigning severity to an error, and in this regard systemic phonology provides a framework for formalizing this aspect. Other more recent phonological theories—such as cognitive phonology, systemic gestural phonology, and optimality theory applied to phonology—could all be used to develop severity metrics, and this could be an area of interesting research in the future.

Our final point concerning a phonological analysis that provides guidance to intervention depends on analyses that group together errors into common patterns, and provide measures of severity. So, if we know that a client realizes target /ɹ/ as [w], and target fricatives as plosives, our knowledge of normal development and functional load immediately tells us that the latter problem needs to be prioritized over the former.

These desiderata, of course, do not override the need—described above—to identify whether you are describing in your phonological analysis the perceived phonology of the listener or (if possible to discover) the intended phonology of the speaker.

EXERCISE 15.3

The functional load of a sound derives not only from how often it is used to contrast with other sounds, but whether it also has a morphological function in terms of inflectional and derivational affixes. Give examples of the affix usage of the following sounds in English, and note whether they are inflectional or derivational: /s/, /d/, /θ/, /z/, /t/, /i/.

INTERLUDE: COMPARING PHONOLOGICAL ANALYSES

The chapters in this book have outlined several fundamental aspects of phonology, and then a series of theoretical approaches that we have described and illustrated with data from normal and disordered speech (together with reviews of studies that have applied the theory to clinical data). What we will do in this section is to look at a clinical case of progressive speech degeneration, and compare how two current phonological theories would account for some of the processes identified in the client's speech (see Ball, Rutter, & Code, 2008, for more details).

Participant

CS is a right-handed, 63-year-old male (at the time of testing, February and March 2002), who first noticed speech problems in November 1994. A structural MRI scan report a year before our data were collected showed no focal damage, and the corpus callosum and brainstem were normal. However, scanning in October 2003 showed significant generalized, bilateral atrophy, more prominent in the left frontotemporal area.

CS's cognitive and memory abilities were mainly intact. Language assessments showed problems with phonology and naming, though other aspects of language and writing appeared unimpaired. A motor speech examination demonstrated no significant motor weakness or sensory loss, a mild dysarthria, but clear nondysarthric problems initiating laryngeal and oral movement (for example, coughing and producing vowels to command). Full details of the assessments undertaken and results are given in Ball et al., (2004).

In summary, CS showed particular problems with initiation of laryngeal, tongue, and lip movements; little or no apparent groping and searching; and problems with control of voicing and coordination of laryngeal with oral articulation.

Materials

The analyses are based on verbal tasks undertaken over a five-week period, approximately seven years after CS's speech difficulties were first noticed, and some six months before his speech deteriorated to become unintelligible and not amenable to analysis. The tasks were reading and repetition of increasingly complex English words, uttering sustained vowels in isolation, counting from 1 to 30, picture naming, reading a phonetically balanced passage ("The Grandfather Passage"), and a variety of diadochokinetic tasks.

Results

Fuller results are given elsewhere, but the main findings showed a range of problems, including intrusive schwa, devoicing voiced and voicing unvoiced obstruents and loss of aspiration, some vowel distortions, anticipation of phones, and increasing errors on repetition, but mainly additions. Unusual addition processes included the addition of bilabials preceding /ɹ/ initial words, and [l] following words ending in /u/. The automatic counting tasks showed increased initiation problems and pausing between words with progress through the series. "The Grandfather Passage" demonstrated significant initiation problems and pausing—with an overall duration of 180 seconds (norm 48 seconds), together with examples of denasalization.

Discussion

Space allows us to examine only three of the speech processes exhibited by CS in this proposal, and will compare how two current phonological approaches account for them. These two approaches are optimality theory (see Chapter 11) and articulatory phonology (Chapter 12). These two approaches were chosen because the first is dominant in current phonology, and the second is especially suited to the analysis of speech implementation. The processes examined were the loss of aspiration in voiceless plosives, denasalization, and the addition of bilabials to /ɹ/ initial words.

Recent developments in theoretical phonology have centered on constraint-based approaches to the description of sound systems. As noted in Chapter 11, constraint-based phonology (as found within the overall framework of optimality theory (OT)) has constraints only and is overtly nonderivational. By this last point we mean that phonological descriptions do not set out to derive a surface realization from an underlying general phonological description through a set of rules, as in the various versions of traditional generative phonology, but rather the relation between the input and the output of the phonology is mediated by the ranking of a set of constraints. The set of phonological constraints is deemed universal; their ranking (and possible violability) is language specific. As applied to disordered speech (e.g., Dinnsen & Gierut, 2008), constraints can be reordered to account for the client's differences from the target phonology.

There are no overall agreed constraints in OT, but one approach to aspiration is given in Beckman and Ringen (2004). Following their terminology, the [–voi] is [spread] constraint is changed from inviolable to violable, thus allowing nonaspirated voiceless stops. If CS had no nasal consonants at all, then an inventory constraint could be invoked; however, CS has variable use of nasals. Assuming from this that he has nasal consonants at the underlying level, and denasalizes some of them, we can use a faithfulness constraint that can now be violable—thus **Faith [Nasal]**. Finally, the labial consonant addition process can only be accounted for in OT through the *ad hoc* addition of a violable constraint requiring such addition (and, presumably, needed only for CS).

The analysis units of gestural phonology are actual gestures of the articulators. As we noted in Chapter 12, the theory posits five main subsystems or gestures: laryngeal, velum, tongue-tip, tongue-body, and lip. A gestural score (or constellation) describes the degree and direction of the movements of these subsystems and how they are coordinated in time. Such a gestural score gives a straightforward account of the loss of aspiration, as a retiming of the stop release and voice onset time, as shown in Figure 15.2 for target [tʰu] *two*, realized as [t⁼u]. Similarly, the denasalization of target [mɔ] *more* to [bɔ] can be captured via a score that decouples the velum gesture from the utterance (see Figure 15.3).* The addition of labials to /ɹ/ initial targets (as in [bɹæp] for /ɹæp/) is also amenable to a gestural account. English /ɹ/ is noted as having a considerable degree of lip-rounding in its production (see, for example, Ball & Müller, 2005), and if the timing of that labial gesture is readjusted such that it commences earlier than the approximant, then a labial consonant will perforce precede the target /ɹ/. This is illustrated in Figure 15.4.

Conclusion

As we noted earlier in this chapter about many phonological theories, it is unclear whether users of OT (especially clinically) are attempting solely to provide a parsimonious and elegant account of phonological data, or also a psycholinguistic description.† If the latter, then OT is clearly aimed at a level of phonological organization in the brain. An OT account of CS's speech, therefore, could be taken as a claim that he has reorganized the hierarchies of phonological constraints in his speech. Gestural phonology, on the other hand, is overtly claiming to model speech processes, and applying this approach to CS's speech would suggest that the problem lies at the level of implementation of phonological planning (in particular, coordination of gestures). It is our view that this latter approach is best suited as a description of CS's speech degeneration, both theoretically and psycholinguistically, and that the data support the notion that CS's main problems are with speech implementation rather than phonological organization.

---

* The gestural scores shown here differ slightly in how they are drawn from those in Chapter 12; this is done to illustrate the current different traditions.

† The requirement that the GEN component of OT generates an infinite number of possible inputs to the EVAL component would seem to disqualify the theory from being a realistic attempt to model actual speech production. As noted earlier, McCarthy (2002) directly addresses this point, and notes that OT is not intended to model speech performance.

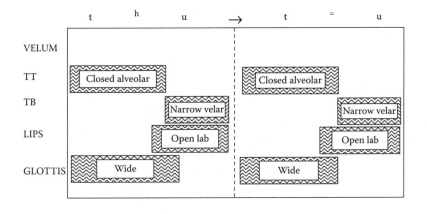

Figure 15.2 Gestural scores for aspirated and unaspirated realizations of *two*.

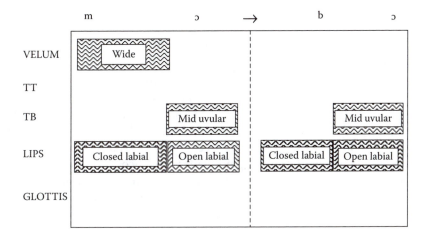

Figure 15.3 Gestural scores for the nasal and denasal realizations of *more*.

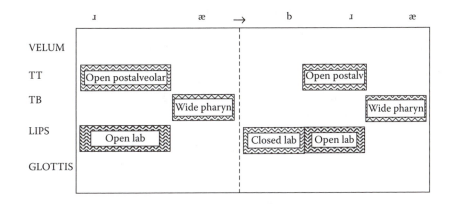

Figure 15.4 Gestural scores for the realizations of *ra(p)* with and without a preceding labial stop.

CONCLUSION

In this book we have surveyed a wide range of current and recent approaches to phonology, pointing—where relevant—to their applications with clinical data. The current state of theoretical phonology provides a wealth of approaches that may be of use to the clinical phonologist. Rather than committing to only one theory, it may prove that a range of approaches can inform the researcher and clinician dealing with disordered speech data. For example, if data analysis only is the focus, even highly unintelligible speech could be described in terms of phonological approaches that stress economy of description (such as nonlinear phonology and optimality theory, though such a restricted focus would, we contend, be of limited use); explanations for patterns seen in the data might be better couched in approaches that are based more strongly on phonetic considerations (such as Firthian prosodic phonology or gestural phonology). Finally, if the planning of remediation is the focus, then approaches such as natural phonology or cognitive phonology may have important insights to offer.* We hope that the range of models presented in this book will spur readers to experiment with different analyses of clinical data, and that they may themselves play a part in the development of clinical phonology.

FURTHER READING

More information on the application of phonology in the clinical context can be found in some earlier texts, such as Grunwell (1981, 1987, 1990), Elbert and Gierut (1986), and the papers in Ball and Kent (1997). More recently, Bernhardt and Stemberger (1998, 2000) have applied a constraint-based nonlinear phonological model to disordered data. Newer material can be found in Howard and Heselwood (2007), and in the relevant chapters of Ball et al., (2008). There have been many journal articles that have used different models of clinical phonology, and readers are encouraged to consult the leading journals in the field (e.g., *Clinical Linguistics and Phonetics* and *Journal of Speech, Language and Hearing Research*) to find current and recent research in clinical phonology. Finally, the discussion on clinical phonology in Ball and Müller (2009) should prove useful.

REVIEW QUESTIONS AND STUDY TOPICS

Review Questions

1. What are the two approaches that linguistic theory can take?
2. What suggestion is made to resolve the problem in the use of the traditional terms *substitution* and *distortion*?
3. What suggestion is made to resolve the problem of using *phonetics* versus *phonology* in the description of neurological disorders?
4. What suggestion is made to resolve the problem of listener versus speaker orientation in sound error description?
5. How can the three suggested changes in descriptive labels be unified into a procedure?

---

* Some might complain that an approach that uses several models is incoherent and, as an anonymous reviewer put it, "would be met with great disdain." As we have stressed in this book, there is no one correct model of phonology, and a refusal to use the best insights from several approaches strikes us as a greater folly.

6. What are desirable aspects of a clinical phonology?
7. What two theories are used in the description of CS's data?
8. In what way did one of the theories applied to CS's data appear superior to the other?

Study Topics and Projects

1. Using your own clinical data, attempt an analysis of the error patterns in terms of the analysis procedure shown in Figure 15.1. How easy was it to do this, and what insights (if any) do you feel it gave?
2. From your reading of this book and others in the area of theoretical phonology, describe the approach that most appeals to you in terms of its usefulness in analysis, diagnosis, and remediation. Critically evaluate the approach, outlining both strengths and weaknesses, and use clinical data to illustrate your arguments.

REFERENCES

Adi-Bensaid, L., & Bat-El, O. (2004). The development of the prosodic word in the speech of a hearing impaired child with a cochlear implant device. *Journal of Multilingual Communication Disorders, 2,* 187–206.

Anderson, J. M. (1969). Syllabic or non-syllabic phonology. *Journal of Linguistics, 5,* 136–143.

Anderson, J., & Durand, J. (1986). Dependency phonology. In J. Durand (Ed.), *Dependency and non-linear phonology* (pp. 1–54). London: Croom Helm.

Anderson, J., & Durand, J. (Eds.). (1987). *Explorations in dependency phonology.* Dordrecht: Foris.

Anderson, J., & Ewen, C. (1987). *Principles of dependency phonology.* Cambridge, England: Cambridge University Press.

Anderson, S. R. (1985). *Phonology in the twentieth century.* Chicago: Chicago University Press.

Archangeli, D. (1984). *Underspecification in Yawelmani phonology and morphology.* PhD dissertation, MIT, Cambridge, MA. (Published by Garland Press, New York, 1988)

Archangeli, D. (1988). Aspects of underspecification theory. *Phonology, 5,* 183–208.

Archangeli, D. (1997). Optimality theory: An introduction to linguistics in the 1990s. In D. Archangeli & D. T. Langendoen (Eds.), *Optimality theory: An overview* (pp. 1–32). Cambridge, MA: Blackwell.

Archangeli, D., & Langendoen, D. T. (Eds.). (1997). *Optimality theory: An overview.* Oxford: Blackwell.

Archangeli, D., & Pulleyblank, D. (1994). *Grounded phonology.* Cambridge, MA: MIT Press.

Armstrong, E. (2005). Language disorder: A functional linguistic perspective. *Clinical Linguistics and Phonetics, 19,* 137–153.

Baker, E. (2000). *Changing nail to snail: A treatment efficacy study of phonological impairment in children.* Unpublished doctoral thesis, University of Sydney, Sydney.

Ball, M. J. (1996). An examination of the nature of the minimal phonological unit in language acquisition. In B. Bernhardt, J. Gilbert, & D. Ingram (Eds.), *Proceedings of the UBC International Conference on Phonological Acquisition* (pp. 240–253). Somerville, MA: Cascadilla Press.

Ball, M. J. (1997). Monovalent phonologies: Dependency phonology and an introduction to government phonology. In M. J. Ball & R. D. Kent (Eds.), *The new phonologies* (pp. 127–161). San Diego: Singular.

Ball, M. J. (2002). Clinical phonology of vowel disorders. In M. J. Ball & F. Gibbon (Eds.), *Vowels and vowel disorders* (pp. 187–216). London: Butterworth-Heinemann.

Ball, M. J. (2003). Clinical applications of a cognitive phonology. *Phoniatrics, Logopedics, Vocology, 28,* 63–69.

Ball, M. J. (2008). Government phonology and speech impairment. In M. J. Ball, M. Perkins, N. Müller, & S. Howard (Eds.), *Handbook of clinical linguistics* (pp. 452–466). Oxford: Blackwell.

Ball, M. J., & Code, C. (Eds.). (1997). *Instrumental clinical phonetics.* London: Whurr.

Ball, M. J., Code, C., Tree, J. J., Dawe, K., & Kay, J. (2004). Phonetic and phonological analysis of progressive speech degeneration: A case study. *Clinical Linguistics and Phonetics, 18,* 447–462.

Ball, M. J., & Gibbon, F. (Eds.). (2002). *Vowel disorders.* Woburn, MA: Butterworth-Heinemann.

Ball, M. J., & Kent, R. D. (Eds.). (1997). *The new phonologies: Developments in clinical linguistics.* San Diego: Singular.

Ball, M. J., Lowry, O. and McInnis, L. (2006). Distributional and stylistic variation in /r/-misarticulations: A case study. *Clinical Linguistics and Phonetics, 20,* 119-124.

Ball, M. J., & Müller, N. (2002). The use of the terms phonetics and phonology in the description of disordered speech. *Advances in Speech-Language Pathology, 4,* 95–108.

Ball, M. J., & Müller, N. (2005). *Phonetics for communication disorders.* Mahwah, NJ: Lawrence Erlbaum.

Ball, M. J., & Müller, N. (2009). Clinical phonology. In L. Wei & V. Cook (Eds.), *Linguistics in the real world.* (pp. 202–222) London: Continuum Press.

Ball, M. J., Müller, N., & Damico, H. (2003). Double onset syllable structure in a speech disordered child. *Advances in Speech-Language Pathology, 5,* 37–40.

Ball, M. J., Perkins, M., Müller, N., & Howard, S. (Eds.). (2008). *Handbook of clinical linguistics.* Oxford: Blackwell.

Ball, M. J., & Rahilly, J. (1999). *Phonetics. The science of speech.* London: Edward Arnold.

Ball, M. J., Rutter, B., & Code, C. (2008). Phonological analyses of a case of progressive speech degeneration. *Asia-Pacific Journal of Speech, Language and Hearing, 11,* 305–312.

Barlow, J., & Gierut, J. (1999). Optimality theory in phonological acquisition. *Journal of Speech, Language and Hearing Research, 42,* 1482–1498.

Barlow, J. A., & Gierut, J. A. (2002). Minimal pair approaches to phonological remediation. *Seminars in Speech and Language, 23,* 57–68.

Bauman-Waengler, J. (2000). *Articulatory and phonological impairments: A clinical focus.* Boston: Allyn and Bacon.

Bauman-Waengler, J. (2003). *Articulatory and phonological impairments: A clinical focus* (2nd ed.). Boston: Allyn and Bacon.

Beckman, J., & Ringen, C. (2004). Contrast and redundancy in OT. In B. Schmeiser, V. Chand, A. Kelleher, & A. Rodriguez (Eds.), *Proceedings of WCCFL 23* (pp. 101–114). Somerville, MA: Cascadilla Press.

Béland, R., Caplan, D., & Nespoulous, J. (1990). The role of abstract phonological representation in word production: Evidence from phonemic paraphasias. *Journal of Neurolinguistics, 5,* 125–164.

Bernhardt, B. (1992a). Developmental implications of nonlinear phonological theory. *Clinical Linguistics and Phonetics, 6,* 259–281.

Bernhardt, B. (1992b). The application of nonlinear phonological theory to intervention with one phonologically disordered child. *Clinical Linguistics and Phonetics, 6,* 283–316.

Bernhardt, B., & Gilbert, J. (1992). Applying linguistic theory to speech-language pathology: The case for non-linear phonology. *Clinical Linguistics and Phonetics, 6,* 123–145.

Bernhardt, B., & Stemberger, J. P. (1998). *Handbook of phonological development.* San Diego: Academic Press.

Bernhardt, B. H., & Stemberger, J.P. (2000). *Workbook in nonlinear phonology for clinical application.* Austin, TX: Pro-Ed.

Bernhardt, B., & Stoel-Gammon, C. (1997). Grounded phonology: Application to the analysis of disordered speech. In M. J. Ball & R. D. Kent (Eds.), *The new phonologies* (pp. 163–210). San Diego: Singular.

Bloomfield, L. (1933). *Language.* New York: Henry Holt.

Boersma, P. (2000). Learning a grammar in functional phonology. In J. Dekkers, F. van der Leeuw, & J. van de Weijer (Eds.), *Phonology, syntax, and acquisition in optimality theory* (pp. 465–523). Oxford: Oxford University Press.

Bradford, A., & Dodd, B. (1996). Do all speech-disordered children have motor deficits? *Clinical Linguistics and Phonetics, 10,* 77–101.

Braine, M. (1974). On what might constitute learnable phonology. *Language, 50,* 270–299.

Browman, C. P., & Goldstein, L. (1986). Towards an articulatory phonology. *Phonology Yearbook, 3,* 219–252.

Browman, C. P., & Goldstein, L. (1989). Articulatory gestures as phonological units. *Phonology, 6,* 201–251.

Browman, C. P., & Goldstein, L. (1990). Tiers in articulatory phonology, with some implications for casual speech. In T. Kingston & M. E. Beckman (Eds.), *Papers in laboratory phonology I: Between the grammar and physics of speech* (pp. 341–376). Cambridge, England: Cambridge University Press.

Browman, C. P., & Goldstein, L. (1992). Articulatory phonology: An overview. *Phonetica, 49,* 155–180.

Browman, C. P., & Goldstein, L. (1995). Dynamics and articulatory phonology. In R. F. Port & T. van Gelder (Eds.), *Mind as motion* (pp. 175–194). Cambridge, MA: MIT Press.

Brown, C., & Matthews, J. (1997). The role of feature geometry in the development of phonemic contrasts. In S. J. Hannahs & M. Young-Scholten (Eds.), *Focus on phonological acquisition* (pp. 67–112). Amsterdam: John Benjamins.

Buckingham, H. (1986). The scan-copier mechanism and the positional level of language production: Evidence from phonemic paraphasia. *Cognitive Science, 10,* 195–217.

Buckingham, H. (1990). Principle of sonority, doublet creation, and the checkoff monitor. In J. Nespoulous & P. Villiard (Eds.), *Phonology, morphology and aphasia* (pp. 193–205). New York: Springer.

Butterworth, B. (1992). Disorders of phonological encoding. *Cognition, 42,* 261–286.

Bybee, J. (1985). *Morphology: A study of the relation between meaning and form.* Amsterdam: John Benjamins.

Bybee, J. (2001). *Phonology and language use.* Cambridge, England: Cambridge University Press.

Carnochan, J. (1960). Vowel harmony in Igbo. *African Language Studies, 1,* 155–160.

Carr, P. (1993). *Phonology.* London: Macmillan.

Chin, S. B. (1996). The role of the sonority hierarchy in delayed phonological systems. In T. Powell (Ed.), *Pathologies of speech and language: Contributions of clinical phonetics and linguistics* (pp. 109–117). New Orleans: International Clinical Phonetics and Linguistics Association.

Chin, S. B., & Dinnsen, D.A. (1991). Feature geometry in disordered phonologies. *Clinical Linguistics and Phonetics, 5,* 329–337.

Chin, S. B., & Dinnsen, D. A. (1992). Consonant clusters in disordered speech: Constraints and correspondence patterns. *Journal of Child Language, 19,* 259–285.

Chomsky, N. (1975). *Reflections on language.* New York: Pantheon Books.

Chomsky, N. (1981). *Lectures on government and binding.* Dordrecht: Foris.

Chomsky, N. (1986). *Knowledge of language.* New York: Praeger.

Chomsky, N., & Halle, M. (1968). *The sound pattern of English.* New York: Harper and Row.

Chomsky, N., & Lasnik, H. (1993). The theory of principles and parameters. In J. Jacobs, A. von Stechow, W. Sternefeld, & T. Vannemann (Eds.), *Syntax: An international handbook of contemporary research* (pp. 506–569). Berlin: Walter de Gruyter.

Christman, S. (1992a). Abstruse neologism formation: Parallel processing revisited. *Clinical Linguistics and Phonetics, 6,* 65–76.

Christman, S. (1992b). Uncovering phonological regularity in neologisms: Contributions of sonority theory. *Clinical Linguistics and Phonetics, 6,* 219–248.

Christman, S. (1994). Target-related neologism formation in jargonaphasia. *Brain and Language, 46,* 109–128.

Clark, J., & Yallop, C. (1990). *An introduction to phonetics and phonology.* Oxford: Blackwell.

Clements, G. N. (1985). The geometry of phonological features. *Phonology Yearbook, 2,* 225–252.

Clements, G. N. (1988). Toward a substantive theory of feature specifications. In *Proceedings of the Eighteenth Meeting of the Northeastern Linguistic Society* (pp. 79–93). Amherst, MA: Northeastern Linguistic Society.

Clements, G. N. (1990). The role of the sonority cycle in core syllabification. In J. Kingston & M. Beckman (Eds.), *Papers in Laboratory Phonology I* (pp. 283–333). Cambridge, England: Cambridge University Press.

Clements, G. N. (1992). Phonological primes: Features or gestures? *Phonetica, 49,* 181–193.

Clements, G. N. (2006). Feature organization. In K. Brown (Ed.), *The encyclopedia of language and linguistics* (2nd ed., Vol. 4, pp. 433–441). Oxford: Elsevier Limited.

Clements, G. N., & Hume, E. (1995). The internal organization of speech sounds. In J. Goldsmith (Ed.), *Handbook of phonological theory* (pp. 245–306). Oxford: Blackwell.

Clements, G. N., & Keyser, S. J. (1983). *CV-phonology: A generative theory of the syllable.* Cambridge, MA: MIT Press.

Code, C., & Ball, M. J. (1982). Fricative production in Broca's aphasia: A spectrographic analysis. *Journal of Phonetics, 10,* 325–331.

Code, C., & Ball, M. J. (1988). Apraxia of speech: The case for a cognitive phonetics. In M. J. Ball (Ed.), *Theoretical linguistics and disordered language* (pp. 152–167). London: Croom Helm.

Code, C., & Ball, M. J. (1994). Syllabification in aphasic recurring utterances: Contributions of sonority theory. *Journal of Neurolinguistics, 8,* 257–265.

Coleman, J. S. (1998). *Phonological representations: Their names, forms and powers.* Cambridge, England: Cambridge University Press.

Compton, A. (1970). Generative studies of children's phonological systems. *Journal of Speech and Hearing Disorders, 35,* 315–339.

Compton, A. (1975). Generative studies of children's phonological disorders: A strategy for therapy. In S. Singh (Ed.), *Measurement procedures in speech, hearing and language* (pp. 55–90). Baltimore: University Park Press.

Compton, A. (1976). Generative studies of children's phonological disorders: Clinical ramifications. In D. Morehead & A. Morehead (Eds.), *Normal and deficient child language* (pp. 61–96). Baltimore: University Park Press.

Compton, A., & Hutton, J. (1976). *Compton-Hutton phonological assessment.* San Francisco: Carousel House.

Creaghead, N., Newman, P., & Secord, W. (1989). *Assessment and remediation of articulatory and phonological disorders* (2nd ed.). Columbus, OH: Merrill.

Cruttenden, A. (2001). *Gimson's pronunciation of English* (6th ed.). London: Edward Arnold.

Davenport, M., & Hannahs, S. (1998). *Introducing phonetics and phonology.* Oxford: Oxford University Press.

Dean, E., Howell, J., Hill, A., & Waters, D. (1990). *Metaphon resource pack.* Windsor, UK: NFER-Nelson.

Dekkers, J. R. M., van der Leeuw, F. R. H., & van de Weijer, J. M. (Eds.). (2000). *Optimality theory: Phonology, syntax and acquisition.* Oxford: Oxford University Press.

Dinnsen, D. (1996). Context-sensitive underspecification and the acquisition of phonemic contrasts. *Journal of Child Language, 23,* 57–79.

Dinnsen, D. (1997). Nonsegmental phonologies. In M. J. Ball & R. D. Kent (Eds.), *The new phonologies* (pp. 77–125). San Diego: Singular.

Dinnsen, D. A. (1999). Some empirical and theoretical issues in disordered child phonology. In W. C. Ritchie & T. K. Bhatia (Eds.), *Handbook of child language acquisition* (pp. 647–674). New York: Academic Press.

Dinnsen, D. A. (2001). New insights from optimality theory for acquisition. *Clinical Linguistics and Phonetics, 15,* 15–18.

Dinnsen, D. A. (2002). A reconsideration of children's phonological representations. In B. Skarabela, S. Fish, & A. H.-J. Do (Eds.), *Proceedings of the 26th Annual Boston University Conference on Language Development* (pp. 1–23). Somerville, MA: Cascadilla Press.

Dinnsen, D., & Barlow, J. (1998). On the characterization of a chain shift in normal and delayed phonological acquisition. *Journal of Child Language, 25*, 61–94.

Dinnsen, D., & Gierut, J. (2008). Optimality theory: A clinical perspective. In M. J. Ball, M. Perkins, N. Müller, & S. Howard (Eds.), *Handbook of clinical linguistics* (pp. 439–451). Oxford: Blackwell.

Dodd, B. (1995). *The differential diagnosis and treatment of children with speech disorder.* London: Whurr.

Donegan, P. (1985). *On the natural phonology of vowels (Outstanding dissertations in linguistics).* New York: Garland.

Elbert, M., & Gierut, J. A. (1986). *Handbook of clinical phonology: Approaches to assessment and treatment.* San Diego: College-Hill.

Ewen, C. J., & van der Hulst, H. (2001). *The phonological structure of words: An introduction.* Cambridge, England: Cambridge University Press.

Fee, E. (1997). The prosodic framework for language learning. *Topics in Language Disorders, 17,* 53–62.

Ferguson, C., Perzer, D. and Weeks, T. (1973). Model and replica phonological grammar of a child's first words. *Lingua, 31,* 35-65.

Firth, J. R. (1936). Alphabets and phonology in India and Burma. *Bulletin of the Society for Oriental Studies, 8,* 517–546.

Firth, J. R. (1948). Sounds and prosodies. *Transactions of the Philological Society, 1948,* 127–152.

Firth, J. R. (1957). *Papers in Linguistics 1934-1957.* London: Oxford University Press.

Fudge, E. (1969). Syllables. *Journal of Linguistics, 5,* 253–286.

Gafos, A. (1999). *The articulatory basis of locality in phonology.* New York: Garland.

Gibbon, F. (1990). Lingual activity in two speech disordered children's attempts to produce velar and alveolar stop consonants: Evidence from electropalatographic (EPG) data. *British Journal of Disorders of Communication, 25,* 329–340.

Gibbon, F. E. (1999), Undifferentiated lingual gestures in children with articulation/phonological disorders. *Journal of Speech, Language and Hearing Research, 42,* 382–397.

Gibbon, F. E. (2007). Research and practice in developmental speech disorders. In M. C. Pennington (Ed.), *Phonology in context* (pp. 245–273). Basingstoke: Palgrave Macmillan.

Giegerich, J. (1992). *English phonology. An introduction.* Cambridge, England: Cambridge University Press.

Gierut, J. A. (1989). Maximal opposition approach to phonological treatment. *Journal of Speech and Hearing Disorders, 54,* 9–19.

Gierut, J. A. (1990). Differential learning of phonological oppositions. *Journal of Speech and Hearing Research, 33,* 540–549.

Gierut, J. A. (1998). Natural domains of cyclicity in phonological acquisition. *Clinical Linguistics and Phonetics, 12,* 481–499.

Gierut, J. A. (1999). Syllable onsets: Clusters and adjuncts in acquisition. *Journal of Speech, Language and Hearing Research, 42,* 708–726.

Gierut, J. A. (2001). Complexity in phonological treatment: Clinical factors. *Language, Speech, and Hearing Services in Schools, 32,* 229–241.

Gierut, J. A., & Champion, A. (2001). Syllable onsets II: Three-element clusters in phonological treatment. *Journal of Speech, Language, and Hearing Research, 44,* 886–904.

Gierut, J. A., Cho, M.-H., & Dinnsen, D. A. (1993). Geometric accounts of consonant-vowel interactions in developing systems. *Clinical Linguistics and Phonetics, 7,* 219–236.

Gimson, A. (1989). *An introduction to the pronunciation of English* (4th ed.). London: Edward Arnold.

Gleason, H. (1956). *An introduction to descriptive linguistics.* New York: Holt, Rinehart, and Winston.

Goad, H. (1997). Consonant harmony in child language: An optimality-theoretic account. In S.-J. Hannahs & Martha Young-Scholten (Eds.), *Focus on phonological acquisition* (pp. 113–142). Amsterdam: John Benjamins.

Goldsmith, J. (1976). *Autosegmental phonology*. PhD thesis, MIT, Cambridge, MA.

Goldsmith, J. (1990). *Autosegmental and metrical phonology*. Oxford: Blackwell.

Goldsmith, J. (1994). Disentangling autosegments: A response. *Journal of Linguistics, 30*, 449–507.

Goldsmith, J. (Ed.) (1995). *The Handbook of Phonological Theory*. Oxford: Blackwell.

Goldsmith, J. (Ed.) (1999). *Phonological Theory: The Essential Readings*. Oxford: Blackwell.

Goldsmith, J. (1992). A note on the genealogy of research traditions in modern phonology. *Journal of Linguistics, 28*, 149-163.

Goozee, N., Purcell, A., & Baker, E. (2001). Sonority and the acquisition of consonant clusters in a child with a cleft lip and palate. In L. Wilson & S. Hewatt (Eds.), *Proceedings of the 2001 Speech Pathology Australia National Conference (Melbourne)* (pp. 119–126). Melbourne: Speech Pathology Australia.

Grunwell, P. (1977). *The analysis of phonological disability in children*. Unpublished PhD thesis, University of Reading, UK.

Grunwell, P. (1981). *The nature of phonological disability in children*. London: Academic Press.

Grunwell, P. (1985). *The phonological assessment of child speech (PACS)*. Windsor: NFER-Nelson.

Grunwell, P. (1987). *Clinical phonology* (2nd ed.). London: Chapman & Hall.

Grunwell, P. (Ed.). (1990). *Developmental speech disorders*. Edinburgh: Churchill Livingstone.

Grunwell, P. (1992a). Assessment of child phonology in the clinical context. In C. Ferguson, L. Menn, & C. Stoel-Gammon (Eds.), *Phonological development: Models, research, implications* (pp. 457–483). Timonium, MD: York Press.

Grunwell, P. (1992b). Principled decision-making in the remediation of children with developmental phonological disorders. In P. Fletcher & D. Hall (Eds.), *Specific speech and language disorders in children* (pp. 215–240). London: Whurr.

Grunwell, P. (1997). Natural phonology. In M. J. Ball & R. D. Kent (Eds.), *The new phonologies* (pp. 35–75). San Diego: Singular.

Gussenhoven, C., & Jacobs, H. (1998). *Understanding phonology*. London: Edward Arnold.

Gussmann, E. (2002). *Phonology: Analysis and theory*. Cambridge, England: Cambridge University Press.

Halle, M. 1992. Phonological features. In W. Bright (Ed.), *Oxford international encyclopedia of linguistics* (pp. 207–212). New York: Oxford University Press.

Halle, M., & Clements, N. (1983). *Problem book in phonology*. Cambridge, MA: MIT Press.

Halle, M., & Mohanan, K. (1985). Segmental phonology of modern English. *Linguistic Inquiry, 16*, 57–116.

Halle, M., & Vergnaud, J.-R. (1981). Harmony processes. In W. Klein & W. Levelt (Eds.), *Crossing the boundaries in linguistics* (pp. 1–22). Dordrecht: Reidel.

Halliday, M. A. K. (1961). Categories of the theory of grammar. *Word, 17*, 241–292.

Halliday, M. A. K. (1967). *Intonation and grammar in British English*. The Hague: Mouton.

Halliday, M. A. K. (2005). Guest contribution. A note on systemic functional linguistics and the study of language disorders. *Clinical Linguistics and Phonetics, 19*, 133–135.

Halliday, M. A. K., & Matthiessen, C. M. I. M. (2004). *An introduction to functional grammar* (3rd ed.). London: Arnold.

Hardcastle, W., & Gibbon, F. (1997). Electropalatography and its clinical applications. In M. J. Ball & C. Code (Eds.), *Instrumental clinical phonetics* (pp. 149–193). London: Whurr.

Harris, J. (1990). Segmental complexity and phonological government. *Phonology, 7*, 255–300.

Harris, J. (1994). *English sound structure*. Oxford: Blackwell.

Harris, J. (2005). Vowel reduction as information loss. In P. Carr, J. Durand, & C. J. Ewen (Eds.), *Headhood, elements, specification and contrastivity* (pp. 119–132). Amsterdam: Benjamins.

Harris, J., & Cottam, P. (1985). Phonetic features and phonological features in speech assessment. *British Journal of Disorders in Communication, 20,* 61–74.

Harris, J., & Gussmann, E. (2002). Word final onsets. *University College London Working Papers in Linguistics, 14,* 1–42.

Harris, J., & Lindsey, G. (1995). The elements of phonological representation. In J. Durand & F. Katamba (Eds.), *Frontiers of phonology* (pp. 34–79). London: Longmans.

Harris, J., & Lindsey, G. (2000). Vowel patterns in sound and mind. In N. Burton-Roberts, P. Carr, & G. Docherty (Eds.), *Phonological knowledge, conceptual and empirical issues* (pp. 185–205). Oxford: Oxford University Press.

Harris, J., Watson, J., & Bates, S. (1999). Prosody and melody in vowel disorder. *Journal of Linguistics, 35,* 489–525.

Harris, Z. S. (1944). Simultaneous components in phonology. *Language, 20,* 181–205.

Harrison, P. (1996). *The acquisition of melodic primes in infancy.* Paper presented at the 4th Phonology Meeting, University of Manchester.

Hawkins, S. (2003). Roles and representations of systematic fine phonetic detail in speech understanding. *Journal of Phonetics, 31,* 373–405.

Hawkins, S. and Smith, R. (2001). Polysp: a polysystemic, phonetically-rich approach to speech understanding. *Italian Journal of Linguistics – Rivista di Linguistica, 13,* 99–188.

Hayes, B. (1981). *A metrical theory of stress rules.* Doctoral dissertation, MIT, Cambridge, MA.

Hayes, B. (1995). *Metrical stress theory: Principles and case studies.* Chicago: Chicago University Press.

Henderson, E. J. A. (1949). Prosodies in Siamese. *Asia Major, 1,* 189–215.

Heselwood, B. (1997). A case of nasal clicks for target sonorants: A feature geometry account. *Clinical Linguistics and Phonetics, 11,* 43–61.

Hewlett, N. and Waters, D. (2004). Gradient change in the acquisition of phonology. *Clinical Linguistics and Phonetics, 18,* 6-8.

Hockett, C. (1958). *A course in modern linguistics.* New York: Macmillan.

Hodson, B. (1980). *The assessment of phonological processes.* Danville, IL: Interstate Inc.

Hodson, B., & Paden, E. (1991). *Targeting intelligible speech: A phonological approach to remediation* (2nd ed.). Austin, TX: Pro-Ed.

Hooper, J. B. (1976). *An introduction to natural generative phonology.* New York: Academic Press.

Howard, S. (2004). Connected speech processes in developmental speech impairment: Observations from an electropalatographic perspective. *Clinical Linguistics and Phonetics, 18,* 407-417.

Howard, S., & Heselwood, B. (2007). *Clinical phonetics and phonology: Analyzing speech in a clinical context.* New York: Academic Press.

Howard, S., Wells, B. and Local, J. (2008). Connected speech. In Ball, M. J., Perkins, M., Müller, N. And Howard, S. (Eds.), *The Handbook of Clinical Linguistics* (pp. 583-602). Oxford: Blackwell.

Hume, E. (1994). *Front vowels, coronal consonants and their interaction in nonlinear phonology.* New York: Garland. (1992 Cornell dissertation)

Hurch, B., & Rhodes, R. A. W. (Eds.). (1996). *Natural phonology: The state of the art* (Trends in Linguistics). Berlin: Mouton de Gruyter.

Hyman, L. (1975). *Phonology: Theory and analysis.* New York: Holt, Rinehart, and Winston.

Ingram, D. (1981). *Procedures for the phonological analysis of children's language.* Baltimore: University Park Press.

Ingram, D. (1997). Generative phonology. In M. J. Ball & R. Kent (Eds.), *The new phonologies: Developments in clinical linguistics* (pp. 7–33). San Diego: Singular.

Jakobson, R., Fant, C. G. M., & Halle, M. (1952). *Preliminaries to speech analysis: The distinctive features and their correlates.* Technical Report 13. Cambridge, MA: Acoustics Laboratory, MIT.

Jakobson, R., & Halle, M. (1956). *Fundamentals of language.* The Hague: Mouton.

Jones, D. (1957). *The history and meaning of the term "phoneme."* London: International Phonetic Association.

Jones, D. (1976). *The phoneme. Its nature and its use.* Cambridge, England: Cambridge University Press.

Kager, R. (1999). *Optimality theory.* Cambridge, England: Cambridge University Press.

Katamba, F. (1989). *An introduction to phonology.* London: Longmans.

Kaye, J. (1990). Coda-licensing. *Phonology, 7,* 301–330.

Kaye, J., & Lowenstamm, J. (1984). De la syllabicité. In F. Dell, J. Hirst, & J.-R. Vergnaud (Eds.), *Forme sonore du langage* (pp. 123–160). Paris: Herman.

Kaye, J., Lowenstamm, J., & Vergnaud, J.-R. (1985). The internal structure of phonological elements: A theory of charm and government. *Phonology Yearbook, 2,* 305–328.

Kaye, J., Lowenstamm, J., & Vergnaud, J.-R. (1990). Constituent structure and government in phonology. *Phonology, 7,* 193–232.

Kenstowicz, M. (1994). *Phonology in generative grammar.* Oxford: Blackwell.

Kent, R. D. (1996). Developments in theoretical understanding of speech and its disorders. In M. J. Ball & M. Duckworth (Eds.), *Advances in clinical phonetics* (pp. 1–26). Philadelphia: Benjamins.

Kent, R. D. (1997). Gestural phonology: Basic concepts and applications in speech-language pathology. In M. J. Ball & R. D. Kent (Eds.), *The new phonologies* (pp. 247–268). San Diego: Singular.

Khan, L., & Lewis, N. (2002). *Khan-Lewis Phonological Analysis* (2nd ed., KLPA-2). Bloomington, MN: Pearson Assessments.

Kingston, J., & Cohen, A. H. (1992). Extending articulatory phonology. *Phonetica, 49,* 194–204.

Kiparsky, P. (1973). "Elsewhere" in phonology. In S. Anderson & P. Kiparsky (Eds.), *A Festschrift for Morris Halle* (pp. 93–106). New York: Holt.

Kiparsky, P. (1982a). Lexical morphology and phonology. In I.-S. Yang (Ed.), *Linguistics in the morning calm* (pp. 3–91). Seoul: Hanshin.

Kiparsky, P. (1982b). From cyclic phonology to lexical phonology. In H. van der Hulst & N. Smith (Eds.), *The structure of phonological representations* (Part I, pp. 131–175). Dordrecht: Foris.

Kiparsky, P. (1985). Some consequences of lexical phonology. *Phonology Yearbook, 2,* 83–138.

Kula, N. (2002). *The phonology of verbal derivation in Bemba.* PhD dissertation, Leiden University, Netherlands.

Ladefoged, P. (1971). *Preliminaries to linguistic phonetics.* Chicago: University of Chicago Press.

Ladefoged, P. (1993). *A course in phonetics* (3rd ed.). Orlando: Harcourt Brace.

Lakoff, G. (1993). Cognitive phonology. In J. Goldsmith (Ed.), *The last phonological rule* (pp. 117–145). Chicago: Chicago University Press.

Lass, R. (1984). *Phonology.* Cambridge, England: Cambridge University Press.

Leben, W. (1973). *Suprasegmental phonology.* Unpublished PhD dissertation, MIT, Cambridge, MA.

Levelt, C. (1995, September). *Unfaithful kids: Place of articulation patterns in early child language.* Paper presented at the Department of Cognitive Science, Johns Hopkins University, Baltimore.

Levin, J. (1985). *A metrical theory of syllabicity.* PhD dissertation, MIT, Cambridge, MA.

Liberman, M. (1975). *The intonational system of English.* New York: Garland Publishing.

Liberman, M., & A. Prince (1977). On stress and linguistic rhythm. *Linguistic Inquiry, 8,* 249–336.

Local, J. K. (2003). Variable domains and variable relevance: Interpreting phonetic exponents. *Journal of Phonetics, 31,* 321–339.

Lorentz, J. P. (1976). An analysis of some deviant phonological rules of English. In D. M. Morehead & A. E. Morehead (Eds.), *Normal and deficient child language* (pp. 29–60). Baltimore: University Park Press.

Maddieson, I. (1984). *Patterns of sound.* Cambridge, England: Cambridge University Press.

McCarthy, J. (1979). *Formal problems in semitic phonology and morphology.* PhD dissertation, MIT, Cambridge, MA. (Published by Garland Publishers, New York)

McCarthy, J. (1988). Feature geometry and dependency: A review. *Phonetica, 43,* 84–108.

McCarthy, J. (2002). *A thematic guide to optimality theory* (Research Surveys in Linguistics). Cambridge, England: Cambridge University Press.

McCarthy, J., & Prince, A. (1993). Generalized alignment. In G. Booij & J. van Marle (Eds.), *Yearbook of morphology* (pp. 79–153). Dordrecht: Kluwer.

McMahon, A. (2000). *Change, chance and optimality.* Oxford: Oxford University Press.

Miccio, A. (2002). Clinical problem solving: Assessment of phonological disorders. *American Journal of Speech-Language Pathology, 11,* 221–229.

Müller, N., Ball, M. J., & Rutter, B. (2006). A profiling approach to phonological disorder. *Advances in Speech-Language Pathology, 8,* 176–189.

Müller, N., Ball, M. J., & Rutter, B. (2008). An idiosyncratic case of /r/ disorder: Application of principles from systemic phonology and systemic functional linguistics. *Asia-Pacific Journal of Speech Language and Hearing, 11,* 269–281.

Nespor, M., & Vogel, I. (1986). *Prosodic phonology.* Dordrecht: Foris.

Nickels, L., & Howard, D. (1999). Effects of lexical stress on aphasic word production. *Clinical Linguistics and Phonetics, 13,* 269–294.

Niemi, J., Koivuselka-Sallinen, P., & Hanninen, R. (1985). Phoneme errors in Broca's aphasia: Three Finnish cases. *Brain and Language, 26,* 28–48.

Oetting, J., & Rice, M. (1993). Plural acquisition in children with specific language impairment. *Journal of Speech, Language and Hearing Research, 36,* 1236–1248.

Ogden, J. A. (1995). *An exploration of phonetic exponency in Firthian prosodic analysis: Form and substance in Finnish phonology.* DPhil thesis, University of York.

Ogden, R. (1999). A declarative account of strong and weak auxiliaries in English. *Phonology, 16,* 55–92.

Ogden, R. A., & Local, J. K. (1994). Disentangling prosodies from autosegments: A note on the misrepresentation of a research tradition. *Journal of Linguistics, 30,* 477–498.

Ogden, R., Hawkins, S. House, J. Huckvale, M., Local, J., Carter, P, Dankovicova, J. and Heid, S. (2000). ProSynth: an integrated prosodic approach to device-independent, natural-sounding speech synthesis. *Computer Speech and Language, 14,* 177-210.

Ohala, D. (1999). *Journal of Communication Disorders, 32,* 397–422.

Ohala, J. (1990). *Alternatives to the sonority hierarchy for explaining segmental sequential constraints.* Paper presented at the Parasession on the Syllable in Phonetics and Phonology, Chicago Linguistics Society.

Oller, K. (1973). Regularities in abnormal child phonology. *Journal of Speech and Hearing Disorders, 38,* 35–46.

Palmer, F. R. (Ed.). (1970). *Prosodic analysis.* London: Oxford University Press.

Pan, N., & Roussel, N. (2008). Do /s/-initial clusters imply CVCC sequences? Evidence from disordered speech. *Clinical Linguistics and Phonetics, 22,* 127–135.

Pandeli, H., Eska, J., Ball, M. J., & Rahilly, J. (1997). Problems of phonetic transcription: The case of the Hiberno-English flat alveolar fricative. *Journal of the International Phonetic Association, 27,* 65–75.

Pater, J. (1997). Minimal violation and phonological development. *Language Acquisition, 6,* 201–253.

Pater, J. and Werle, A. (2000). Direction of assimilation in child consonant harmony. *The Canadian Journal of Linguistics, 48,* 385-408.

Patte, D. S., Safran, E. M., & Martin, N. (1987). Specifying the nature of the production deficit in conduction aphasia: A case study. *Language and Cognitive Processes, 2,* 43–84.

Pike, K. L. (1947). *Phonemics: A Technique for Reducing Language to Writing.* Ann Arbor: University of Michigan Press.

Prince, A. (1980). A metrical stress theory for Estonian quantity. *Linguistic Inquiry, 11,* 511–562.

Prince, A. (1983). Relating to the grid. *Linguistic Inquiry, 14,* 19–100.

Prince, A., & Smolensky, P. (1993). *Optimality theory: Constraint interaction in generative grammar.* Technical Report 2, Rutgers University Center for Cognitive Science. Cambridge, MA: MIT Press.

Reynolds, J. (1990). Abnormal vowel patterns in phonological disorder: Some data and a hypothesis. *British Journal of Disorders of Communication, 25,* 115–148.

Robins, R. H. (1957). Aspects of prosodic analsysis. *Proceedings of the University of Durham Philosophical Society, Series B, 1.* 1-12. (Reprinted in Palmer, F. (Ed) (1970) *Prosodic Analysis* (pp. 188-200), Oxford: Oxford University Press.)

Roca, I. (1994). *Generative phonology.* London: Routledge.

Roca, I., & Johnson, W. (1999). *A workbook in phonology.* Oxford: Blackwell.

Romani, C., & Calabrese, A. (1998). Syllabic constraints in the phonological errors of an aphasic patient. *Brain and Language, 64,* 83–121.

Rutter, B. (2008). Repair sequences in dysarthric conversational speech: A study in interactional phonetics. Unpublished Ph.D. dissertation, the University of Louisiana at Lafayette.

Sagey, E. (1986). *The representation of feature and relations in nonlinear phonology.* Unpublished PhD dissertation, MIT, Cambridge, MA.

Sagey, E. (1990). *The representation of features in non-linear phonology: The articulator node hierarchy.* New York: Garland.

Saltzman, E., & Kelso, J. A. S. (1987). Skilled actions: A task dynamic approach. *Psychological Review, 94,* 84–106.

Saltzman, E. L., & Munhall, K. G. (1989). A dynamical approach to gestural patterning in speech production. *Ecological Psychology, 1,* 333–382.

Selkirk, E. (1984). *Phonology and syntax: The relationship between sound and structure.* Cambridge, MA: MIT Press.

Shriberg, L., & Kwiatkowski, J. (1980). *Natural process analysis.* New York: Wiley.

Smith, N. (1973). *The acquisition of phonology: A case study.* Cambridge, England: Cambridge University Press.

Smolensky, P. (1996). *The initial state and 'richness of the base' in optimality theory.* Technical Report, Department of Cognitive Science, Johns Hopkins University. Baltimore.

Sosa, A.V., & Bybee, J. (2008). A cognitive approach to clinical phonology. In M. J. Ball, M. Perkins, N. Müller, & S. Howard (Eds.), *Handbook of clinical linguistics* (pp. 480–490). Oxford: Blackwell.

Spencer, A. (1984). A non-linear analysis of phonological disability. *Journal of Communication Disorders, 17,* 325–348.

Spencer, A. (1996). *Phonology.* Oxford: Blackwell.

Sprigg. K. (2005). Types of r prosodic piece in a Firthian phonology of English, and their vowel and consonant systems. *York Papers in Linguistics, Series 2, 4,* 125-156.

Sprigg, R. K. (1957). Junction in spoken Burmese. In W. S. Allen (Ed.), *Studies in linguistic analysis* (pp. 104–138). Special volume of the Philological Society. Oxford: Blackwell.

Stampe, D. (1969). The acquisition of phonetic representation. In *Proceedings of the 5th Regional Meeting of the Chicago Linguistics Society* (pp. 443–454). Chicago: University of Chicago Press.

Stampe, D. (1979). *A dissertation on natural phonology.* New York: Garland.

Stemberger, J. P., & Bernhardt, B. (1997). Optimality theory. In M. J. Ball & R. D. Kent (Eds.), *The new phonologies* (pp. 211–245). San Diego: Singular.

Stemberger, J. P., & Bernhardt, B. H. (1999). The emergence of faithfulness. In B. MacWhinney (Ed.), *The emergence of language* (pp. 417–446). Mahweh, NJ: Erlbaum.

Steriade, D. (1982). *Greek prosodies and the nature of syllabification.* PhD dissertation, Department of Linguistics Dissertation Series, MIT, Cambridge, MA.

Steriade, D. (1987). Redundant values. In A. Bosch, B. Need, & E. Schiller (Eds.), *Papers from the parasession on autosegmental and metrical phonology* (pp. 339–362). Chicago: Chicago Linguistics Society.

Steriade, D. (1990). Gestures and autosegments. In J. Kingston & M. Beckman (Eds.), *Papers in laboratory phonology I* (pp. 382–397). Cambridge, England: Cambridge University Press.

Studdert-Kennedy, M., & Goodell, E. (1995). Gestures, features and segments in early child speech. In B. deGelder & J. Morais (Eds.), *Speech and reading: A comparative approach* (pp. 65-88). Oxford: Erlbaum UK.

Sussman, H. (1984). A neuronal model for syllable representation. *Brain and Language, 22,* 167–177.

Tatham, M. (1984). Towards a cognitive phonetics. *Journal of Phonetics, 12,* 37–47.

Tench, P. (1992a). From prosodic analysis to systemic phonology. In P. Tench (Ed.), *Studies in systemic phonology* (pp. 1–18). London: Pinter.

Tench, P. (1992b). *Studies in systemic phonology.* London: Pinter.

Tesar, B., & Smolensky, P. (1998). Learnability in optimality theory. *Linguistic Inquiry, 29,* 229–268.

Tesar, B., & Smolensky, P. (2000). *Learnability in optimality theory.* Cambridge, MA: MIT Press.

Trubetzkoy, N. S. (1969). *Principles of phonology* (C. A. M. Baltaxe, Trans.). Berkeley: University of California Press. (Original work published 1939)

Van Riper, C. (1978). *Speech Correction: Principles and Methods.* Englewood Cliffs, N.J.: Prentice-Hall.

Velleman, S. L., & Shriberg, L. D. (1999). Metrical analysis of children with suspected developmental apraxia of speech and inappropriate stress. *Journal of Speech Language and Hearing Research, 42,* 1444–1460.

Vergnaud, J.-R.(1977). Formal properties of phonological rules. In R. Butts & J. Hintikka (Eds.), *Basic problems in methodology and linguistics.* Amsterdam: Reidel.

Waterson, N. (1970). Some aspects of the nominal forms of the Turkish word. In F. R. Palmer (Ed.), *Prosodic analysis* (pp. 174–187). London: Oxford University Press. (Original work published 1956)

Waterson, N. (1970). Some speech forms in an English child: A phonological study. *Transactions of the Philological Society, 1970,* 1–24.

Waterson, N. (1971). Child phonology: A prosodic view. *Journal of Linguistics, 7,* 179–211.

Waterson, N. (1987). *Prosodic phonology: The theory and its application to language acquisition and speech processing.* Newcastle upon Tyne: Grevatt and Grevatt.

Weiner, F. (1979). *Phonological process analysis.* Baltimore: University Park Press.

Weismer, G., Tjaden, T., & Kent, R. D. (1995). Can articulatory behavior in speech disorders be accounted for by theories of normal speech production? *Journal of Phonetics, 23,* 149–164.

Wheeler, D., & Touretzky, D. (1993). A connectionist implementation of cognitive phonology. In J. Goldsmith (Ed.), *The last phonological rule* (pp. 146–172). Chicago: Chicago University Press.

Williams, A. L., & Dinnsen, D. A. (1987). A problem of allophonic variation in a speech disordered child. *Innovations in Linguistics Education, 5,* 85–90.

Wyllie-Smith, L., McLeod, S., & Ball, M. J. (2006). Normally developing and speech impaired children's adherence to the sonority hypothesis. *Clinical Linguistics and Phonetics, 20,* 271–291.

Yavaş, M. (2000, August 16–19). *Sonority effects of vowel nuclei in onset duration.* Poster presented at VIIIth International Clinical Phonetics and Linguistics Association Conference, Edinburgh.

Yavaş, M., & Core, C. (2001). Phonemic awareness of coda consonants and sonority in bi-lingual children. *Clinical Linguistics and Phonetics, 15,* 35–39.

Yavaş, M., & Gogate, L. (1999). Phoneme awareness in children: A function of sonority. *Journal of Psycholinguistic Research, 28,* 245–260.

Young, D. (1992). English consonant clusters: A systemic approach. In P. Tench (Ed.), *Studies in systemic phonology* (pp. 44–69). London: Pinter.

ANSWERS TO EXERCISES

CHAPTER 1

Exercise 1.1

The data suggest the following belong to separate phonemes:

a. /ɑɨ/, /aɪ/, /aɨ/, /aʊ/, /əɪ/, /ɛʊ/

b. /p/, /t/, /k/, /b/, /s/, /l/, /ʃ/, /ʁ/, /d/, /m/, /f/, /n/

Exercise 1.2

The data suggest that allophones pattern as follows:

a. /p/-[p˭] syllable initial following /ʃ/; [pʰ] syllable initial otherwise.

/t/-[t˭] syllable initial following /ʃ/; [tʰ] syllable initial otherwise.
/k/-[k˭] syllable initial following /s/; [kʰ] syllable initial otherwise.

b. /b/-[b] word initially and medially following a nasal; elsewhere [β].

/d/-[d] word initially and medially following a nasal; elsewhere [ð].
/g/-[g] word initially and medially following a nasal; elsewhere [ɣ].

Exercise 1.3

The target realization map for this client is as follows:

Target	Realization
/p/	[b]
/t/	[d]
/k/	[d]
/b/	[b]
/d/	[d]
/g/	[d]
/m/	[m]
/n/	[n]
/ŋ/	[n]

Exercise 1.4

Street

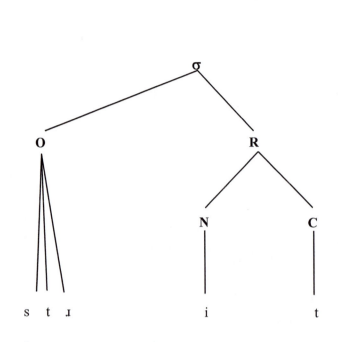

Restrict

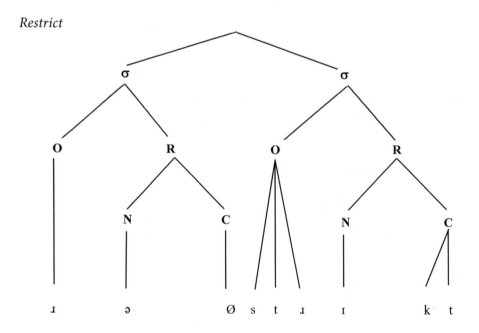

Racetrack

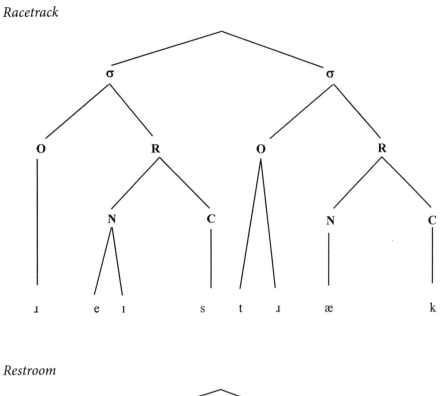

Restroom

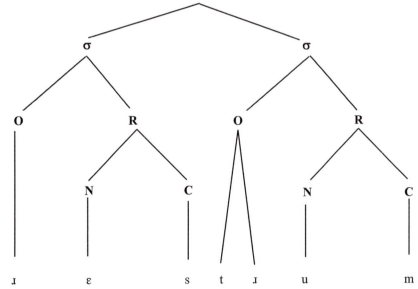

Extract

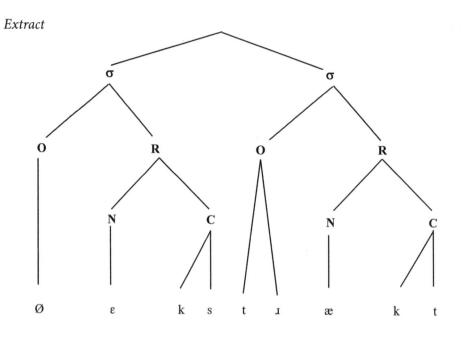

Exercise 1.5

Syllable tree diagrams will show that this client's realizations of /ɹ/ are as follows:

    i. In word initial onset position we find either [ɥ] or [w].
   ii. In word internal onset position we find [ʋ].
  iii. In coda position /ɹ/ is deleted.

CHAPTER 2

Exercise 2.1

Onset

Trap	1-4
Brush	1-4
Play	1-4
Muse	3-5
Dwell	1-5
Twice	1-5
Drain	1-4
Claim	1-4
Green	1-4
Quick	1-5

Coda

Help	4-1
Task	2-1
Hand	3-1

Delve	4-2
Part	4-1
Aft	2-1
Harm	4-3
Lamp	3-1
Malt	4-1
Turf	4-2

Findings: The outermost consonant is always lower than the inner one; with onsets, the difference between values is at least 2, often 3; with codas, the difference can be as low as 1.

Exercise 2.2

Onset

Stop	2-1
Scrape	2-1-4
Splash	2-1-4
Scar	2-1
Spin	2-1
Strike	2-1-4
Spread	2-1-4
Squeak	2-1-5
Sphere	2-2

Coda

Cats	1-2
Ox	1-2
Dogs	1-2
Width	1-2
Hides	1-2
Eighth	1-2
Helps	4-1-2
Six	1-2
Act	1-1

With onsets, if the outermost consonant is greater or equal to the second consonant, it is always /s/. Third consonants in onsets are always greater than the second. In codas, final consonants may be greater than penultimate ones, but in this case they are usually morphemes (plural, etc.). Monomorphemic examples can be found, however, also with the two consonants of equal value.

Exercise 2.3

Adjuncts shown by plus sign:

Spray	/s+pɹeɪ/
Texts	/tɛk+st+s/
Strong	/s+tɹɒŋ/
Lacked	/læk+t/
Scrape	/s+kɹeɪp/
Sculpts	/s+kʌlp+t+s/

Sixths	/sɪk+s+θ+s/	
Split	/s+plɪt/	

Exercise 2.4

Item	Target	Realization	
Swim	/swɪm/	[fɪm]	2-5 > 2
Snail	/sneɪl/	[n̥eɪl]	2-3 > 3
Slow	/sloʊ/	[ɬoʊ]	2-4 > 2
Smile	/smaɪl/	[m̥aɪl]	2-3 > 3
Slight	/slaɪt/	[ɬaɪt]	2-4 > 2
Sweet	/swit/	[fit]	2-5 > 2
Snow	/snoʊ/	[n̥oʊ]	2-3 > 3
Smoke	smoʊk/	[m̥oʊk]	2-3 > 3

The realization combines the voiceless/friction of the /s/ with the place/manner of the second consonant.

CHAPTER 3

Exercise 3.1

a. Hindi

/p, t̪, ʈ, k, pʰ, t̪ʰ, ʈʰ, kʰ, b, d̪, ɖ, g, bʱ, d̪ʱ, ɖʱ, gʱ/

	p	t̪	ʈ	k	pʰ	t̪ʰ	ʈʰ	kʰ	b	d̪	ɖ	g	bʱ	d̪ʱ	ɖʱ	gʱ
sonorant	−	−	−	−	−	−	−	−	−	−	−	−	−	−	−	−
syll	−	−	−	−	−	−	−	−	−	−	−	−	−	−	−	−
cons	+	+	+	+	+	+	+	+	+	+	+	+	+	+	+	+
ant	+	+	−	−	+	+	−	−	+	+	−	−	+	+	−	−
cor	−	+	+	−	−	+	+	−	−	+	+	−	−	+	+	−
high	−	−	−	+	−	−	−	+	−	−	−	+	−	−	−	+
low	−	−	−	−	−	−	−	−	−	−	−	−	−	−	−	−
back	−	−	−	+	−	−	−	+	−	−	−	+	−	−	−	+
dist	−	−	+	−	−	−	+	−	−	−	+	−	−	−	+	−
nas	−	−	−	−	−	−	−	−	−	−	−	−	−	−	−	−
lat	−	−	−	−	−	−	−	−	−	−	−	−	−	−	−	−
cont	−	−	−	−	−	−	−	−	−	−	−	−	−	−	−	−
voice	−	−	−	−	−	−	−	−	+	+	+	+	+	+	+	+
tense	−	−	−	−	+	+	+	+	−	−	−	−	−	−	−	−
h.s.p.	−	−	−	−	−	−	−	−	−	−	−	−	+	+	+	+

Note: Some of the features not needed to contrast this set of consonants are omitted.
h.s.p. = heightened subglottal pressure.

b. Turkish

/i, y, u, ɯ, e, ø, o/

	i	y	u	ɯ	e	ø	o
sonorant	+	+	+	+	+	+	+
syll	+	+	+	+	+	+	+
cons	–	–	–	–	–	–	–
high	+	+	+	+	–	–	–
low	–	–	–	–	–	–	–
back	–	–	+	+	–	–	+
round	–	+	+	–	–	+	+
cont	+	+	+	+	+	+	+
voice	+	+	+	+	+	+	+
tense	+	+	+	+	+	+	+

Note: Some of the features not needed to contrast this set of vowels are omitted.

c. Russian

/f, fʲ, v, vʲ, s, sʲ, z, zʲ, z, zʲ, ʃ, ʒ, x, xʲ/

	f	fʲ	v	vʲ	s	sʲ	z	zʲ	ʃ	ʒ	x	xʲ
sonorant	–	–	–	–	–	–	–	–	–	–	–	–
syll	–	–	–	–	–	–	–	–	–	–	–	–
cons	+	+	+	+	+	+	+	+	+	+	+	+
ant	+	+	+	+	+	+	+	+	–	–	–	–
cor	–	–	–	–	+	+	+	+	+	+	–	–
high	–	+	–	+	–	+	–	+	+	+	+	+
low	–	–	–	–	–	–	–	–	–	–	+	–
back	–	–	–	–	–	–	–	–	–	–	+	–
nas	–	–	–	–	–	–	–	–	–	–	–	–
lat	–	–	–	–	–	–	–	–	–	–	–	–
cont	+	+	+	+	+	+	+	+	+	+	+	+
voice	–	–	+	+	–	–	+	+	–	+	–	–

Note: Some of the features not needed to contrast this set of consonants are omitted.

Exercise 3.2

Reexamine the clinical data from Exercise 1.3. Draw up a list of distinctive features used by the client for this set of consonants. Draw up a list of distinctive features of the target set not used correctly by the client. What problems do you encounter in making this analysis?

Features used by client:

[±son, –syll, +cons, +ant, ±cor, –high, –low, –back, +voice, ±nasal, –cont]

(We have omitted from this list some features not needed to contrast the set of consonants concerned.)

Features not used correctly:

[–voice, –ant, +high, +back, –voice]

The main problem is that listing the features separately does not indicate that it is combinations of features that the client is using incorrectly in the realization of velar targets as alveolars. Also, this one place change involves errors to three different features.

Exercise 3.3

i. [i e æ ɑ o u]

	i	e	æ	ɑ	o	u
high	*u*	*m*	*u*	*u*	*m*	*u*
low	*u*	*u*	*m*	*u*	*u*	*u*
back	–	–	*m*	*u*	+	+
round	*u*	*u*	*u*	*u*	*u*	*u*
Complexity	1	2	2	0	2	1

Complexity value: 8.

ii. [i e æ ɑ o u]

	i	e	æ	ɑ	o	u
high	*u*	*m*	*u*	*u*	*u*	*u*
low	*u*	*u*	*m*	*u*	*m*	*u*
back	–	–	*u*	*u*	*u*	+
round	*u*	*u*	*u*	*u*	*m*	*u*
Complexity	1	2	1	0	2	1

Complexity value: 7.

Exercise 3.4

Set 1 changes voiceless obstruents to voiced. Obstruents are unmarked if voiceless, so this voicing change moves from unmarked to marked for voice for all eight consonants.

Set 2 changes obstruents to nasals. Nasals are marked, so all six consonants have changed from unmarked to marked for nasality. Nasals (being sonorants) are unmarked when voiced, marked when voiceless. So the change of /p, t, k/ to [m̥, n̥, ŋ̊] creates marked nasals.

Therefore, the realizations in Set 1 are less marked than those in Set 2.

CHAPTER 4

Exercise 4.1

Variants of the regular past tense suffix in English: /-t/, /-d/, /-ɪd/.

Exercise 4.2

A phonological rule that expresses obstruents become rounded when preceding a rounded vowel:

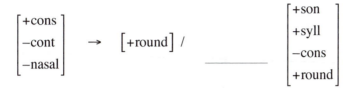

$$\begin{bmatrix} +\text{cons} \\ -\text{cont} \\ -\text{nasal} \end{bmatrix} \rightarrow [+\text{round}] / \underline{\hspace{2cm}} \begin{bmatrix} +\text{son} \\ +\text{syll} \\ -\text{cons} \\ +\text{round} \end{bmatrix}$$

Exercise 4.3

A phonological rule that expresses that /t/ deletes when second member of final three consonant clusters.

$$/t/ \quad \rightarrow \quad \emptyset / \quad C \underline{\hspace{2cm}} C \#$$

Exercise 4.4

A phonological rule that expresses the pattern in Turkish that high vowels in suffixes agree in terms of [back] and [round] with the preceding vowel (assuming there is a consonant between the preceding vowel and the suffix vowel). Note use of Greek lowercase notation.

$$\begin{bmatrix} +\text{son} \\ +\text{syll} \\ -\text{cons} \\ +\text{high} \end{bmatrix} \rightarrow \begin{bmatrix} \alpha \text{ back} \\ \beta \text{ round} \end{bmatrix} / \begin{bmatrix} +\text{son} \\ +\text{syll} \\ -\text{cons} \\ \alpha \text{ back} \\ \beta \text{ round} \end{bmatrix} C \underline{\hspace{2cm}}$$

Exercise 4.5

Rule ordering account for Canadian raising and voicing of intervocalic /t/ in Canadian English.

	write	writer	ride	rider
	raɪt	raɪtɚ	raɪd	raɪdɚ
Canadian raising	ʌɪ	ʌɪ	n.a.	n.a.
Intervocalic voicing	n.a.	d	n.a.	n.a.
	rʌɪt	rʌɪdɚ	raɪd	raɪdɚ

Note: If the rules were reversed, the intervocalic voicing would block the raising.

Exercise 4.6

The set of rules to account for the disordered data, using the target form as the input.

Rule 1: Aspirated fortis plosives become ejectives.

$$\begin{bmatrix} +\text{cons} \\ -\text{cont} \\ -\text{voice} \\ -\text{nasal} \\ +\text{tense} \end{bmatrix} \rightarrow \begin{bmatrix} +\text{eject} \\ -\text{tense} \end{bmatrix}$$

Rule 2: Voiced plosives become fortis aspirated.

$$\begin{bmatrix} +\text{cons} \\ -\text{cont} \\ +\text{voice} \\ -\text{nasal} \end{bmatrix} \rightarrow \begin{bmatrix} -\text{voice} \\ +\text{tense} \end{bmatrix}$$

Rule 3: /s/ + /p, t, k/ loses /s/.

$$/\text{s}/ \quad \rightarrow \quad \varnothing \ / \ \underline{\hspace{2cm}} \begin{bmatrix} +\text{cons} \\ -\text{cont} \\ -\text{nasal} \end{bmatrix}$$

Rule 1 must be ordered before Rule 2, to avoid target voiced stops becoming ejectives.

CHAPTER 5

Exercise 5.1

a. Hindi

/p, ṭ, t̪, k, pʰ, t̪ʰ, ṭʰ, kʰ, b, ḍ, d̪, g, bʱ, d̪ʱ, ḍʱ, gʱ/

		p	ṭ	t̪	k	pʰ	t̪ʰ	ṭʰ	kʰ	b	ḍ	d̪	g	bʱ	d̪ʱ	ḍʱ	gʱ
sonorant		−	−	−	−	−	−	−	−	−	−	−	−	−	−	−	−
approx		−	−	−	−	−	−	−	−	−	−	−	−	−	−	−	−
cons		+	+	+	+	+	+	+	+	+	+	+	+	+	+	+	+
LABIAL		✓				✓				✓				✓			
	Round	−				−				−				−			
CORONAL			✓	✓			✓	✓			✓	✓			✓	✓	
anterior	Ant		+	−			+	−			+	−			+	−	
distributed	Dist		−	−			−	−			−	−			−	−	
DORSAL					✓				✓				✓				✓
	High				+				+				+				+
	Low				−				−				−				−
	Back				+				+				+				+
nas		−	−	−	−	−	−	−	−	−	−	−	−	−	−	−	−
lat		−	−	−	−	−	−	−	−	−	−	−	−	−	−	−	−
cont		−	−	−	−	−	−	−	−	−	−	−	−	−	−	−	−
voice		−	−	−	−	−	−	−	−	+	+	+	+	+	+	+	+
sprd gl		−	−	−	−	+	+	+	+	−	−	−	−	+	+	+	+
con gl		−	−	−	−	−	−	−	−	−	−	−	−	−	−	−	−

Note: Some of the features not needed to contrast this set of consonants are omitted.

b. Turkish
/i, y, u, ɯ, e, ø, o/

		i	y	u	ɯ	e	ø	o
sonorant		+	+	+	+	+	+	+
approx		–	–	–	–	–	–	–
cons		–	–	–	–	–	–	–
Labial			✓	✓			✓	✓
	Round		+	+			+	+
Coronal								
Dorsal		✓	✓	✓	✓	✓	✓	✓
	High	+	+	+	+	–	–	–
	Low	–	–	–	–	–	–	–
	Back	–	–	+	+	–	–	+
nas		–	–	–	–	–	–	–
cont		+	+	+	+	+	+	+
voice		+	+	+	+	+	+	+

Note: Some of the features not needed to contrast this set of vowels are omitted.

c. Russian
/f, fʲ, v, vʲ, s, sʲ, z, zʲ, ʃ, ʒ, x, xʲ/

		f	fʲ	v	vʲ	s	sʲ	z	zʲ	ʃ	ʒ	x	xʲ
sonorant		–	–	–	–	–	–	–	–	–	–	–	–
approx		–	–	–	–	–	–	–	–	–	–	–	–
cons		+	+	+	+	+	+	+	+	+	+	+	+
Labial		✓	✓	✓	✓								
	Round	–	–	–	–								
Coronal						✓	✓	✓	✓	✓	✓		
	Ant					+	+	+	+	–	–		
	Dist					–	–	–	–	+	+		
Dorsal			✓		✓		✓		✓			✓	✓
	High		+		+		+		+			+	+
	Low		–		–		–		–			–	–
	Back		–		–		–		–			+	–
nas		–	–	–	–	–	–	–	–	–	–	–	–
lat		–	–	–	–	–	–	–	–	–	–	–	–
cont		+	+	+	+	+	+	+	+	+	+	+	+
strident		+	+	+	+	+	+	+	+	+	+	–	–
voice		–	–	+	+	–	–	+	+	–	+	–	–
sprd gl		–	–	–	–	–	–	–	–	–	–	–	–
con gl		–	–	–	–	–	–	–	–	–	–	–	–

Note: Some of the features not needed to contrast this set of consonants are omitted.

Exercise 5.2

Changing from velar to alveolar would involve decoupling the [DORSAL] node and coupling in the [CORONAL] one. This compares with having to change four feature values in a purely binary system.

Exercise 5.3

Fully specified target:

	ɪ	ɛ	æ	ɔ	ʊ
high	+	–	–	–	+
low	–	–	+	–	–
back	–	–	–	+	+
tense	–	–	–	–	–
round	–	–	–	+	+

Fully specified realization:

	ɪ	æ	ɑ	ɒ	u
high	+	–	–	–	+
low	–	+	+	+	–
back	–	–	+	+	+
tense	+	–	+	–	+
round	–	–	–	+	+

Feature errors: 6.

Realization using markedness conventions:

	i	æ	ɑ	ɒ	u
high	+			–	+
low		+	+	+	
back	–	–			+
tense		–		–	
round				+	

Feature errors: 2.

Realization using radical underspecification:

	i	æ	ɑ	ɒ	u
high					
low		+		+	
back	–				+
tense					
round				+	

Feature errors: 1.

CHAPTER 6

Exercise 6.1

Allophonic alternations and derived environment rules:

  a. Allophonic alternations
  b. Derived environment rules
  c. Allophonic alternations
  d. Derived environment rules

Exercise 6.2

	happy	**wide**	**total**
Level 1		wid+th	
Level 2	happy +ness		total+ity+arian
Level 3	un+happiness	width+s	totalitarian+ism
	unhappiness	widths	totalitarianism

	ject	junct	mouse
Level 1	ob+ject	ad+junct	mice
Level 2			
Level 3	object+ing	adjuncts	
	objecting	adjuncts	mice's

Exercise 6.3

  a. Analysis into feet and syllables:

    [an-ti]_F [dis-e]_F [stab-lish-ment]_F [ar-ian-ism]_F
    (*-ism* may also count as two syllables)

  b. Analysis into phonological words and phrases:

    [Mary broke]_{PhP}[the Japanese [tea]_W [pot]_W]_{PhP}

  c. Two different IP analyses showing differences of meaning:

    [Thank you very much]_{IP}   sincere
    [Thank you]_{IP} [very much]_{IP} sarcastic

CHAPTER 7

Exercise 7.1

The process demonstrated in Exercise 7.1 is that of compensatory lengthening. With the nasal and stop consonants forming a singleton, and thus occupying a single timing slot, the vowel spreads to fill this slot.

Exercise 7.2

The underlying form of the nasal must be /n/ because it surfaces as this when preceding a vowel. A rule capturing the process could be any simple place assimilation rule, as shown in (19).

Exercise 7.3

The data in this exercise exhibit the spreading of the unified place features of [labial] and [coronal] from vowel to preceding consonant.

CHAPTER 8

Exercise 8.1

The following metrical grids represent the primary and secondary stressed syllables of the words in this exercise.

```
| x    .   |   | .    x   |   primary stress
| x    .   |   | .    x   |   secondary stress
| x    x   |   | x    x   |   syllables
   'merger'        'persuade'
```

```
| .   x   .   . | | .   .   x   . |   primary stress
| .   x   .   x | | x   .   x   . |   secondary stress
| x   x   x   x | | x   x   x   x |   syllables
    'investigate'        'horizontal'
```

Exercise 8.2

The following examples are usually treated as compounds, with stress on the first word: *carrot cake, snooker table, an Englishman*. On the other hand, the following are usually treated as simply nouns modified by an adjective: *apple pie, an English man, a leather jacket*.

Exercise 8.3

The first list of words involves the addition of the suffix *-ence*, which does not cause a shift in stress. In the second list of words, however, when the suffix *-ion* is added, a shift in stress to the penultimate syllable should be detected.

CHAPTER 9

Exercise 9.1

The client seems to be realizing /s/ and /z/ in a variety of ways: [j b d̥ d̥ x d ç h]. However, [j b] appears syllable initially word initial (SIWI), [d̥ d] syllable initially within the word (SIWW), and [ç h] syllable finally.

Exercise 9.2

The labial-velar approximant is limited to a prevocalic position in English. In this sense it always occupies a syllable onset. For this reason we have good reason to abstract it as a prosody of the vowel itself, rather than regard it as being in the same system as such freely distributed sounds as /s/.

Exercise 9.3

The words *home* and *room* certainly feature lip-rounding for the majority of the word, while nasality can be treated as a prosody of the word in *man*, and of the syllable rhyme in *sink*, *room*, and *lamp*. Place of articulation is generally paradigmatic; however, the places of velarity and bilabiality could be treated as prosodies of the coda in *sink* and *lamp*, respectively.

CHAPTER 10

Exercise 10.1

a. Plural *mouse-mice, louse-lice*: rule, as this change is not phonetically natural.
b. Plural *cat* + *[s]*, *dog* + *[z]*: process, as the agreement of voicing is natural.
c. Juxtapositional assimilation: *te[n] dogs, te[m] men, te[m] boys, te[ŋ] cups, te[ŋ] kids*: process, as the agreements in place are natural.
d. Vowel change: *prof[eɪ]ne–prof[æ]nity, obsc[i]ne–obsc[ɛ]nity*: rule, as this change is not phonetically natural.

Exercise 10.2

Which of the following processes effect systemic simplification, and which structural simplification?

a. Weak syllable deletion, for example, *umbrella* → ['bwɛlə]: structural
b. Reduplication, for example, *bottle* → [bɒbɒ]: structural
c. Consonant harmony, for example, *doggy* → [gɒgi]: structural
d. Context-sensitive voicing, where obstruents are voiced initially and voiceless finally: systemic (because all pairs of contrastive voiced-voiceless obstruents are reduced by 50% since the contrast has disappeared)

Exercise 10.3

K is deviant (systemic sound preference): Fricative preference in syllable final position; /d/ preference in syllable intial position (coinciding also with cluster reduction).
S is delayed (persisting normal processes): Cluster reduction, fricative stopping, consonant harmony, and context-sensitive voicing.
J is uneven (chronological mismatch): Showing velar consonant harmony, despite having clusters developed.

Exercise 10.4

Normal acquisition: Velar fronting; final consonant deletion; /s/ cluster reduction; liquid gliding to /ɹ/.
Functional load order: Final consonant deletion (also has morphological consequences); /s/ cluster reduction; velar fronting, liquid gliding to /ɹ/.

CHAPTER 11

Exercise 11.1

The candidate set and constraint violations for *spit* are shown below.

spɪt/	DEP-IO	MAX-IO	ONSET	NO-CODA	*COMPLEX
☞ [spɪt]				*	*
[sɪt]		*!		*	
[spɪ]		*!			*
[sə.pɪt]	*!	*		*	
[sə.pɪ]	*!	**			

Exercise 11.2

In order for both /bæθ/ and /sup/ to be correctly generated, the constraint FAITH would need to outrank all the output constraints, guaranteeing an alignment between the input forms and the surface form. This gradual promotion of faithfulness constraints over output constraints is the proposed model of language acquisition in OT.

Exercise 11.3

The following constraint ranking would bring about an optimal form of [kæti]:

No-Coda > Max-IO > Dep-IO

Equally, an equal ranking for the first two constraints would achieve the same effect. The crucial fact is that the constraint **DEP-IO** is ranked the lowest. The table below demonstrates how this would surface.

/kæt/	NO-CODA	MAX-IO	DEP-IO
[kæt]	*!		
[kæ]		*!	
☞ [kæti]			*

CHAPTER 12

Exercise 12.1

A gestural score for [bʰukʰ] should look like the following:

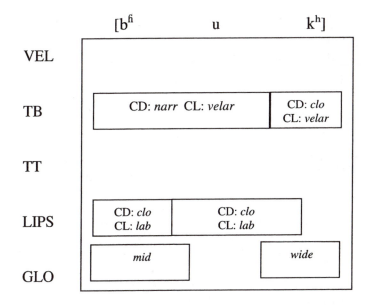

Here, *mid* is taken to represent breathy voice; *narrow* might be an alternative.

Exercise 12.2

A gestural score for *man* should look something like the following. It succinctly captures the fact that one single nasal gesture spans for the entire word.

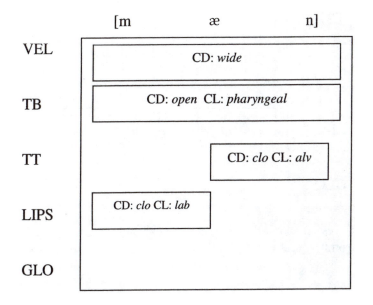

Exercise 12.3

The score for target *booth* is as follows:

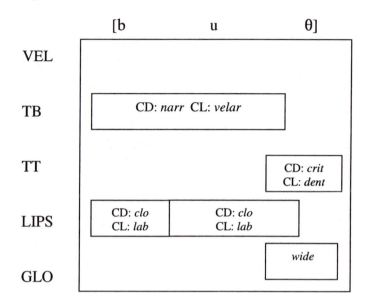

The score for realization [bup] is as follows:

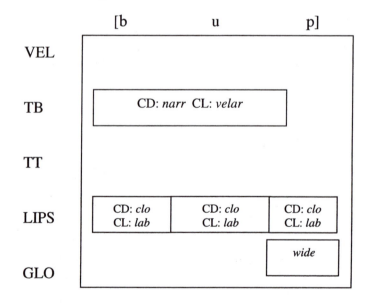

The gestural scores show that the final segment exhibits progressive assimilation of place and manner from the first.

CHAPTER 13

Exercise 13.1

GovP diagrams showing the constituency of the following English words:

go, got, goat:

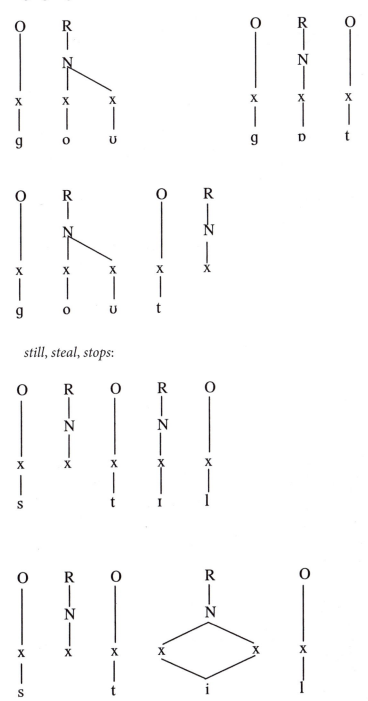

still, steal, stops:

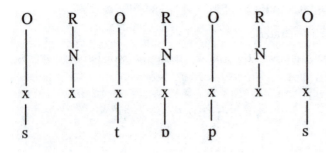

pelt, peeled, pest, pets:

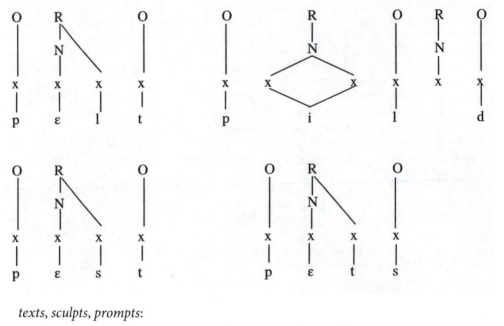

texts, sculpts, prompts:

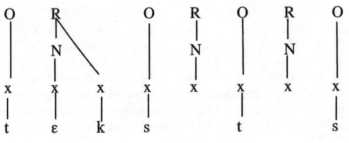

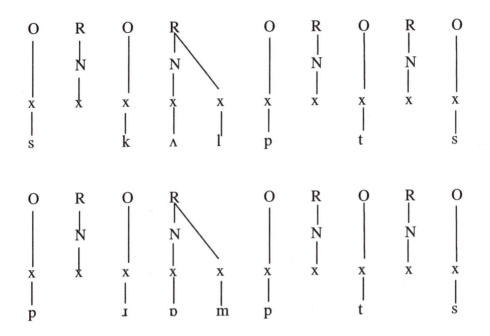

Exercise 13.2

The governing constituent units:

creep—/p/ governs /kri/.
now—only one constituent.
kept—/t/ governs /kɛp/.
stand—/tæn/ governs /s/; /d/ governs /tæn/.

The governing segment in the branching onsets and rimes:

creep—/k/ governs /r/.
now—no branching onsets or rimes.
kept—/p/ governs /t/.
stand—/æ/ governs /n/.

Exercise 13.3

Element combinations and governing relation for:

Lax vowel: [ʏ]   **[I, U, @]**
Long vowel: [ø]

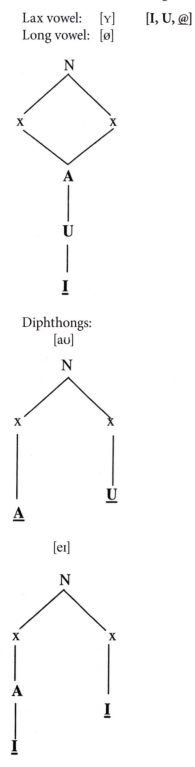

Diphthongs:
[aʊ]

[eɪ]

Exercise 13.4

Element combinations and governing relation for:

Plosives:	[c]	[**h**, **I**, **ʔ**] [q]	[**h**, <u>A</u>, **ʔ**]
Fricatives:	[ç]	[<u>h</u>, **I**] [ɸ]	[**h**, <u>U</u>]
Approximants:	[ʎ]	[**I**, **ʔ**] [ɥ]	[**I**, <u>U</u>]

Exercise 13.5

Element counting:	[aɪ, aʊ, iə, eɪ]	1-1, 1-1, 1-1, 2-1
Element counting:	[ae, io, uo]	1-2, 1-2, 1-2

The second sets all have a greater number of elements in second place.

Exercise 13.6

Dental fricatives replaced by either labiodental fricatives or alveolar stops. The change to alveolar stops is simpler as one element is added; for labiodental fricatives an element is changed and the governing element is altered.

$$[\theta] \quad \rightarrow \quad [f]$$

$$\theta \quad \rightarrow \quad f$$

$$
\begin{array}{ccc}
x & & x \\
| & & | \\
h & & \underline{h} \\
| & & | \\
\underline{R} & & U
\end{array}
$$

$$[\theta] \quad \rightarrow \quad [t]$$

$$\theta \quad \rightarrow \quad t$$

$$
\begin{array}{ccc}
x & & x \\
| & & | \\
h & & h \\
| & & | \\
\underline{R} & & \underline{R} \\
& & | \\
& & ?
\end{array}
$$

Exercise 13.7

Consonant fortition: /l/ to [d], /dʒ/ to [d], /z/ to [d], and /ð/ to [d]?

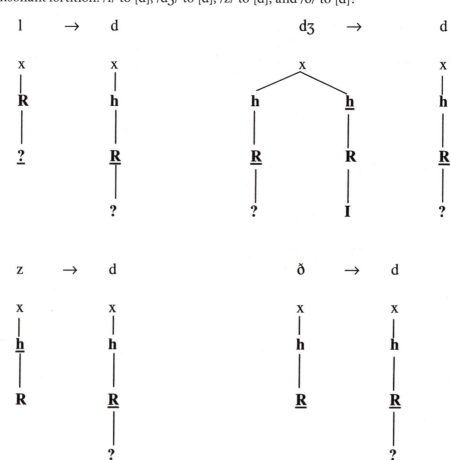

Exercise 13.8

The realization of /ɹ/ as [w]:

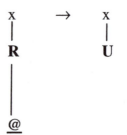

CHAPTER 14

Exercise 14.1

a)

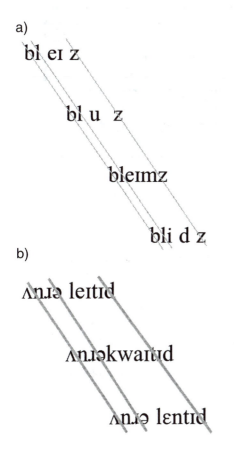

bl eɪ z

bl u z

bleɪmz

bli d z

b)

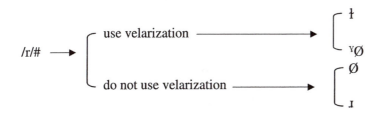

brɪtəl erʌv

brɪtəkwarɪtd

brɪtəl erʌv

Exercise 14.2

Syllable final, word final, cluster

/r/C# ⟶ use velarization ——————— ˠØ

do not use velarization ——————— Ø

Syllable final, word final, singleton

/r/# ⟶ use velarization ⟶ ⎡ ɫ
⎣ ˠØ

do not use velarization ⟶ ⎡ Ø
⎣ ɹ

Exercises 14.3

Maasai Rightward [+ATR] Spread

Argument:	+ATR	Default	Nondefault
Parameters	Function	INSERT	
	Type	PATH	
	Direction	LEFT TO RIGHT	
	Iteration	ITERATIVE	
Structure requirements	A-structure	NONE	
	T-structure	FREE	
Other requirements	A-condition		
	T-condition		

CHAPTER 15

Exercise 15.1

Target	Realization	Category
Soap	[ɫoʊp]	Distortion
Goat	[doʊt]	Substitution
Loop	[ɫup]	Distortion
Shoe	[çu]	Distortion
Key	[ti]	Substitution
Me	[mʷi]	Distortion

Exercise 15.2

Target	Realization	Category
Soap	[ɫoʊp]	External phonetic
Goat	[doʊt]	Internal phonemic
Loop	[ɫup]	Internal allophonic
Shoe	[çu]	External phonetic
Key	[ti]	Internal phonemic
Me	[mʷi]	Internal allophonic

Exercise 15.3

Affix	Category	Example
/s/	Inflectional	cat + /s/, plural, possessive
		walk + /s/, third person singular, present
/d/	Inflectional	open + e/d/, past tense/particple
/θ/	Derivational	wid(e) + /θ/ adjective to noun
/z/	Inflectional	dog + /z/, plural, possessive
		run + /z/, third person singular, present
/t/	Inflectional	walk + /t/, past tense/participle
/i/	Derivational	chalk + /i/, noun to adjective

APPENDIX

THE INTERNATIONAL PHONETIC ALPHABET (revised to 2005)

CONSONANTS (PULMONIC)

	Bilabial	Labiodental	Dental	Alveolar	Postalveolar	Retroflex	Palatal	Velar	Uvular	Pharyngeal	Glottal
Plosive	p b			t d		ʈ ɖ	c ɟ	k g	q ɢ		ʔ
Nasal	m	ɱ		n		ɳ	ɲ	ŋ	N		
Trill	B			r					R		
Tap or Flap		ⱱ		ɾ		ɽ					
Fricative	ɸ β	f v	θ ð	s z	ʃ ʒ	ʂ ʐ	ç ʝ	x ɣ	χ ʁ	ħ ʕ	h ɦ
Lateral fricative				ɬ ɮ							
Approximant		ʋ		ɹ		ɻ	j	ɰ			
Lateral approximant				l		ɭ	ʎ	ʟ			

Where symbols appear in pairs, the one to the right represents a voiced consonant. Shaded areas denote articulations judged impossible.

CONSONANTS (NON-PULMONIC)

Clicks	Voiced implosives	Ejectives
ʘ Bilabial	ɓ Bilabial	ʼ Examples:
ǀ Dental	ɗ Dental/alveolar	pʼ Bilabial
ǃ (Post)alveolar	ʄ Palatal	tʼ Dental/alveolar
ǂ Palatoalveolar	ɠ Velar	kʼ Velar
ǁ Alveolar lateral	ʛ Uvular	sʼ Alveolar fricative

VOWELS

	Front	Central	Back
Close	i y	ɨ ʉ	ɯ u
	ɪ ʏ		ʊ
Close-mid	e ø	ɘ ɵ	ɤ o
		ə	
Open-mid	ɛ œ	ɜ ɞ	ʌ ɔ
	æ	ɐ	
Open	a ɶ		ɑ ɒ

Where symbols appear in pairs, the one to the right represents a rounded vowel.

OTHER SYMBOLS

- ʍ Voiceless labial-velar fricative
- w Voiced labial-velar approximant
- ɥ Voiced labial-palatal approximant
- ʜ Voiceless epiglottal fricative
- ʢ Voiced epiglottal fricative
- ʡ Epiglottal plosive
- ɕ ʑ Alveolo-palatal fricatives
- ɺ Voiced alveolar lateral flap
- ɧ Simultaneous ʃ and x

Affricates and double articulations can be represented by two symbols joined by a tie bar if necessary.

k͡p t͡s

SUPRASEGMENTALS

- ˈ Primary stress
- ˌ Secondary stress ˌfoʊnəˈtɪʃən
- ː Long eː
- ˑ Half-long eˑ
- ˘ Extra-short ĕ
- | Minor (foot) group
- ‖ Major (intonation) group
- . Syllable break ɹi.ækt
- ‿ Linking (absence of a break)

DIACRITICS Diacritics may be placed above a symbol with a descender, e.g. ŋ̊

̥	Voiceless	n̥ d̥	̤	Breathy voiced	b̤ a̤	̪	Dental t̪ d̪
̬	Voiced	s̬ t̬	̰	Creaky voiced	b̰ a̰	̺	Apical t̺ d̺
ʰ	Aspirated	tʰ dʰ	̼	Linguolabial	t̼ d̼	̻	Laminal t̻ d̻
̹	More rounded	ɔ̹	ʷ	Labialized	tʷ dʷ	̃	Nasalized ẽ
̜	Less rounded	ɔ̜	ʲ	Palatalized	tʲ dʲ	ⁿ	Nasal release dⁿ
̟	Advanced	u̟	ˠ	Velarized	tˠ dˠ	ˡ	Lateral release dˡ
̠	Retracted	e̠	ˤ	Pharyngealized	tˤ dˤ	̚	No audible release d̚
̈	Centralized	ë	̴	Velarized or pharyngealized	ɫ		
̽	Mid-centralized	e̽	̝	Raised	e̝ (ɹ̝ = voiced alveolar fricative)		
̩	Syllabic	n̩	̞	Lowered	e̞ (β̞ = voiced bilabial approximant)		
̯	Non-syllabic	e̯	̘	Advanced Tongue Root	e̘		
˞	Rhoticity	ɚ a˞	̙	Retracted Tongue Root	e̙		

TONES AND WORD ACCENTS

LEVEL		CONTOUR	
e̋ or ˥	Extra high	ě or ˩˥	Rising
é ˦	High	ê ˥˩	Falling
ē ˧	Mid	e᷄ ˦˥	High rising
è ˨	Low	e᷅ ˩˨	Low rising
ȅ ˩	Extra low	e᷈ ˧˦˧	Rising-falling
↓	Downstep	↗	Global rise
↑	Upstep	↘	Global fall

extIPA SYMBOLS FOR DISORDERED SPEECH

(Revised to 2008)

CONSONANTS (other than on the IPA Chart)

	bilabial	labiodental	dentolabial	labioalv.	linguolabial	interdental	bidental	alveolar	velar	velophar.
Plosive		p̪ b̪	p͆ b͆	p͇ b͇	t̼ d̼	t̪͆ d̪͆				
Nasal			m͆	m͇	n̼	n̪͆				
Trill					r̼	r̪͆				
Fricative median			f͆ v͆	f͇ v͇	θ̼ ð̼	θ̪͆ ð̪͆	h̪͆ ɦ̪͆			ʩ
Fricative lateral+median								ʪ ʫ		
Fricative nareal	m͋							n͋	ŋ͋	
Percussive	ʬ						ʭ			
Approximant lateral					l̼	l̪͆				

Where symbols appear in pairs, the one to the right represents a voiced consonant. Shaded areas denote articulations judged impossible.

DIACRITICS

͍	labial spreading	s͍	͈	strong articulation	f͈	͊	denasal	m͊
͆	dentolabial	v͆	͉	weak articulation	v͉	͌	nasal escape	v͋
̪͆	interdental/bidental	n̪͆	\	reiterated articulation	p\p\p	͌	velopharyngeal friction	s͌
͇	alveolar	t͇	͎	whistled articulation	s͎	↓	ingressive airflow	p↓
̼	linguolabial	d̼	→	sliding articulation	θ͢s	↑	egressive airflow	!↑

CONNECTED SPEECH

(.)	short pause
(..)	medium pause
(...)	long pause
f	loud speech [{$_f$ laʊd $_f$}]
ff	louder speech [{$_{ff}$ laʊdɚ $_{ff}$}]
p	quiet speech [{$_p$ kwaɪət $_p$}]
pp	quieter speech [{$_{pp}$ kwaɪətɚ $_{pp}$}]
allegro	fast speech [{$_{allegro}$ fɑst $_{allegro}$}]
lento	slow speech [{$_{lento}$ sloʊ $_{lento}$}]
crescendo, ralentando, etc. may also be used	

VOICING

ˬ	pre-voicing	ˬz
ˬ	post-voicing	zˬ
₍̥₎	partial devoicing	₍z̥₎
₍̥	initial partial devoicing	₍z̥
̥₎	final partial devoicing	z̥₎
₍̬₎	partial voicing	₍s̬₎
₍̬	initial partial voicing	₍s̬
̬₎	final partial voicing	s̬₎
=	unaspirated	p⁼
ʰ	pre-aspiration	ʰp

OTHERS

( ), (Ç̲), (V̲)	indeterminate sound, consonant, vowel	ʞ	velodorsal articulation
(P̅l̅.v̅l̅s̅), (N̲)	indeterminate voiceless plosive, nasal, etc	¡	sublaminal lower alveolar percussive click
( )	silent articulation (ʃ), (m)	!¡	alveolar and sublaminal clicks (cluck-click)
(( ))	extraneous noise, e.g. ((2 sylls))	*	sound with no available symbol

VoQS: Voice Quality Symbols

Airstream Types

Œ	œsophageal speech	И	electrolarynx speech
Ю	tracheo-œsophageal speech	↓	pulmonic ingressive speech

Phonation types

V	modal voice	F	falsetto
W	whisper	C	creak
V̈	whispery voice (murmur)	V̰	creaky voice
Vʰ	breathy voice	C̡	whispery creak
V!	harsh voice	V!!	ventricular phonation
V̰!!	diplophonia	V̈!!	whispery ventricular phonation
V̪	anterior or pressed phonation	W̲	posterior whisper

Supralaryngeal Settings

L̝	raised larynx	L̞	lowered larynx
Vᵒᵉ	labialized voice (open round)	Vʷ	labialized voice (close round)
V̫	spread-lip voice	Vᵛ	labio-dentalized voice
V̺	linguo-apicalized voice	V̻	linguo-laminalized voice
Vˆ	retroflex voice	V̪	dentalized voice
V̳	alveolarized voice	Vʲ	palatoalveolarized voice
Vʲ	palatalized voice	Vˠ	velarized voice
Vᴮ	uvularized voice	Vˤ	pharyngealized voice
V̡ˤ	laryngo-pharyngealized voice	Vꟸ	faucalized voice
Ṽ	nasalized voice	Ṽ	denasalized voice
J̞	open jaw voice	J̝	close jaw voice
J̪	right offset jaw voice	J̫	left offset jaw voice
J̟	protruded jaw voice	Θ	protruded tongue voice

USE OF LABELED BRACES & NUMERALS TO MARK STRETCHES OF SPEECH
AND DEGREES AND COMBINATIONS OF VOICE QUALITY:

[ˈðɪs ɪz ˈnɔɹməl ˈvɔɪs {3V! ˈðɪs ɪz ˈveɹi ˈhɑɹʃ ˈvɔɪs 3V} ˈðɪs ɪz ˈnɔɹməl ˈvɔɪs wʌns
ˈmɔɹ {L̝ 1V! ˈðɪs ɪz ˈlɛs ˈhɑɹʃ ˈvɔɪs wɪð ˈloʊɚd ˈlæɹɪŋks 1V!L̝}]

INDEX